The Double Cure

Echoes from national camp meetings

First Fruits Press
Wilmore, Kentucky
c2016

The double cure, or, Echoes from national camp meetings.

First Fruits Press, ©2016
Revised and enlarged edition previously published by McDonald & Gill Co., [189-?]..

ISBN: 9781621716105 (print), 9781621716112 (digital), 9781621716129 (kindle)

Digital version at http://place.asburyseminary.edu/firstfruitsheritagematerial/136/

First Fruits Press is a digital imprint of the Asbury Theological Seminary, B.L. Fisher Library. Asbury Theological Seminary is the legal owner of the material previously published by the Pentecostal Publishing Co. and reserves the right to release new editions of this material as well as new material produced by Asbury Theological Seminary. Its publications are available for noncommercial and educational uses, such as research, teaching and private study. First Fruits Press has licensed the digital version of this work under the Creative Commons Attribution Noncommercial 3.0 United States License. To view a copy of this license, visit http://creativecommons.org/licenses/by-nc/3.0/us/.

For all other uses, contact:

First Fruits Press
B.L. Fisher Library
Asbury Theological Seminary
204 N. Lexington Ave.
Wilmore, KY 40390
http://place.asburyseminary.edu/firstfruits

The double cure, or, Echoes from national camp meetings -- Wilmore, Kentucky : First Fruits Press, ©2016.
    8, 442 pages [39] leaves of plates : portraits ; 21 cm.
    Contents: 1. Holiness / J.M. Pike -- 2. Personal fellowship and divine cleansing / W. Jones -- 3. A divided congregation / John Thompson -- 4. Christian perfection, explained and defended / Wm. McDonald -- 5. Suffering as Christians / G.W. Brindell -- 6. Perfect in God's will / E.I.D. Pepper -- 7. Sanctify them / C.J. Fowler – 8. Holiness / C.S. Nusbaum -- 9. Unity with God / M.D. Collins -- 10. Supreme love to God / J.A. Wood -- 11. Christian perfection / G.W. Wilson -- 12. The children of God / G.A. McLaughlin -- 13. Ezekiel's vision of the holy waters / B. Carradine -- 14. Growth in grace / H.N. Brown -- 15. Light, the basis and measure of responsibility / J.N. Short -- 16. Be ye holy / I Simmons -- 17. God near in the valley of decision / Alex. McLean -- 18. Help through unexpected channels / Isaiah Reid -- 19. The holiness of God: our assimilation to Him / L.R. Dunn -- 20. Perfect loyalty to God / Bishop Taylor -- 21. The Sanctifier and the sanctified / Andrew Cather -- 22. John the Baptist, or, Holiness staggering under trials / A.J. Jarrell -- 23. The true tabernacle, or, The three epochs of experience / J.B. Foote -- 24. Full Salvation / H.C. Morrison -- 25. Complete consecration necessary to entire sanctification / D. Cobb -- 26. Baptism with the Holy Ghost / P.F. Bresee -- 27. Be ye holy / W.L. Gray -- 28. History of the Holiness Movement in the church / C. Munger -- 29. Bible measure of love to God and man / M.L. Haney -- 30. Fullness of Christ / Joseph H. Smith -- 31. After regeneration, what? / C.A. Van Anda -- 32. Freedom from sin and the law / J.H. Senseney -- 33. Salvation / Joshua Gill.
    Reprint. Previously published: Boston : McDonald & Gill Co., [189-?].
    ISBN - 13: 9781621716105 (pbk.)

    1. Evangelistic sermons. 2. Holiness -- Sermons. 3. Sanctification -- Sermons. I. Title. II. Echoes from national camp meetings.
BT767 .D69 2016   1/.8

Cover design by Jon Ramsay

asburyseminary.edu
800.2ASBURY
204 North Lexington Avenue
Wilmore, Kentucky 40390

First Fruits Press
The Academic Open Press of Asbury Theological Seminary
204 N. Lexington Ave., Wilmore, KY 40390
859-858-2236
first.fruits@asburyseminary.edu
asbury.to/firstfruits

BISHOP KEY.

WILLIAM NAST.

CONTENTS.

1. HOLINESS 1
   J. M. Pike.
2. PERSONAL FELLOWSHIP AND DIVINE CLEANSING . . 26
   W. Jones.
3. A DIVIDED CONGREGATION 45
   John Thompson.
4. CHRISTIAN PERFECTION, EXPLAINED AND DEFENDED . 56
   Wm. McDonald.
5. SUFFERING AS CHRISTIANS 77
   G. W. Brindell.
6. PERFECT IN GOD'S WILL 90
   E. I. D. Pepper.
7. SANCTIFY THEM 102
   C. J. Fowler.
8. HOLINESS 115
   C. S. Nusbaum.
9. UNITY WITH GOD 130
   M. D. Collins.
10. SUPREME LOVE TO GOD 139
    J. A. Wood.
11. CHRISTIAN PERFECTION 149
    G. W. Wilson.
12. THE CHILDREN OF GOD 159
    G. A. McLaughlin.
13. EZEKIEL'S VISION OF THE HOLY WATERS 169
    B. Carradine.
14. GROWTH IN GRACE 180
    H. N. Brown.
15. LIGHT, THE BASIS AND MEASURE OF RESPONSIBILITY 192
    J. N. Short.

CONTENTS.

16. BE YE HOLY 207
    I. Simmons.

17. GOD NEAR IN THE VALLEY OF DECISION 223
    Alex. McLean.

18. HELP THROUGH UNEXPECTED CHANNELS 234
    Isaiah Reid.

19. THE HOLINESS OF GOD — OUR ASSIMILATION TO HIM 242
    L. R. Dunn.

20. PERFECT LOYALTY TO GOD 254
    Bishop Taylor.

21. THE SANCTIFIER AND THE SANCTIFIED 267
    Andrew Cather.

22. JOHN THE BAPTIST; OR, HOLINESS STAGGERING UNDER TRIALS 279
    A. J. Jarrell.

23. THE TRUE TABERNACLE; OR, THE THREE EPOCHS OF EXPERIENCE 290
    J. B. Foote.

24. FULL SALVATION 301
    H. C. Morrison.

25. COMPLETE CONSECRATION NECESSARY TO ENTIRE SANCTIFICATION 313
    D. Cobb.

26. BAPTISM WITH THE HOLY GHOST 326
    P. F. Bresee.

27. BE YE HOLY 337
    W. L. Gray.

28. HISTORY OF THE HOLINESS MOVEMENT IN THE CHURCH 352
    C. Munger.

29. BIBLE MEASURE OF LOVE TO GOD AND MAN . . . 371
    M. L. Haney.

30. FULLNESS OF CHRIST 384
    Joseph H. Smith.

31. AFTER REGENERATION, WHAT? 394
    C. A. Van Anda.

32. FREEDOM FROM SIN AND THE LAW 405
    J. H. Senseney.

33. SALVATION 416
    Joshua Gill.

W. B. OSBORN.

INTRODUCTION.

A NATIONAL CAMP MEETING, for the special promotion of entire sanctification or Christian perfection, as a definite experience, was never heard of in the modern Christian church until the year of our Lord, 1867, when such a meeting was inaugurated in Vineland, N.J.

The first suggestion in regard to holding such a meeting was made by Rev. John A. Wood in 1865, while on his way to a camp meeting in New Jersey. The suggestion was made to a Christian lady of means, who at once, such was her deep interest in the subject, promised, if such a meeting could be arranged for, that she would become responsible for half the expenses. Brother Wood, while at the camp meeting, made mention of the sister's promise to Rev. W. B. Osborn, who, with his usual enthusiasm, entertained the suggestion, and during the following winter named the subject to Rev. John S. Inskip, then pastor of the Green-street M. E. Church, New York City. The idea seemed to take full possession of this, if possible, more enthusiastic man, who was all on fire with his new-found experience of perfect love. After earnest prayer it was agreed that such a meeting should be held during the following summer, if only two tents were erected on the grounds.

A call was issued to all who were in favor of holding such a meeting to convene in the city of Philadelphia, June 13, to consider the subject.

INTRODUCTION.

A company of brave, devout men assembled in response to the "call," headed by that earnest lover of holiness, Dr. George M. C. Roberts of Baltimore, who presided at the meeting, and who poured out his soul to God in the opening prayer, in devout thanksgiving that he was permitted to see that favored hour. He seemed, it is said, like one of the old prophets talking face to face with God.

The venerable Anthony Atwood moved that a camp meeting for the special promotion of Christian holiness be held. Then the saintly Alfred Cookman moved that it be called "The National Camp Meeting for the Promotion of Holiness" — a name which it has always retained. It was decided to hold the first meeting at Vineland, commencing July 17, 1867.

This was a bold move, and met with much adverse criticism at the time, and some of the brethren were threatened with church discipline for favoring the movement. But Vineland, Manheim, and Round Lake turned the tide, and national camp meetings became the most mighty and attractive gatherings in the nation. It was the holiness era of the nineteenth century.

There have been eighty-four national camp meetings held in different sections of the land, and eleven tabernacle meetings in the leading cities of the country. Many of these tabernacle meetings have been quite equal to the "nationals." These meetings have been held in twenty-one States of the Union, one Territory, and one in Canada. In New York, 10; Illinois, 10; Maine, 8; Pennsylvania, 8; New Jersey, 6; Ohio, 6; Iowa, 6; Massachusetts, 4; Maryland, 2; Tennessee, 2; Michigan, 3; Indiana, 3; Nebraska, 2; California, 2; in New Hampshire, West Virginia, Wisconsin, Kansas, Minnesota, Delaware, Vermont, Georgia, Utah, one each, and one in Canada. The taber-

A. W. BUNKER.

nacle meetings have been held as follows: in California, 3; in Baltimore, 2; in Salt Lake City, 1; in Indianapolis 1; and 2 in India — Poonah and Bombay.

These meetings have been held annually as follows: —

1867. Vineland, N.J.
1868. Manheim, Pa.
1869. Round Lake, N.Y.
1870. Hamilton, Mass., Oakington, Md., and Des Plaines, Ill.
1871. Round Lake, N.Y., Urbana, O., and five tabernacle meetings, California, Salt Lake, and Indianapolis.
1872. Oaks Corners, and Sea Cliff, N.Y., Richmond, Me., Urbana, O., Williamsville, Ill., and Knoxville, Tenn.
1873. Cedar Rapids, Ia., Landisville, Pa., Moundsville, W. Va., Knoxville, Tenn., and a tabernacle meeting in Baltimore.
1874. Sterling, Mass., Old Orchard, Me., Joliet, Ill., and a tabernacle meeting in Baltimore, and in Washington.
1875. Fernwood, Pa., Cedar Rapids, Ia., Urbana, O., Old Orchard, Me., Newburg, N.Y., and a tabernacle meeting in Washington.
1876. Bennett, Neb., Milwaukee, Wis., Loveland, O., Shelter Island, N.Y., Newburg, N.Y., and Old Orchard, Me.
1877. Clear Lake, Ia., Chester Heights, Pa., and Framingham, Mass.
1878. Clear Lake, Ia., New Castle, Pa., and Epping, N.H.
1879. Lawrence, Kan., Bennett, Neb., Sewickley, Pa., Douglas, Mass., Summit Grove, Md., Urbana, O., and New Castle, Pa.
1880. Round Lake, N.Y., and India.
1881. Round Lake, N.Y., and Warsaw, Ind.
1882. Round Lake, N.Y., and Lincoln, Neb.
1883. Pitman Grove, N.J., and Old Orchard, Me. This was Bro. Inskip's last national camp meeting.
1884. Lansing, Mich., Pitman Grove, N.J., and Old Orchard, Me.
1885. Lansing, Mich., Red Rock, Minn., Ocean City, N.J., Warsaw, Ind., Old Orchard, Me., Jacksonville, Ill., and Augusta, Ga.
1886. Clear Lake, Ia., Joanna Heights, Pa., Murdock, Ill., and Wesley Park, Can.
1887. Pitman Grove, N.J.
1888. Mt. Taber, N.J.
1889. Des Plaines, Ill., Old Orchard, Me., and Beulah Park, Cal.

1890. Camden, Del., and Decatur, Ill.
1891. Northfield, Vt., and Linwood Park, O.
1892. Linwood Park, O., Ogden, Utah, Des Moines, Ia., Des Plaines, Ill.
1893. Hackley Park, Mich., Des Plaines, Ill., Long Beach, Cal.
1894. Silver Heights, Ind., Decatur, Ill.

Rev. John S. Inskip presided at forty-nine national camp meetings and eleven tabernacle meetings, making sixty in all. The writer has attended eighty-two of these meetings.

There are at present forty-six members of the National Association, — thirty-nine ministers and seven laymen, — whose portraits are found in this volume. These thirty-nine ministers are not all represented in this book of sermons. Some, being out of the country, could not be reached, and a few, for other causes, have not responded. But the volume, as a whole, is a splendid presentation of the different aspects of holiness from the Bible standpoint.

The fruit of national camp meetings in the spiritual uplift of the churches from a state of almost utter backsliding as the result of the Rebellion, in the inspiration it has given to the work of evangelization and missionary zeal, in the valuable holiness literature it has given to the churches, and in the new era of spiritual song with which it has flooded the land, — in these and other almost unnumbered blessings, — their influence for good has been unprecedented in modern times. The whole church has cause for thankfulness to God for national camp meetings. Through their instrumentality many thousands have been converted, and many more have been entirely sanctified; and their saving influence has been felt in every land. Indeed, "their sound has gone out into all the earth, and their words unto the end of the world."

W. McDONALD.

THE DOUBLE CURE.

I.

HOLINESS.

J. M. PIKE, OCALA, FLA.

"Holiness becometh thine house, O Lord, forever" (Ps. 93 : 5).

THIS declaration of the Psalmist was applicable to the tabernacle which Moses was commanded to erect in the wilderness, to the tent which David pitched on Mount Zion, and to the temple which was afterwards erected by Solomon. Everything about those buildings. was sacredly and solemnly set apart for holy purposes. They contained the holy place, which was daily accessible for devotional exercises, and the most holy place, where God specially manifested His presence, and which was entered only once a year, and then by the high priest alone. Everything about the sanctuary was in keeping with the inscription engraved upon the plate of the holy crown of pure gold — "Holiness to the Lord" — which the high priest wore upon his mitre.

The words are applicable to any church building sacredly set apart for purposes of divine worship.

Nothing but the direst necessity should permit the sacredness of the sanctuary to be infringed upon by the introduction of worldly expedients for the purposes of gain or amusement. The motto, "Holiness to the Lord," should be the standing test for all expedients to raise money for church purposes, or for instruction, or for recreation.

The term "house" is used to designate God's people. "Ye also, as lively stones, are built up a spiritual house, an holy priesthood" (1 Peter 2:5). "But Christ as a Son over his own house; whose house are we" (Heb. 3:6). "In whom all the building fitly framed together groweth unto an holy temple in the Lord: In whom ye also are builded together for an habitation of God through the Spirit" (Eph. 2:21, 22). This spiritual house is composed of individual members; and while "God does not dwell in temples made with hands," He has promised to dwell in man. "I will dwell in them and walk in them." John says, "If we love one another, God dwelleth in us." So, also, Paul, "Know ye not that ye are the temple of God, and that the Spirit of God dwelleth in you? If any man defile the temple of God, him shall God destroy; for the temple of God is holy, which temple ye are" (1 Cor. 3:16, 17). If then we are God's building, His habitation, His temple, His house, these words are peculiarly applicable — "Holiness becometh thine house, O Lord, forever."

The term "holy" is applied in the Scriptures not only to God, to angels, to heaven, to priests, and to sacrifices; but to men and women. We read of holy prophets, holy apostles, holy brethren. Of John the Baptist it is said, "Herod feared John, knowing that he was a just man and an holy" (Mark 6 : 20). "Holy men of God spake as they were moved by the Holy Ghost" (2 Pet. 1 : 21). "In the old time the holy women also, who trusted in God, adorned themselves" (1 Pet. 3 : 5).

The one great design of our holy religion is to make men holy. We have a holy Bible, written by holy men who were inspired by the Holy Ghost; it points out a holy way, to a holy heaven, where we are to meet a holy God, dwell amid holy associations, and engage in holy services for evermore. Hence, we "are called, not unto uncleanness, but unto holiness" (1 Thess. 4 : 7). We are "to put on the new man, which, after God, is created in righteousness and true holiness." "Being made free from sin, and become servants to God, ye have your fruit unto holiness." The chastisements of life are sent "that we might be made partakers of His holiness." We are commanded "to be holy in all manner of living;" and "to follow . . . holiness, without which no man shall see the Lord." Thus we see that the design of Christ's atoning work, the chastisements of life, the invitations, the promises, the commands of God, as set forth in the Scripture, all point to the holiness of God's people.

The Methodist church, claiming to be Scriptural in its origin and design, is based upon this fundamental truth of the Christian faith. John Wesley says, "In 1729 my brother Charles and I, reading the Bible, saw we could not be saved without holiness; followed after it, and incited others so to do. In 1737 we saw that this holiness comes by faith. In 1738 we saw, likewise, that men are justified before they are sanctified; but still holiness was our object — inward and outward holiness. God then thrust us out to raise up a holy people." After he had preached the doctrine for half a century, and had seen thousands brought into the experience, two years before his death, he wrote, " This doctrine is the grand *depositum* which God has lodged with the people called Methodists ; and for the sake of propagating this chiefly He appears to have raised us up."

This distinctive mission of Methodism was recognized by the bishops of the M. E. Church in 1824, and in the address to the General Conference, they said, " If Methodists give up the doctrine of entire sanctification, or suffer it to become a dead letter, we are a fallen people. Holiness is the main cord that binds us together; relax this, and you loosen the whole system. This will appear more evident if we call to mind the original design of Methodism. It was to raise up and preserve a holy people. This was the principal object which Mr. Wesley had in view. To this end all the doctrines believed and preached by the Methodists tend."

Dr. McClintock said, " Knowing exactly what I say, and taking the full responsibility of it, I repeat we are the only church in history, from the apostles' time until now, that has put forward as its elemental thought the great central idea of the Book of God, from the beginning to the end, *the holiness of the human soul, heart, mind, and will*. Go through all the confessions of all the churches, and you will find this in no other. It may be called fanaticism, but that, dear friends, is our mission. If we keep to that, the next century is ours. Our work is a moral work, that is to say, the work of making men holy. Our preaching is to that; our church agencies are for that; our schools, colleges, universities and theological seminaries are for that. There is our mission. There is our glory. There is our power, and there shall be our triumph."

The Centennial Conference of American Methodism, which met in Baltimore in 1884, reaffirmed this idea of the mission of our church in all its branches, in these words, "We remind you, brethren, that the mission of Methodism is to promote holiness."

It is very evident, then, that this subject is one of immense importance. If the design of the life, teachings, sufferings and death of Jesus was to make men holy; if we are divinely admonished to be holy in all manner of living: if God has called us unto holiness; if without holiness no man shall see the Lord; and if the great, definite mission of the Methodist Church is to spread Scriptural holiness over the land, surely it demands our most careful and prayerful attention, and we should never rest until it is made clear to our understanding, crystallized in our experience, and manifested in our lives.

Almost all really regenerated persons have in their minds an ideal Christian experience, which is far superior to that which they enjoy. Occasionally, under deeply spiritual preaching, or listening to the clear ringing testimony of one who has drunk deeply at the fountain, or during some special devotional exercises, there has come to the spiritual vision heights of such holy rapture, depths of such perfect love, and experiences of such calm, abiding peace, that a great hunger has taken possession of the spirit. No word but "holiness" seems sufficiently comprehensive to define such an ideal experience. The longing soul aspires after it, but there is a shrinking back from it, as though it were too sacred to become the possession of a poor human heart. Mystery environs it; and though we know that it alone can satisfy the longings of our spirit, we fail to grasp it.

Now, the Holy Spirit is the sole author of all religious experience; from its incipiency in conviction, through all the stages of conversion, sanctification, spiritual growth, maturity, until the soul "is presented faultless before the presence of His glory with exceeding joy." Wherever the Spirit is unobstructed in His work in the heart, He will reveal the latent depravity, and will beget such longings for its removal that the soul will "cry out, impatient to be freed." Even those who oppose the idea of an instantaneous removal of inbred sin as a second work of the Spirit, acknowledge that in the heart of the regenerated there is something that gives inward distress, that occasionally beclouds the spiritual vision, that weakens the faith, that begets doubt, that dampens the fervor of our zeal, and sadly interferes with our religious joy. There is a longing still unsatisfied, a vacancy still unfilled. The Holy Spirit reveals the lack, begets the longing, and somehow imparts an assurance that God has made provision to satisfy these holy aspirations. If there be clear, Scriptural teaching, the soul soon finds its satisfying portion, and an unspeakable joy.

This precious gift of God has been variously designated by uninspired writers as "the higher life," "the rest of faith," "the faith of assurance," "the second blessing," etc. We confess to a prejudice in favor of Scripture terms. The writers were holy men, inspired of the Holy Spirit. The Spirit knew what term would best convey the divine meaning; hence He calls it "perfection," "perfect love," "purity," "a clean heart," "the baptism of the Holy Ghost," "being filled with the Spirit," "sanctification," "holiness." The use of these terms, in preference to those of uninspired men, may cause us to bear more of the offence of the cross; but it will honor the Master more, and will bring greater blessing to us. He says, "Whosoever, therefore, shall be ashamed of me, and of *my words*, in this adulterous and sinful generation, of him, also, shall the Son of Man be ashamed when He cometh in the glory of His Father." The term "holiness" has a heavenly origin, and we will glory in its use.

I. *What is holiness?*

1. It is not absolute holiness. This belongs only to the infinitely holy God.

> "Holy as thou, O Lord, is none!
> Thy holiness is all thy own;
> A drop of that unbounded sea
> Is ours, a drop derived from thee."

2. It is not angelic holiness. The holy angels have maintained inviolate the trust reposed in them.

Their obedience has been always perfect; their holiness unsullied.

3. It is not the holiness possessed by Adam previous to the fall. He was, no doubt, as pure as the angels. His obedience was as prompt and as perfect as theirs. There was no defect either in his physical or his spiritual life.

4. It is not a holiness that will result in a perfect life in the estimation of men. God said to Abraham, "Walk *before me*, and be thou perfect." Had he said, "Walk before men, and be perfect," he would have required an impossibility. God said that "Job was a perfect and an upright man." Satan dissented from the divine declaration, and Job's friends joined with Satan in impugning the motives of this man of God. Jesus was holiness personified; but they said He was in league with the devil, and they hated Him unto the death.

5. It will not exempt us from temptation. Perfectly holy angels in heaven were tempted, and fell. Adam, blessed with angelic purity, was tempted, and most grievously fell. The Son of God "was tempted in all points like as we are," and the temptations continued to the latest hour of His life. Men have strong temptations sometimes in their regenerated life, but we really know little of direct conflict with Satan until after we are sanctified. Satan knows that one thoroughly holy man will do more damage to his kingdom than a score of ordinary Christians. Hence all of his hellish power is exercised to effect the overthrow of the holy man. John Wesley says: "It is the doc-

trine that the devil peculiarly hates, and he is all the time stirring up his own children, and some of God's weak children, against it." His hatred is specially directed against those who profess it.

6. It is not a completed experience, but admits of unending growth. It simply places us in a condition where the obstructions to growth are removed. The vegetables in the garden will grow if the soil is fertilized, even in the midst of weeds; but the growth will be retarded, and the crop will be inferior. With all the weeds removed, the growth will be more rapid, and results more satisfactory. Grace will grow amid the weeds of inbred sin; but the best results can only be realized when the heart is made pure. Who can set any limit to the possibilities of growth in a holy soul, even in this life? "The path of the just is as the shining light, that shineth more and more unto the perfect day." As the light is more and more revealing, so the path of the just brings him nearer and nearer to the source of heavenly light. He has clearer revealings of the divine character, of the divine will, of the greatness of his privileges in Christ Jesus, and the wonderful possibilities of a holy soul. "Reflecting as a mirror the glory of the Lord, we are transformed into the same image from glory to glory, even as from the Spirit of the Lord" (2 Cor. 3:18). We presume that this transforming process from glory to glory will be continued forevermore, and we shall be becoming more and more like God, until —

> "Plunged into the Godhead's deepest sea,
> We are lost in His immensity."

What is it? It is the holiness of a fallen, but redeemed human being, and can be enjoyed and lived, by one who is subject to human infirmities and surrounded by all the circumstances incident to human life. It implies a heart thoroughly cleansed from all sin, both inherited and acquired, and filled with the Spirit of purity. Wesley says, "It is the loving God with all our heart, mind, soul and strength. This implies that no wrong temper — none contrary to love — remains in the soul; and that all the thoughts, words and actions are governed by pure love." "The eye is single, and the whole body is full of light." He heeds the admonition, "Whatsoever ye do, whether ye eat or drink, do all to the glory of God." His constant aim is "To show forth the excellencies of Him who hath called us out of darkness into His marvelous light." "He walks worthy of the Lord unto all pleasing." The constant attitude of the soul is "I delight to do thy will, O my God." There is no jar in the spiritual machinery.

> "I have no cares, O blessed will,
> For all my cares are Thine;
> I live in triumph Lord, for Thou
> Hast made Thy triumphs mine."

No commentaries are needed to explain the words, "We which have believed do enter into rest." There is rest, sweet rest, from worry; the past is under the blood. At the present, "I am free from all danger while under His wings." For the future of life I lean upon His promise, "My God shall supply all your need." As for death, my Elder Brother, my unfailing

Friend, holds the key, and He will open the door and let me through at the very best time. As for the judgment, Jesus will be upon the throne. "There is therefore now no condemnation to them that are in Christ Jesus." As I am in Him, and one with Him, He cannot condemn me without condemning Himself. As for eternity, "I have a building of God, a house not made with hands, eternal in the heavens." What a fullness of meaning is now discovered in the words, "The water that I shall give him shall become in him a well of water springing up unto eternal life" (R.V.). Not a suction-pump, which needs special effort to produce the flow of water; but an artesian well which is perpetually flowing. The well of joy is within; "And he need not go abroad for joy who has so much at home."

Holiness is a pure heart. And "as a man thinketh in his heart so is he." The natural outcome is a pure life. Who can paint the beauties of holiness? We love purity. At whatever cost, we must have pure air and pure water. What a relief, after days of traveling amid the dust and filth of crowded railway cars, to enjoy a perfect bath in pure water, get rid of the dusty, soiled garments and enrobe ourselves in those that are spotlessly clean. Holiness means pure thoughts, pure intentions, pure motives, pure words, pure actions. It is the purity of heaven brought down to earth, and deposited for awhile in a human heart, to be exhibited in a pure life. It is the pure Christ re-incarnated in a human life. Paul says, "It is no longer I that live but Christ that liveth in me." Thrice blessed condition! Who would object to it?

II. *Is it possible to obtain it?*

We have been setting forth what we believe to be the normal Christian experience as it is revealed in the Bible. It is not the privilege of a favored few but the common birthright of all God's children. The possibility of its attainment is put beyond a doubt.

1. God commands it. Let us remember that these commands are given to living Christians to be obeyed in this life. "Be ye yourselves also holy in all manner of living; because it is written, Ye shall be holy; for I am holy" (1 Pet. 1:15, 16. R.V.). "Ye therefore shall be perfect, as your heavenly Father is perfect" (Matt. 5:48. R.V.). "Thou shalt love the Lord thy God with all thy heart, and with all thy soul, and with all thy mind" (Matt. 22:37). These are God's commands. Did He ever intend they should be obeyed? Knowing the character of our heavenly Father, would He be likely to issue a command that it was impossible for His children to obey? As an earthly father, would you issue a command to your children which you knew was beyond their power of obedience, and threaten punishment to them if they disobeyed? The question suggests its own answer. Every command of God therefore implies the gracious ability to obey.

2. The promises of God clearly teach the possibility of its attainment. These promises refer to all phases of the subject, but we quote but three, "Then will I sprinkle clean water upon you, and ye shall be clean; from all your filthiness, and from all your idols, will I cleanse you . . . and I will put my Spirit within you, and cause you to walk in my statutes," etc.

(Ez. 36 : 25, 27). Zacharias, the father of John the Baptist, under the inspiration of the Holy Spirit, said, "Blessed be the Lord God of Israel; for he hath visited and redeemed His people," etc. (Luke 1: 68, 72–74). Here we are reminded of the promise and covenant and oath of the Lord God of Israel to deliver us from all our enemies, to impart to us the gift of perfect love, and to enable us to walk before Him in holiness all our days. St. John says, "If we walk in the light as He is in the light, we have fellowship one with another, and the blood of Jesus Christ His Son cleanseth us from all sin" (1 John 1 : 7).

God's ability to fulfill His promises cannot be questioned. "He is able also to save them to the uttermost that come unto God by Him." "He is able to do exceeding abundantly above all that we ask or think." "Is anything too hard for the Lord?" His willingness is equal to His power. "Hath He said it, and will He not perform? Hath He spoken, and will He not make it good?" Will He mock His children? Will He hold in His hand a good which we greatly need, enkindle in our hearts a desire for its possession, offer it freely for our acceptance, and when we reach out our hand to receive the coveted gift say, "No, you cannot have it"? Will He assure me that the blessing of holiness has been secured for me through the atoning death of Jesus, that it will be the delight of His great, loving heart to bestow that gift upon me, and when I ask for it give me something inferior? If I ask bread of Him, will He give me a stone? If I ask a fish, will He give me a serpent?

If I ask an egg, will He offer me a scorpion? No, a thousand times, no! "He wills that I should holy be!" He yearns for the God-like pleasure of bestowing this gift upon me, and making me like Himself. And when I ask Him in simple faith to sanctify me wholly, according to my faith it is done unto me. There is no discount on God's promise to pay.

3. The very purpose of the life and death of Jesus was to make us holy. The name given Him before His birth was indicative of His mission, "Thou shalt call His name Jesus, for He shall save His people from their sins." To save men from hell was but a secondary object. This was but the natural result of being saved from sin. "He gave Himself for us, that He might redeem us from all iniquity, and purify unto Himself a peculiar people, zealous of good works" (Tit. 2 : 14). Not holiness at death, but "vessels unto honor, sanctified and made meet for the Master's use," here and now. "Christ also loved the church, and gave Himself for it; that He might sanctify and cleanse it with the washing of water by the Word, that He might present it to Himself a glorious church, not having spot, or wrinkle, or any such thing; but that it should be holy and without blemish" (Eph. 5 : 25–27). Thus we see that all that Jesus did and suffered was to make His people holy. "According as He hath chosen us in Him before the foundation of the world, that we should be holy and without blame before Him in love" (Eph. 1 : 4).

4. The prayers of inspired men are directed to the same object. Jesus Himself, when praying for His disciples, made this prominent. They were already

branches of the true vine; their names were written in heaven; they had heeded the call of Christ and had left all to follow Him; they were not of the world, even as He was not of the world; they had been commissioned to preach, and had wrought miracles in His name. But for these He prayed, "Sanctify them through Thy truth." Paul's prayer for the Thessalonians was, "The very God of peace sanctify you wholly; and I pray God your whole spirit and soul and body be preserved blameless unto the coming of our Lord Jesus Christ." For the Ephesians He prayed, "That ye might be filled with all the fullness of God." For the Colossians, "That ye might be filled with the knowledge of His will in all wisdom," and "walk worthy of the Lord unto all pleasing." These petitions were inspired of the Holy Spirit, and He would not be the author of a prayer for which there was no answer.

5. In addition to the foregoing arguments, proving the possibility of obtaining complete sanctification, we produce the testimony of individual experience: Enoch walked with God for three hundred years, and we have it from the highest authority that he pleased God. Abraham was commanded to "walk before God and be perfect;" and we are assured that he fully obeyed the divine command, for God made him an example of perfect faith to his children in all the ages. God's testimony of Job was that "he was a perfect and an upright man." Daniel was such a favorite of heaven that the angel Gabriel was commissioned to say to him that he was "a man greatly beloved." Stephen and

Barnabas were "good men, full of faith and the Holy Ghost;" and much people were saved through their instrumentality. Paul said, "I am crucified with Christ: nevertheless I live; yet not I, but Christ liveth in me, and . . . I live by the faith of the Son of God." So complete was his consecration that he said, " Christ shall be magnified in my body, whether it be by life, or by death. For to me to live is Christ, and to die is gain." In the midst of his trials he exclaims, " We glory in tribulations." In poverty and in prison his language is, " I have learned, in whatsoever state I am, therewith to be content." In labors more abundant, " I can do all things through Christ which strengtheneth me." And when the hour of his execution arrived he said, " I am ready to be offered."

All down the ages there have been choice spirits who have witnessed to the possession of this pearl of great price, the influence of whose holy lives has become the heritage of succeeding generations. The persecutions inflicted upon Madam Guyon were not sufficient to quench the glow of the perfect love which filled her heart. Behind the prison bars she wrote, " I passed my time in great peace, content to pass the rest of my life there if such was the will of God. I sang songs of joy, which the maid who served me learned by heart as fast as I made them, and we together sang Thy praises, O my God ! The stones of my prison looked, in my eyes, like rubies. I esteemed them more than all the gaudy brilliancies of the world. My heart was full of that joy Thou givest to them that love Thee in the midst of their greatest crosses."

Faber, though connected with the Roman Catholic church, had a genuine experience. The great spiritual epoch of his life, which brought him complete deliverance, he put into verse—

> "'Twas the labor of minutes, and years of disease
> Fell as fast from my soul as the words from my tongue.
> And now, blest be God and the sweet Lord who died;
> No deer on the mountain, no bird in the sky,
> No bright wave that leaps on the dark bounding tide,
> Is a creature so free or so happy as I."

Frances R. Havergal, one of the sweetest spirits that held connection with the Episcopal church says, "First I was shown that 'the blood of Jesus Christ His Son cleanseth us from all sin,' and then it was made plain to me that He who had thus cleansed me had power to keep. me clean; so I just utterly yielded myself to Him and utterly trusted Him to keep me." Her sister says, "The blessing she had received (to use her own words) lifted her whole life into sunshine, of which all she had previously experienced was but as pale and passing April gleams compared with the fullness of summer glory."

David B. Updegraff, of the Society of Friends, who has recently been translated to his abiding rest in heaven, leaves a blessed testimony to having enjoyed this blessing for years. He says, "With my all upon the altar, I had no sooner reckoned myself 'dead unto sin and alive unto God' than the Holy Ghost fell upon me. Instantly I felt the melting and refining fire of God permeating my whole being. I had entered into rest. I was nothing and nobody, and was glad that it was forever settled that way. . . . The inmost calm and repose in God of that time, that day, that hour, was a wonder to me then, and continues to be so still. It was, and it is, 'the peace of God that passeth understanding.' The witness of the Spirit to entire sanctification was as clear and unmistakable to my own soul as it was in the experience of justification. I have had abundant time and occasion in the nineteen years that have passed to scrutinize and test the reality and nature of the work wrought then and perpetuated by the power of the Holy Ghost. I have learned that this wondrous baptism of the Holy Ghost is the secret of stability in the Christian character as well as success."

Rev. J. O. Peck, who also has recently been called to his reward, has left a written testimony of his experience of this wondrous grace. After relating the stages of conviction and desire and purpose and consecration and faith that must always precede the obtainment of the blessing, he says, "It settled in me deeper and deeper, sweeter and sweeter, till I seemed 'filled with all the fullness of God.' I was ineffably satisfied. . . . The Spirit sealed these words on my heart, which have been ever since the sweetest verse in the Bible to me, 'Thou wilt keep him in perfect peace whose mind is stayed on Thee, because he trusteth in Thee.' . . . This experience I have never lost — not always equally clear and conspicuous, but ever a sacred deposition in my heart." In concluding, he says, "'My soul doth magnify the Lord' for this experience, which has doubled my joys and if I may judge, doubled the effectiveness of my imperfect ministry."

Dr. T. B. Anderson, of California, who was wondrously sanctified at a holiness meeting last winter, has published an account of his experience, from which we extract the following, "My thoughts ran thus, 'Lord, what blessings I have received from Thee here have been good, and I know all about them; but if there are others that would be of service to me, or to my ministry, I want them. I now take the place of the ox on the Greek coin — stand between the altar and the plow — ready for service or sacrifice. I am ready for poverty or riches, friends or foes; but give me what I need.' Suddenly I found myself falling — falling away from everything — the church and the preachers; my family and friends. I went into loneliness and desolation. An horror of great darkness was around me. . . . Just at the end of the darkness, to my surprise I found myself in the arms of the 'Wonderful Man.' He was the whitest man I ever saw; His face was like the sun. For a moment He held me; and such a bracing, buttressing and girding of life I never had before. I was, blessed be God, in the arms of Omnipotence. For hours and hours, wave after wave of glory rolled into my soul. . . . The effect on my life has been peace, quietness, assurance. I found the work wrought in me to be purgative, illuminative, unitive. I love my church, my brethren, my family — the whole world — better than I did before. . . . Everything drops in its place, and my experience is delightful. What effect has it had on my life? It has tranquilized it. The fret, worry, anxiety, all gone; my heart aches no more; my feet so tired, are resting. Indeed, they feel as if they were in the burning path of the Cherubim. Hallelujah!"

To these may be added the testimonies of a countless host, who with united voice declare that, conscious of inward distress of soul caused by inbred sin, they sought definitely, by consecration and faith the blessing of complete deliverance; instantaneously the work was wrought, and the clear, divine testimony was given; and the joy then brought to the soul was "unspeakable and full of glory." Like Thomas Collins, they could say, "I sought it, I found it, I kept it, I have it now, and it is heaven." Many of them lived for years in its enjoyment, shedding the radiance of a holy life upon surrounding darkness, and died shouting " Victory through the blood of the Lamb!" Thousands more all over our broad land, with perfect love to God and man, are bending every energy " to spread Scriptural holiness over the land."

What shall we do with their testimony? Here are intelligent witnesses whose testimony would be accepted in any court of justice. In standing forth as witnesses of holiness they subject themselves to much adverse criticism, to the charge of being righteous overmuch, to being misunderstood and misrepresented, of pretending to be better than their brethren, and of separating from them and dividing the church; but with the consciousness of heaven's approval they keep on telling the story and are happy and useful on the way.

Now then, if God commands us to be holy; if He

promises to make us holy ; if Jesus died to secure this blessing for us ; if inspired men prayed that Christians might partake of this wondrous gift ; and if thousands of the saintliest spirits that ever lived, declared that they possessed it and bear testimony to its preciousness, why may not every child of God enter into its possession at this hour ?

Holiness will be popular in heaven. Its songs, its service, its associations, its very atmosphere will be holy. Without holiness none can enter there. An unholy soul in heaven would be a monstrosity. The light of the holiness that shines there would so reveal his moral deformity that he would be shunned by every pure spirit in that land of light and love. In the midst of heaven's great multitude, and an observer of its perfect bliss, an unholy soul would be lonesome and unhappy. It would be hell's torture in the midst of heaven's joy, and such a soul would seek a way of escape as soon as possible. We must be in harmony with our environment ; we must move in an atmosphere congenial to our tastes, or we cannot be happy. Holiness of heart is the only guarantee of our entrance into heaven, and the only preparation for its enjoyment after we get there.

III. *How may it be obtained?*

This is the most difficult question on the subject to answer. Minds are so variously constituted, and temperaments differ so greatly that the directions given to one may not be applicable to another. There are, however, certain conditions which must be met by all who would secure this pearl of great price. To the man who has complied with those conditions, and who is living in the light which full salvation brings, nothing is more simple. He wonders why every one cannot see the way as clearly as he does. To those about him inquiring the way, he traces the steps that led him into this divine secret so simply that he thinks a child could understand it; yet all is mystery to them.

First, there must be a belief that the blessing is attainable. Being conscious of remaining impurity which disturbs the peace of the soul, interrupts its joy and often engenders doubt, and believing that the atonement of Jesus provides for the entire cleansing of the heart, there must be a conviction that the blessing is your blood-bought privilege, and may be yours by possession. Doubt here clips the wings of desire and places an effectual barrier in the way of attainment. You must believe that there is such a blessing and that it is for you.

Second, there must be an earnest desire for, and a diligent seeking of the blessing. This is the goodly pearl, the pearl of great price. This is the soul's satisfying portion. This is "love that passeth knowledge;" "joy unspeakable and full of glory;" "peace that passeth all understanding;" "hope, as the anchor of the soul, sure and steadfast;" this is, "being blessed with all spiritual blessings in the heavenlies;" this is the highest gift that heaven offers to man on earth — Christ in a pure heart. He will only come to a heart that is aflame with ardent desire for His presence. When holiness is desired more than wealth, more than honor, more than health, more than friends, more than anything else, there is not much delay in obtaining the blessing. "God loves to be longed for; He longs to be sought."

Third, there must be a determination never to rest until the blessing is yours. Many fail just here. There seems to be no lack of earnestness for a little while, but the blessing is not found as easily as was at first supposed; discouragements come, effort is relaxed, desire languishes, and the struggle is given up. But when the mind becomes so thoroughly fixed upon the obtainment of this blessing that you will have it at whatever cost, the battle is more than half gained. If you persevere, it is yours, as sure as that you live, and God is true. All the power and wisdom and cunning of Satan will be exercised to secure your defeat. He hates a holy man. Friends that you love as you love your life, will very likely try to dissuade you from your purpose. The exercise of your mind will react upon your physical being, and will produce feelings the most depressing. But if you keep your eye upon Jesus and persevere, victory will be yours.

Fourth, the complete consecration of yourself and your all to God. This consecration embraces body, soul, spirit, time, talents, reputation, property, friends, all we have or hope to have through time and eternity. It means that we place ourselves at God's disposal, to go where He sends us, to follow where he leads, to do whatever He bids us —

"Thy ransomed servant, I restore to thee thine own,"
And from this moment, live or die, to serve my God alone."

Fifth, you must believe that God receives you and sanctifies you wholly just now. The divine Word says, "If we walk in the light as He is in the light, we have fellowship one with another, and the blood of Jesus Christ His Son cleanseth us from all sin." You have been walking in the light, as the Holy Spirit has led you along step by step, revealing more and more clearly your duty, and you have taken a joyous satisfaction in saying "Yes" to the admonition of that Spirit. And now, as your heart is conscious of fellowship with the Father and the Son, by the blessed Spirit, you are simply to believe the statement, "The blood of Jesus Christ His Son cleanseth from all sin," and you will soon exclaim, "I am every whit made whole. Glory, glory to the Lamb!"

There is sometimes an interval between the exercise of the faith which claims the blessing of holiness and the witness of the Spirit to its possession. The question is asked, "What is the attitude of the soul during that interval?" We reply, "It is in an attitude of calm repose, earnest desire and holy expectancy." No words can more appropriately describe it than those of Wesley,

"Restless, resigned, for God I wait,
For God my vehement soul stands still!"

The good wife, whose husband has been away from home for some time, receives information that he will return on a certain day. The hour is not designated. She prepares for his reception, calmly confident that he will come for he said he would, and she expects him every hour. Soon her faith is rewarded in the joy of his presence. So the soul that has prepared for the coming of the Comforter, by supreme consecration and reliance upon the Word, will not be disappointed.

The truths here presented have been drawn from the Word of God and forged on the anvil of personal experience. I know whereof I affirm. For fourteen years after my conversion I plodded my weary way, in common with many Christians of my acquaintance, with a commingling of light and darkness, faith and doubt, joy and sorrow, victory and defeat, success and failure in my Christian experience. But since that blessed day, now twenty years ago, when the Comforter assured me that He had come to abide, religion has been a luxury, the service of God a delight. It grows brighter and sweeter and better every day, and I am full of expectation that this streak of sunshine will issue into the blaze of eternal day.

> "Oh, that all might catch the flame,
> All partake the glorious bliss."

II.

PERSONAL FELLOWSHIP AND DIVINE CLEANSING.

WM. JONES, M.D., D.D., LL.D., SEDALIA, MO.

"But if we walk in the light, as He is in the light, we have fellowship one with another, and the blood of Jesus Christ His Son cleanseth us from all sin" (1 John 1:7).

A CORRECT exegesis of this Scripture will obviate all difficulty in the development of the vital truths it contains. "This then is the message which we have heard of Him, and declare unto you, that God is light, and in Him is no darkness at all." This text is parallel with the passage that "God is love." Holiness and light and love are equivalents. Light unites in itself purity and clearness and beauty and life and glory, as no other material agent possibly can combine.

Light is the condition of all material life and growth; seeds have been entombed in the stomach of an Egyptian mummy for more than a thousand years, and afterward, when exposed to the light, have germinated and borne fruit. This principle is universal in its application. It embraces every department of the material, moral and spiritual universe. "God is light." He is the fountain of light. Out of His

essential personality flow forth those forces that bless the earth with the elements of fruitfulness and with the institutions of progress, and which give unto a fallen manhood the possibilities of a return to the fellowship of the Father and open to him the portals of eternal life.

In the natural world darkness is the absence of light. In the spiritual realm darkness, untruthfulness, deceit and every species of moral and physical uncleanness indicate the entire or partial absence of God. In Him is no darkness at all. All who are in communion and fellowship with God, and walk with Him, walk in the light. There is no authority in the Word of God, nor in the philosophy of religious experience, for that delusive sentiment —

> "I would rather walk with God in the dark
> Than go alone in the light."

No person can walk with God and be in darkness. "If we say we have fellowship with Him, and walk in darkness, we lie and do not the truth." God is "holiness and righteousness." He not only has no evil in Himself, but He cannot suffer it in His creatures. As in the physical world the air is man's life element, and he lives in it and cannot live out of it, even so in a spiritual sense the divine life and light of God are the element of man's spiritual life, and no man can walk in the fellowship of God without these constituent qualities.

The Christian must live in his element if he lives at all. As a man cannot live in a vacuum, nor under the water, and as a fish cannot live out of the water, because that is its life element, neither can a Christian live in the element of darkness.

There are two propositions affirmed in the text: (*a*) If we walk in the light, as God is in the light, we have fellowship with God and He has fellowship with us. (*b*) While the Christian sustains that divine relationship and walks in the light with God "the blood of Jesus Christ His Son cleanseth him from all sin." These two propositions are both affirmed by the Holy Ghost, and therefore are not debatable. But they suggest two questions: (1) What is implied in walking in the light? (2) What is implied in being cleansed from all sin? In this discourse we produce no arguments to prove that the text is true. The statement is definite and explicit that when a human soul fulfills the conditions of the divine promise, " the blood cleanseth from all sin."

This text is addressed to real Christians; it can have no possible application to unconverted persons. "If we walk in the light as God is in the light." Dead men never walk; unconverted persons cannot have fellowship with God. The text being addressed to living Christians, cannot refer to the process of making alive from spiritual death, but it is an illustration of the divine method of cleansing those who are regenerated from the elements of impurity that linger in the soul after the new birth.

Walking in a spiritual sense is a feat that is possible only to living Christians. Life, of necessity, precedes locomotion. By a law as inflexible as the divine veracity, everything in the realm of nature, whether of matter or of spirit, must have life before it can possess the inherent power of motion. And as the experience of heart purity is obtained while obediently walking with God, and retained only while obediently keeping His commandments, it follows as a logical necessity that the cleansing is not co-etaneous with regeneration but is a specific work of grace, wrought subsequent to that experience.

The word "if" in the text is a very significant term; it clearly indicates that no one can obtain a pure heart that will not fulfill the condition on which the precious experience is promised. In this textual statement we are shown that purification succeeds pardon and is secured by the strictest obedience to the divine command.

Entire sanctification or its equivalent, "full salvation," is neither a mental nor moral idiosyncrasy; it is not a phase of religious experience that is dependent on some peculiarity of temperament. It is a normal, religious experience, obligatory upon all, and is dependent upon the personal adjustment of the individual to the Saviour of men. "If we walk in the light as He is the light," if we keep the personal fellowship of God unbroken; "The blood of Jesus Christ His Son cleanseth us from all sin." Holiness is an experience of fellowship with God. "If we walk in the light, we have fellowship one with another." No person can reach this condition of light and fellowship who continues to linger in the shadow of any former experience or event. Holiness comes after pardon; comes only to those who are walking in the fellowship of God; comes while the soul is pulsating with life and glowing with the brightness which eminates from God.

The light of this divine fellowship with Jesus leads directly to the fountain of cleansing. There is no darkness in the land from whence this light comes. "There is no night there." "The Lord God and the Lamb giveth them light." This light spans like a rainbow of hope the deep, dark chasm that sin has cleft in the moral universe. It has been shining down the ages, and still it pours its radiance on the pathway of a lost race. No enginery of scepticism; no combination of forces from any hostile camp can obscure its brilliancy, or for one single moment intercept its flow into the believing heart. God never designed His children to walk in darkness, with only an occasional ray of light to pierce the moral gloom. It grieves the heavenly Father when His loved ones, for whom Jesus died, prefer to dwell amid the shadows and view the light from afar. He commands us to walk in the light, where the secret impurities of the heart shall be subject to its searching power and disappear forever at the touch of the cleansing blood. Believers sin against their own souls and seriously embarass the progress of the church when they remain in the darkness and bondage of legalism, when God so graciously invites them to walk in the sunlight of His blessed fellowship.

The text says, "If we walk." To realize on this promise there must be an advance movement. If we refuse to obey, or remain passive, we utterly fail. If you succeed beloved, you are to walk — not after your own lusts — but in "the light;" not always where you wish to go, but where the Master may direct. God never loiters. He offers no opportunity the second time. If you walk in the light with Him, you must yield a prompt and perfect obedience.

When I was in the city of Baltimore I ascended the celebrated monument erected to the memory of the immortal Washington. It is built upon a pedestal of solid masonry sixteen feet high. On this solid base is reared a column of white marble of immense height and singular beauty. The ascent is by a spiral stairway inside the shaft. The guide adjusted his lamp and said, "Follow me close." We entered a side door and commenced the ascent. The darkness was so dense that the lamp made but a small circle of light — only enough to enable us to take one step at a time. To hesitate a moment was to be left in impenetrable night. Up this heated column by the aid of this simple light, we passed one day in June, to emerge at the top covered with dust and bathed in prespiration, and almost suffocated from heat and bad air. We stood upon the balcony at the head of the stairway and gazed upon one of the most entrancing scenes that ever greeted the eyes of man. There lay the city far below, with its towers and temples and churches, fretted and gleaming in the morning light; its busy streets thronged with the industries of a great commercial city, and its capacious harbor filled with vessels representing nearly every nation upon the globe. To survey such a prospect, and breathe the uncontaminated air of heaven, was more than enough to repay the adventurer for the time and labor required to make the ascent. The soul was fairly intoxicated with the grandeur and indescribable beauty of its surroundings.

Thus if you would ascend the heights of religious experience; if you would explore the untrodden realm of conscious fellowship with God; if you would enter the land of Beulah, where the sun shines always, you must walk in the light with God; you must keep time to His advancing footsteps. Although the surroundings may be like the darkness of Egypt, "which may be felt;" though toil and self-denial be thy daily lot, place your hand in the hand of Jesus, let Him get fast hold upon you, and wherever He leads follow gladly without debate. He will conduct you up celestial heights where the scenery will partake more of the nature of heaven than of earth; where the landscape of mountain and plain is cleft and chasmed and filled with crystal streams and covered with groves luxuriant in foliage and flora. "Whose rich trees weep odorous gums and healing balm," and pour their fragrance on the burdened air; where your exultant soul can truly sing —

> "How brilliant my pathway when Thou art my light;
> How clear is my vision when Thou art my sight;
> How honored and glorious Thy temple to be,
> And know that Thou dwellest this moment in me.
>
> "When musing of glory with soul all aglow,
> Communing with saints of joys here below, —

> When strong in the faith and the power of Thy might,
> And soaring aloft in the regions of light,
> O Jesus I'll praise Thee by night and by day
> I'll pray without ceasing, so sweet to obey,
> For nothing so pure and so precious to me
> As secret and holy communion with Thee."

But the text contains the positive statement, that when the living Christian walks in the light of holy fellowship with God, "the blood of Jesus Christ His Son cleanseth us from all *sin*." There are two significant terms in this text — "sin" and "cleanseth." The term sin is an emphatic word and is the key to the meaning of this text. It is in the singular number and cannot refer to acts of trangression; to personal violations of the law of God. These were all removed by forgiveness. Pardon is the first act of the divine administrator in the salvation of the guilty. The transgressions are all forgiven before the penitent seeker can have conscious life or peace. Adoption, pardon, regeneration, are all embraced in the fact of sonship. Pardon is the great event in the salvation of one who is in revolt against the King of heaven. When the condemnation is removed and the regenerated soul is made a member of the household of God, all the other aspects of the case follow in their regular order.

The other significant term is "cleanseth." It is never used interchangeably with pardon nor regeneration. It is specific in its application, and implies the act and process of purification — "to complete," "to perfect." It refers to an act of Almighty God, by which He perfects the salvation of the obedient Christian. "The blood of Jesus Christ His Son cleanseth from all sin." As used here, this term can have no possible application, except to the removal of some impurity, some lingering element of defilement remaining in the soul after conversion — some hereditary constituent quality of uncleanness, lying outside of the domain of pardon and regeneration — an impurity lying back of all phenomena of life or action — some essence of being, that could neither be pardoned nor regenerated — that odious thing which the apostle calls "the old man, the body of sin," which is to be destroyed, to be cleansed away.

We perceive therefore, that if this text is true, the completeness of salvation as certainly as its primary stages, is secured through the sacrificial merit of Christ's death, and that this completed salvation is a normal religious experience, obtained through faith, and witnessed to by the Holy Ghost as a present conscious experience.

It is not a declaration that "the blood" did cleanse at a certain date in the past, nor a promise that it will cleanse at the hour of death. It is a clear, definite, unequivocal statement that when the regenerate soul walks in the fellowship of God and keeps that divine relationship with all fidelity, "the blood of Jesus Christ His Son cleanseth from all sin." This verb is in the present tense. It harmonizes with the other part of the sentence.

The "if" comprehends the whole procedure. If we walk in the light with God, we have fellowship with Him; and while we sustain that divine relationship the sacrificial merit of Jesus Christ, through His priestly office, avails for all of our needs; for all the past impurities, both contracted and hereditary. Avails also for the unconscious mistakes and weaknesses of the present. And we not only say with Charles Wesley —

> "Every moment Lord I need
> The merit of Thy death."

But, in the language of a present experience, we say —

> "Every moment Lord we have
> The merit of Thy death."

There is a widely prevalent error in the church to-day — one that has wrought disaster in all the past — a notion that salvation is a thing, an event completed in itself, a form of experience that may be obtained and kept. Under the delusion of this heresy persons fail to keep their fellowship with God. "They lose their experience," and wander in gross darkness, or with broom and candle, make dilligent search for the lost piece of silver.

The text teaches us that salvation is not only a great experimental fact — a spiritual condition of the soul, which is contingent upon its personal relations with God — but that it is a continuous eperience redolent of new manifestations of the divine presence each succeeding day. It implies the daily submission of the soul to the will of God as certainly as it demands the outward obedience to His law. It embraces a conscious experience — a state of fellowship with God; and it is in the recognition of this fellowship alone that the blood of Calvary's offering makes the soul clean and preserves it blameless before God.

This entire cleansing implies more than the complete repression of the evil nature — much more than the strictest conformity to the highest standard of ethics. There is a subtle and dangerous heresy vigorously propagated at the present time, which affirms that the sinful nature of man cannot be extirpated in this life. Those who entertain this doctrine affirm that the utmost the Holy Ghost can do for the soul is to repress hereditary depravity. They affirm that the Adamic nature cannot be crucified. They affirm that Paul was mistaken when he said, "Knowing this, that our old man is crucified, that the body of sin might be destroyed." These public teachers assure us that " the old man was not crucified, that he was not even nailed to the cross — that he was simply repressed." They pervert and destroy the Word of God when they say, " Knowing this, that *our* old man is repressed; he is tied down; he is placed in seclusion, and he whose fallen nature is repressed is freed from sin." There is an unlimited difference between the terms "repression" and "destruction" in their primary signification. Complete repression is consistent with the most vigorous life and the most tremendous purpose. A criminal behind the prison bars, ironed to the floor of his cell, is repressed, but even there he conceives and plans for the execution of crimes of darker hue than those for which he now suffers.

In the Union Depot, at St. Thomas, Canada, I saw an Indian babe strapped to a board, standing in the corner of the room. The incipient warrior was entirely repressed; but from the throne of his repression the young brave made his dusky mother obey the behest of his will. So, again and again, your "old man" that has been repressed asserts himself, and the regenerate manhood goes down before the fierce assault of the Adamic nature.

The conception of holiness by repression is contrary both to human experience and the Bible, and is antagonistic to the fundamental principles of philosophy. Holiness in man is the same in kind as holiness in God. Therefore, as God is essentially holy, saved manhood must be essentially pure. The holiness of God is the pattern for Christian holiness. "He that hath this hope in him purifieth himself even as He is pure." As we study this subject we cannot avoid the conviction that, if any person is dreaming of entering a holy heaven, to dwell in fellowship with a holy God with the carnal nature still in him, though it be held in a state of repression by the Holy Ghost, he will awake to the consciousness of his mistake amid the wailings of the lost.

The idea of salvation from sin by repression obliterates from the mind the natural distinction between virtue and holiness, and substitutes legal morality for the life and purity that are essentially inherent in Jesus Christ. The Bible does not authorize us to say that God is perfectly moral, or that the angels are virtuous. We reject the divinity of Jesus Christ when we ascribe to Him only virtue. He is nowhere in Scripture styled the divine represser; His name "is called Jesus, because He saves His people from their sins." Virtue and holiness are not the same; virtue is the natural excellence of a moral being tested by law. It is the practice of duty according to the established standard of right. Virtue always has reference to actions. Holiness is purity of substance, and always has regard to quality. Holiness, when applied to the Supreme Being, denotes that perfection of purity which is essential to His divine nature. Holiness, when applied to man, is relative, and always derived. It implies that quality of the spiritual nature which exists in him after the Holy Ghost has eliminated from his soul all hereditary impurity and wrought its essential fabric into harmony with the being of God. According to the doctrine of salvation by repression, the distinction between "being" and "action," between "virtue" and "holiness," is eliminated from our thought; and spiritual purity as an essential quality of the human soul emasculated, and salvation is made impossible.

If God can do no more than to repress impurity, polluted human nature can never become holy. The law cannot save, or Christ would not have died. For four thousand years Sinai has smoked and thundered, but no one has been saved by the law. Law applies to actions, but holiness pertains to the essential quality of being. Therefore, if sin exists in the form of pollution, and that defilement is a quality of the fallen nature, giving humanity an impulse toward sinful actions, the repression of that vicious impulse can never exterminate it. If there is in human nature a quality of unholiness — the existence of a carnal principle which is enmity against God — it will have to be eradicated before man can dwell in peace and fellowship with God.

The Scripture affirms that the "carnal mind is enmity against God." It is not at enmity, but is organized, aggressive, eternal enmity. "The carnal mind is not subject to the law of God, neither indeed can be." If the Scripture is true the carnal nature can never be subjugated to the law of God. In the process of salvation it is neither justified nor regenerated; its nature cannot be changed. Because of this fact, it must either be destroyed or remain sin forever, for sin in a state of repression is sin; repression does not change its nature.

The State criminal in the seclusion of his cell burns with revenge. He plots against the peace of the State; he plans for the execution of other crimes; no amount of repression can make him a good citizen; the only forces that can transform his nature cannot reach him through the law.

The carnal mind, though held in a state of repression by the Holy Ghost, "is enmity against God," and while it remains in existence the peace of God's kingdom is imperiled, and the salvation of the soul in which it is fostered is made impossible by its presence. Furthermore, if the Holy Ghost cannot extirpate this impurity now, He can never do it, for Omnipotence does not admit of possible increase; and if the defiled soul cannot be cleansed now the text is not true, for this Scripture affirms that, "If we walk in the light as He is in the light, we have fellowship one with another, and the blood of Jesus Christ His Son cleanseth us from all sin." But if it be true that the Father, Son and Holy Ghost, with the full consent and co-operation of the contrite believer, can do no more than to repress inbred sin, the adversary is now, and always will be, the victor. But the text affirms that the "blood cleanseth." The Holy Ghost honors the blood of atonement, and the seeker after full salvation cannot obtain until he honors Him whose "blood cleanseth from all sin." This is the final test of faith in the process of salvation. No one can realize on the merit of Christ until he accepts that which the Father hath already accepted — the sufficiency of Christ's death — that "He made there, by Himself once offered, a full, perfect and sufficient sacrifice, oblation and satisfaction for the sins of the whole world." The believer is neither cleansed by walking nor by working. His complete salvation is wrought by divine forces and agencies. "The blood of Jesus Christ His Son cleanseth us from all sin."

Another popular error entertained by many prominent scholars of this age is the notion that this state of entire purity is attained by growth. All growth is by accretion. In all the phenomena of growth the vital forces proceed according to the general law of appropriation. All cleansing is by elimination — by removal. The processes and purposes of growth are entirely different from the processes and purposes of cleansing. Growth is for the enlargement of the organism, for maturity and fruitage. Christian growth is for character building, for usefulness in the Master's vineyard — growth is a complex process, and involves the obedience and co-operation of a responsible being; it requires time in which the active forces may produce their desired result. Cleansing is a vital part of man's salvation; and salvation, in all its stages, is God's own personal work and is done at once. Neither time nor growth can in any sense, enter as factors into man's salvation. But growth is not conceivable without time, though time is never a worker. Time gives opportunity for the vital forces to work, it affords space in which the living organisms of plants or animals or spiritual beings, may receive the prepared material from without, and build it into their own respective tissues.

The student of physiology discovers that at every pulsation of the heart millions of the red corpuscles of the blood lose their individuality, but by being thus expended they preserve and perpetuate the organism of the body. This mysterious process is under the control and direction of the life-principle; it is the means by which the life, that invisible and incomprehensible but accomplished architect, which inhabits all living organisms, builds and keeps in repair, each intricate structure. Man's daily food, the air he breathes and the water he drinks, all combine to vitalize and replenish the blood, and send it forward on its energizing mission, so that as the blood goes on its ceaseless round of duty, every part of the system takes up and appropriates to its own use, the elements it requires for its own renovation and growth. Thus we preceive that as man does not grow by labor, but by the use of wholesome food, neither do Christians become spiritually strong by religious exercise. As in the material world men live, and are healthy and strong, able to endure the vicissitudes of heat and cold, able to perform almost unlimited toil because they have an abundance of wholesome food and a pure atmosphere, even so is the spiritual sustentation from food, and not from labor; and from healthful environments and proper conditions come forth those grand achievements in the field of Christian activity, that have filled the earth with light and life and power, through all the ages.

If we examine the physical organism, we discover that as the circulating current approaches each organ of the body, the prepared particles that are in the blood leave the stream and mingle with the substance of the organ, and are incorporated into its own nature and essence. If you place a fractured bone or an open wound under a powerful glass during the process of healing, you will discover that as the prepared particles leave the stream of blood, the bones and muscles and nerves are in a state of expectancy, and at once receive and assimilate the portion designed for each delicate tissue. "If it were not for this wise arrangement of divine providence, the constant friction of life, the perpetual toil, the consuming care, would soon exhaust the vital forces of the system and send the entire human family to premature decay."

The Christian's life is "hid with Christ in God." The Christian sustenance is the divine fellowship, and that it may not cease to invigorate and energize him, he is commanded to walk in the light of personal fellowship with God, to dwell in Christ, who poured His life-blood into the veins of an expiring world to rescue it from the dominion of sin, and who now gives Himself in the fullness of His purity and strength to every obedient believer who walks in the light of His fellowship.

Christians in their individual capacity are the conserving forces of the moral world. They are to invigorate society and preserve it from decay, but their power and energy would soon become exhausted if they were not constantly replenished from on high.

Every day, Christians have to stand in the presence of the enemies of Jesus; they have to mingle in the activities of business and social life; they have to do with politics; they have to go to the fields and shops and marts of trade. Every breath of worldly atmosphere chills them; every unconverted person, each backslider, every indifferent or formal professor with whom they come in contact, takes away from them a portion of their vitality. And in order to preserve them from spiritual death and avert disaster to the church, and enable them to continually exert an influence for good, they must receive a continuous supply of power and energy by an unbroken fellowship with Him who is "the way, the truth and the life."

The significance of this text is seen only in the light of these truths. Living Christians only, are able to walk; obedient Christians cheerfully and gladly walk in the light, and honest inquirers walk up to the advance line of the light they have received; and walking in this fellowship God fulfills His promise, and the purified Christian shares in the rapture of Bernard Barton, who has taught us to sing —

> "Walk in the light, so shalt thou know
> That fellowship of love,
> His Spirit only can bestow
> Who reigns in light above.
>
> "Walk in the light, and thou shalt own
> Thy heart made truly His
> Who dwells in cloudless light enthroned,
> In Whom no darkness is.
>
> "Walk in the light, and thou shalt find
> Thy darkness passed away,
> Because that light on thee has shined,
> In which is perfect day.
>
> "Walk in the light, and e'en the tomb
> No fearful shades shall wear;
> Glory shall chase away its gloom,
> For Christ hath conquered there.
>
> "Walk in the light, thy path shall be
> Peaceful, serene and bright,—
> For God, by grace, shall dwell in thee,
> And God Himself is light."

III.

A DIVIDED CONGREGATION.

JOHN THOMPSON, PHILADELPHIA, PA.

"For there were many in the congregation that were not sanctified" (2 Chron. 30 : 17).

THERE never was a time when both secular and religious papers abounded with reports of meetings as now. Reports of meetings of corporations, reports of political meetings, reports of business meetings and reports of religious meetings, are published extensively and read with avidity. It is especially true that reports of sermons and religious meetings were never so numerous in secular papers as now. My memory takes me back to a time when religious papers were very few compared with the present, and when it was a rare thing to see a sermon or extensive reports of religious meetings in secular papers.

Now the daily as well as the weekly papers are keenly on the lookout, not only for sermons, but they must also furnish a photograph of the minister. They not only want to tell who preached the sermon, but they want to give a glimpse of the preacher. In this way religious information is disseminated as never before. The text that I have announced forms a part of a report of a religious meeting that was held a great while ago. Reports of most religious meetings are by human authority, but this meeting was reported by divine authority. Most reports of religious meetings are read and then cast away, but, by divine authority, the report of this meeting was to be preserved for all time to come, so that it might be read and studied and digested by all coming generations.

We will invite your attention —

I. TO THE MEETING.

1. *It was an extra meeting.* The time for holding the regular Passover service had passed without being observed. This was an evidence of the lukewarmness and backslidden condition of both priests and people, but especially of the priests. The heart of Hezekiah was greatly stirred at this state of things, which led him to call an extra meeting.

Churches that are cold and lukewarm, backslidden and dead, are seldom quickened and resurrected by the ordinary means of grace. Ministers and church members who oppose extra efforts for the quickening of dead churches, as a rule, are disappointed. When trade becomes dull, business men and merchants put on the pressure and make extra efforts to give a new impetus to business. They are willing for anything that is honorable rather than stagnation or bankruptcy. Surely, ministers and churches should not be less wise and energetic than men of this world. If your church is lukewarm and dead, by all means have extra meetings. Some seem to think that, in order to revive a lukewarm and backslidden church, they should secure a popular preacher, who will attract the crowds. Others think they would get along all right if they only had a new church. Still others think that the church would come up all right, if they only had first-class singers to attract the young people. Hezekiah did not allow himself to be switched off by any of these subterfuges. He saw that what the church needed was extra salvation services, and, in great earnestness, he sat himself to work in arranging for such services as would reclaim the backslidden and enliven the lukewarm, and right well did he succeed, as will be shown by the results.

2. *The call was for a seven days' meeting.* Seven days of extra services. As far as possible, all business was suspended. It was seven days in succession of all-day services. It would be a courageous thing now for a pastor to urge his church to suspend all business as far as possible for seven days of revival services, but if he could succeed in having his church enter into an arrangement of this kind, he would be quite sure at the end of the seven days, to find himself the pastor of an enlivened and resurrected church.

3. *It was a protracted meeting.* The meeting was called for seven days, but at the end of the seven days, they were all of one accord, in the thought that the meeting should not close, and by unanimous consent they resolved to continue it another week. Our extra services should be protracted until a glorious victory is gained. Sometimes there is a yielding to discouragement, and a meeting is closed just when victory is near at hand. If seven days is not enough, continue

another seven days, and if need be, still another seven days. Resolve to fight it out on this line. Stand by your guns until the enemy surrenders. Victory will be the reward of perseverance.

4. *It was a consecration meeting.* Hezekiah's text was, "Yield yourselves unto the Lord" (verse 8). Yielding ourselves to God takes in all that is implied in an unconditional, perpetual and absolute consecration of ourselves to God. That one word, "yield," if taken in its full meaning, is nothing short of a desperate consecration of ourselves to God. Hezekiah certainly meant nothing short of this. This was the subject of *the* sermon of this meeting. This is something more than that aimless consecration of which we hear so much in the so-called consecration meetings of these times. A thorough, genuine, desperate consecration is the essential, preparatory step to entire sanctification. A consecration that does not have for its aim entire sanctification, is defective and comes short of the consecration that God requires of us. No unprejudiced one will read the account of this meeting, without being satisfied that the aim of Hezekiah was to lead the people of God into the Canaan of heart purity.

II. WE WILL CALL ATTENTION TO THE CONGREGATION.

1. *The congregation was large.* "A very great congregation" (verse 13). There was nothing exclusive in this meeting. All were invited. No one could say, "This meeting is not for me." The postmen who

were sent out to give the invitation were authorized to invite everybody to attend this meeting, and a great many accepted the invitation. There was something of novelty in this call, and probably some were moved by curiosity to attend. Some probably went from a sense of duty, fearing to disobey the call. Others felt the need of such a meeting, and felt what it would be to them. Well, it is a good thing to have a good congregation, not because a large congregation is essential to a good meeting but because a large congregation affords a greater opportunity for usefulness.

2. *It was a congregation of professors of religion.* Everyone who attended the meeting was a member of some one of the tribes, and all the tribes were professors of religion. Some were very inconsistent, but still they held on to their profession. Some were lukewarm, but still they had not given up their profession. Some were backsliders, but still they were church members. Others, like Hezekiah, were not only professors, but they were possessors, and glad to be privileged to attend such a meeting. They who hunger and thirst after righteousness are sure to be on hand when they are invited to attend one of Hezekiah's meetings.

3. *It was a congregation of heroes.* This meeting, as might have been expected, met with strong opposition, and it was just that kind of opposition that always intimidates the faint-hearted. "So the posts passed from city to city through the country of Ephraim and Manasseh, even unto Zebulun; but they

laughed them to scorn, and mocked them " (verse 10). Timid souls cannot bear to be laughed at, and their courage fails when they are mocked and ridiculed. The devil has laughed many a poor soul out of his religion, but those who attended this meeting were not to be moved by the scoffs of the enemies of God and men.

The demand of the times is for men and women who cannot be laughed out of their convictions. The cause of Christ is in need of heroes who have in them the stuff out of which martrys are made. We want men and women who will meekly and humbly, but firmly and persistently, stand up for pure and undefiled religion. Courage, my brother! Courage, my sister! Get on the whole armor, and stand up for Jesus.

The opposition to this meeting came from professors of religion, the very ones who should have been most earnest for its success. But we must keep in mind that all professors are not possessors. If people are only professors, and not in the enjoyment of experimental religion, they sometimes become the most bitter persecutors of the saints of the Most High. John Wesley's most bitter persecutors were professors of religion, and we do not forget that our Christ was murdered by professors of religion. Many of the saints of God have been condemned and burned at the stake by persons professing Godliness. If we are walking in the narrow way, we must not be surprised if cold-hearted, lukewarm, backslidden professors become our persecutors.

If we should meet with opposition from this source,

let us heed the words of our blessed Christ, "Love your enemies, bless them that curse you, do good to them that hate you, and pray for them which despitefully use you and persecute you."

4. *It was a divided congregation.* How many churches have been rent and torn asunder by internal quarrels and dissensions. But it is not of such divisions that I wish to speak now. The division to which I wish to call your attention is a division of religious character. This is the division spoken of in our text, "There were many in the congregation who were not sanctified." No difference what interpretation is given to the word "sanctified" in the text, the charge is of a very serious character. Let us bear in mind that it is the Lord Himself who brings this charge against this congregation. This, of course, magnifies its importance. It was the great God who said, "There were many in the congregation that were not sanctified." The Lord Himself draws this line, and He makes but two classes — the sanctified and the unsanctified. Let us get the thought clearly in our minds that this is the Lord's own classification. It is not said that none in the congregation were sanctified, but that many were not sanctified. Of course, the sanctified were in the minority, as is the case in most congregations. If we would be pure and holy, we must be content to be associated with the minority, but it is much better to be with the minority, and be right, than with the majority and be disloyal to God. Christ warned His followers not to go with the multitude to do evil. The Lord has not promised to be

with the multitude, but with those who walk in the narrow way.

Possibly the Lord is still looking down on many churches, and giving utterance to the lamentable language of the text, "There are many in the congregation that are not sanctified." How is it in the congregation where you worship? How is it with you personally? Are you sanctified? I hope the time will come when we can say, "*Many* in the congregation were sanctified."

The Lord hasten the day. Let all who love our Lord Jesus Christ stop reading long enough to give utterance to a good hearty "Amen!"

III. THE RESULT OF THIS MEETING.

This is the all-important question in reference to all of our religious services. When the doxology has been sung and the benediction pronounced, the question of importance is, Well, what has been accomplished? In reference to this meeting, we notice —

1. *The scoffers.* In reference to them the sacred historian gives a sad account. Their end was indeed dreadful, but just what might have been expected. The tribes that scoffed and mocked and made sport of this meeting, were soon taken captive by the king of Assyria. This, we are sure, would never have been permitted if they had been true and loyal to God. Those who ridicule pure religion and make sport of the saints of God, would do well to remember the doom of these scoffers.

2. *The prayers of the congregation were answered.* "And their prayers came up to His holy dwelling place, even unto heaven" (ver. 27). Very many of the congregation probably did not attend the prayer meeting, but the faithful few were on hand from day to day, and God hearkened and heard their prayers. God not only answered their prayers in behalf of themselves, but in behalf of the lukewarm and backslidden.

3. *The priests were blessed.* Special mention is made of this. Again and again we are told of the rich blessings that came on the priests. For this Hezekiah prayed perseveringly and earnestly. "Hezekiah prayed for them, saying, The good Lord pardon every one" (verse 18). "The Lord hearkened to Hezekiah" (verse 20). When the priests were blessed, they did not hesitate to let it be known. "The priests praised the Lord day by day, singing with loud instruments unto the Lord" (verse 21). They not only praised the Lord, but they kept it up from day to day. When they once got started there seemed to be no stopping them. When the priests were blessed they were not afraid of a little noise. It was then that they got out their loud instruments. The time to get out our loud instruments is when God sends His rich blessings on our souls. When the church is cold and lukewarm, the clamor is for ritualistic services. Then the beautiful instruments are in demand. But when God visits the church with rich blessings, then there is a demand for the loud instruments. If the loud instruments have been laid aside,

let us get them out and have them ready for use when the showers of blessings shall come on the church.

It looks as though some of the priests failed to get into the spirit of the meeting. It is said that "a great number of the priests sanctified themselves" (verse 24). A great number in this case does not mean all. Possibly some of the dignified ones took a back seat and contented themselves with criticisms of the meeting. Poor fellows, no blessing came to their souls, and, of course, they were not made a blessing to others. A sainted man of God, now in heaven, used to pray, "Lord, bless me, that I may be a blessing to others."

4. *After the priests were blessed the work went on gloriously.* Let it be remembered that, if the work of God does not prosper in our churches, it is not always the fault of the preacher. Sometimes it is true that the preachers are to blame. At other times it is the fault of the hearers, and sometimes the fault is with both preachers and hearers. In this case it is quite clear that the preachers were stumbling-blocks in the way of the revival of God's work. When the priests were blessed the work went on gloriously. So it would be in some other congregations. If the priests were baptized the people would fall in line and dead churches would come to life.

5. *The meeting seems to have closed with a praise service.* "So there was great joy in Jerusalem; for since the time of Solomon, the son of David, king of Israel, there was not the like in Jerusalem" (verse 26).

This sounds like the closing service of a good old-fashioned camp meeting.

Those of us who were not present at that meeting may be permitted, even at this late date, to raise our shouts of praise with the shouts of Hezekiah for this glorious meeting.

IV

CHRISTIAN PERFECTION, EXPLAINED AND DEFENDED.

REV. W. McDONALD, BOSTON, MASS.

"Therefore leaving the principles of the doctrine of Christ, let us go on unto perfection; not laying again the foundation of repentance from dead works, and of faith toward God,

"Of the doctrine of baptisms, and of laying on of hands, and of resurrection of the dead, and of eternal judgment.

"And this will we do, if God permit" (Heb. 6:1-3).

DELITZCH, the great German exegete, has rendered the first verse of this text thus, "Wherefore, leaving the first elementary doctrines of Christ, let us go on unto perfection."

It may be properly said, that what a foundation is to a building, and what an alphabet is to a language, these elementary doctrines of Christ are to the perfection at which we are to aim. But a foundation is not a building, though an essential part of it, and without which the building could not be carried on to a safe completion. An alphabet is not a language, though no language can be perfected without it. So these elementary doctrines of Christ are valuable mainly as putting us into the Christian way, and giving us the elements of Christian life and character.

I. Let us proceed to a consideration of these

CHRISTIAN PERFECTION. 57

"principles," and the perfection to which they lead us. These principles are here given under six heads, viz., "repentance from dead works," "faith towards God," "the doctrine of baptisms," "the laying on of hands," "the resurrection of the dead," and "eternal judgment."

These must not be understood as embracing all the "principles of the doctrine of Christ," but a careful consideration of them will reveal the fact that they embrace examples of them in every department of life. For instance, "repentance from dead works, and faith towards God," relate to the *inner* spiritual life. The "doctrine of baptisms," whatever that may mean, and "the laying on of hands," whatever that may include, have reference to what may be denominated the *ceremonial* life of the Christian, for religion has its ceremonials as well as its doctrines.

"The resurrection of the dead," and "eternal judgment," relate to the *future* life of a believer, so that together they cover the inner life, the outer life and the future life of the Christian; and beyond this there is no life.

We are exhorted to "leave" these principles, or "elementary doctrines," and "go on unto perfection."

1. We are not to understand by this that we are to abandon these principles, so as no longer to hold them as essential doctrines of the Christian faith, or teach them as gospel requirements, or practice them in our lives.

It will always be necessary to urge upon all classes the necessity of repentance and faith. In the present state of the church it will be needful to press upon believers the importance of church ordinances, and to thunder in the ears of saint and sinner the doctrine of "the resurrection of the dead and eternal judgment." We must never cease to hold, teach and practice these elementary truths, for without this the gateway to perfection is never found.

2. But by leaving these principles I understand that we are not to make them the end of our religious attainments.

The great majority of professed believers never get beyond the foundation, if, indeed, they succeed in holding to that. They never get beyond the alphabet. After years of experience, they seem never to have grasped the thought clearly, that "it is better farther on." They talk and sing of the time of their "first love," and even sigh for the days of their espousal, and mourn that they are not as happy as when they were first converted. They sing —

> "I then rode on the sky,
> Freely justified I,
>   Nor did envy Elijah his seat:
> My glad soul mounted higher
> In a chariot of fire,
>   And the world it was under my feet."

But now the wail is often heard —

> "Oh, that I were as heretofore,
>   When warm in my first love."

This is, but ought not to be, the average experience of the Christian church. But the gospel has something better for discouraged, sin-baffled souls than this. They are to come up higher.

3. By leaving these elementary doctrines, I understand that we are to make them the stepping-stones to a higher Christian life. These principles are furnished for the purpose of lifting the soul higher and aiding honest believers in the pursuit of holiness.

Of what use is a foundation except to erect upon it a superstructure? Indeed, if it is not so utilized, it becomes worthless, and often worse than worthless; for, "if the salt have lost its savor, it is thenceforth good for nothing but to be cast out and trodden under foot of men."

Of what possible use is an alphabet except to study and perfect a language? Were we able to repeat the alphabets of all the babbling tongues of earth and stopped there, it would be labor lost. I know of no value that a primary Christian experience can be to a Christian except to put him in possession of a power to conquer sin in his nature; and if he does not employ it for that purpose, sin will conquer him. It is a sad mistake to suppose that an elementary Christian experience secures to the believer the "white stone" and the "new name."

As John Wesley says, " Something more will have to be done for them before they are prepared for a holy heaven." I do not say that a justified soul will be lost, but, if the Word of God is to be believed, that "without holiness no man shall see the Lord," unless believers move forward to the attainment of "that sanctification without which no man shall see the Lord," they will never see Him in His glory.

Mr. Fletcher says, "Should it be objected that no Christian is safe till he has obtained Christian perfection, we reply that all Christian believers are safe who either stand in it [Christian perfection], or are pressing after it. And if they do neither, we are prepared to prove that they rank among fallen believers."

We therefore plead with professing Christians to begin the march for holiness, or Christian perfection. Without this there is no safety for any soul. This is —

> "The land of rest from inbred sin —
> The land of perfect holiness."

II. Having briefly noted the "principles of the doctrine of Christ," and what is implied in leaving them, let us now consider that *perfection* to which these principles conduct us.

The term *perfection* has greatly troubled many honest minds. It is a term offensive to many, and objected to by most, and all from a misapprehension of its meaning.

"A single hour," says Mr. Wesley to a friend, "spent in free conversation, would convince you that none can rationally or Scripturally say anything against the perfection I have preached for thirty years." "Let Christian perfection appear in its own shape," he continues, "and who can fight against it? It must be disguised before it can be opposed. It must be covered with a bear skin first, or even the wild beasts of the people will scarce be induced to worry it."

We are told that this term describes a religious attainment not possible in this life, and the urging it as a possible experience becomes a stumbling-block to honest people. If that be so, it is to be regretted, and the more so because (we speak it reverently) the Holy Spirit is responsible for putting it in our way. It is not a term of human invention. It came through holy men who were inspired of God to write it. It would be well for such objectors to make their objections at headquarters. We are not responsible for the mistake, if it be a mistake.

Mr. Wesley very forcibly says, "As to the word perfection, it is Scriptural, therefore neither you nor I can in conscience object to it unless we would send the Holy Spirit to school and teach Him to speak who made the tongue." It would seem that He, who understands all the possibilities of human nature and its capabilities of enjoyment, has employed the term *perfection* more frequently to describe a state of religious experience than any other single word. For the term perfection and its equivalents are employed with greater frequency in the Scriptures than any other single term in this connection.

We are gravely told that there is nothing perfect in this world, and that we are not to look for perfection in man. But such people talk of things which they claim are perfect. The well-formed beast is pronounced perfect. The flower with its brilliant hues, we say is perfect. The faultless gem that sparkles in the sunlight is pronounced perfect. Nature, from the "cedar that grows on Lebanon to the hyssop that springs from under the wall," presents a charming perfection. Men claim that the products of their shops and factories are perfect. Merchants pronounce their goods perfect. Music has its perfect cadence and its perfect cord. Mathematics has its perfect number, and grammar its perfect tense. Why, then, should not salvation have its perfect love?

I was seated in a parlor conversing with a friend who repudiated the idea of perfection, saying that there was nothing perfect in this world. After a little diversion, I drew his attention to a portrait of himself hanging on the wall. I remarked, "You have a most excellent portrait. It is a striking likeness. What is the judgment of your friends in regard to it?" He replied, "They all pronounce it a *perfect* likeness." "It is true then," I said, "that there is something *perfect* in this life." It is common to say of a likeness which bears a strong resemblance to the original, that it is a perfect likeness.

It is equally proper to say that a faith which does not doubt God but trusts Him implicitly in all things, is perfect faith; humility which ascribes all glory to God, taking none to itself, is perfect humility; meekness which saves from all irritability is perfect meekness; resignation which says, exalted or abased, "Not as I will, but as Thou wilt," is perfect resignation; love which expels all hatred and tormenting fear, is perfect love. These graces are simply *complete*, not in the sense of being *mature*, so as not to admit of increase, but complete up to the full measure of our present light and capacity. It is simply to "love God with all the heart and our neighbor as ourselves."

There are several mistakes made in regard to Christian perfection.

1. Some confound it with *absolute perfection.* This is done by many, who we must believe are honest, though misguided. They insist that we teach *absolute* perfection. A thousand times we have insisted that no such doctrine is ever taught; that absolute perfection belongs alone to God. It is called *absolute* because nothing can be added to it. It is complete in *quality* and *quantity*, and is underived. Christian perfection is derived, and wholly dependent on the merits of Jesus. It is like the perfection of God in *quality*, but not in *quantity*. We are to be "perfect as our Father in heaven is perfect," and "As He is, so are we, in this world." A drop of water is like the ocean, and yet not the ocean; so Christian perfection may be like God's; in quality they may be the same, for we may have the "mind of Christ," but the latter admits of eternal increase.

Absolute perfection implies freedom from errors, mistakes and every form of ignorance. "But the highest perfection to which man can attain, while the soul dwells in the body, does not exclude ignorance and error and a thousand infirmities" (Wesley). It is simply moral perfection, having its seat in the heart, not in the intellect. Hence it may exist with a thousand mistakes and infirmities. There is not an angel in heaven who is absolutely perfect; God alone is perfect in this sense.

The term, when properly understood, has none of the objectionable characteristics which some imagine. They are more imaginary than real. A simple definition of perfection will settle this question.

Richard Hooker, an old English divine, defines perfection thus; "We count those things perfect which want nothing requisite to the end whereunto they were instituted." In other words, if a thing answers the end for which it was made, it is perfect. The machinery which propels a railroad train, and the machinery which keeps in motion a thousand spindles in a cotton factory, and the machinery which runs my watch are very unlike, and yet in their places they are perfect. They do what they were made to do. But change them, and you would witness great imperfection in their application. In like manner, man, for the end for which God made him, may be perfect, but for any other work or place he may be an imperfect adjustment. He could not be, in his present state, a perfect angel or a perfect Adam, but he may be "perfect in love," for "herein is our love made perfect," and this was the end for which God made him, to love Him with all his heart.

Take another definition of perfection. We say that is perfect which simply has what properly belongs to it and nothing else. As an illustration, take the lamb which was offered in sacrifice. It must be a perfect lamb. Its perfection consisted in its being free from all blemishes, and not lacking in any of its parts or members. "It might have been fatter or leaner than some other lamb, younger or older, larger or smaller, but still the test of perfection was, that it had what belonged to a lamb, and nothing else." So the Christian is perfect in that he has what belongs to a Christian and nothing else. He is not in his religious character a compound; he is not a perfect angel, as we have before said; he may not be possessed of the same measure of grace that another enjoys, or manifest the same degree of external sanctity in word and look; but if the one test of perfection is found in him, if his heart is emptied of sin and filled with love, and love only, if he "loves God with *all* his heart and his neighbor as himself," he has "perfected holiness in the fear of the Lord."

2. Another mistake is made, in regarding Christian perfection as a blessing attained subsequent to entire sanctification, and confounding it with maturity or ripeness of Christian character. It is proper to say that this is not the Methodistic view of the subject. From Wesley down, Methodists have always held that entire sanctification and Christian perfection are one and the same. A recent writer says, "Not a few well-meaning people confound the two [entire sanctification and Christian perfection], and speak of them as identical, and use terms describing them as interchangeable. Hence follow confusion, distraction and fanaticism" (Bishop Merrill, in *Zion's Herald*). He further says, "The old divines, and the broader and clearer view — the real Methodistic view — escape this baneful and ruinous perversion of precious truth by distinguishing between purity and perfection as between purity and maturity!"

We are forced to say that this is a baseless assumption. The Methodist fathers never did any such thing as their writings clearly prove.

Mr. Wesley says, " Entire sanctification, or Christian perfection, is neither more nor less than pure love; love expelling sin and governing both the heart and life of a child of God." Here " Christian perfection " and the "expulsion of sin from the heart" are identical. " This," says Mr. Wesley, " is the doctrine which we preached from the beginning, and which we preach to this day."

He further says, " Christian perfection is that love of God and our neighbor which implies deliverance from all sin." Here " Christian perfection " and " deliverance from sin," which occur at the time the soul is entirely sanctified, are declared by Wesley to be one and the same.

Dr. Adam Clark says, " When I speak of the purification of the heart, or the doctrine of Christian perfection, I use sanctification in the sense in which it has been generally understood among Methodists." Here " Christian perfection," " purification " and " sanctification," are used interchangeably.

Richard Watson says, " We have spoken of justification, adoption, regeneration and the witness of the Holy Spirit, and we now proceed to another as distinctly marked and as graciously promised in the Holy Scriptures. This is the entire sanctification or the *perfected holiness* of believers."

Here the " entire sanctification " and the " perfected holiness of believers " are spoken of as one and the same. Mr. Fletcher says, "If Christian perfection implies a forsaking all *inward* as well as outward sin; and if true repentance is a grace 'whereby we forsake sin,' it follows that, to attain Christian perfection, we must so follow our Lord's evangelical precept, 'Repent, for the kingdom of heaven is at hand,' as to leave no sin, no bosom sin, no heart sin, no indwelling sin, unrepented of, and consequently, unforsaken."

Here Mr. Fletcher is speaking of ridding the heart of all "sin," all "indwelling sin," all "bosom sins," all "inward and outward sin;" and all this in order to secure "Christian perfection." But all these, says the writer to which we refer, are removed when the soul is entirely sanctified, and this, he claims, is not perfection. Let it be understood that Mr. Fletcher is speaking of repentance in believers and not unbelievers. Methodism has never made a distinction between purity and perfection, and whenever the term *maturity* has been employed, which is seldom, it has always had reference to entire sanctification.

All believers in the doctrine of Christian perfection, believe also in the maturity of Christian character. But they believe that it is a gradual, steady, progressive work for all time, and perhaps for all eternity.

A pure heart is one in which the graces are unmixed. Love is without hate, faith is without doubt, humility is without pride, meekness is without anger. *Maturity* has the sense of ripeness by time and natural growth. In this state love is not more pure but more intensified, faith is not freer from doubt but of greater compass and force.

Purity is a proper preparation for growth; *maturity* is the gradual perfecting of growth. Purity is instantaneous, *maturity* is gradual. *Purity* respects quality, *maturity* quantity.

"The heart may be cleansed from all sin," says Bishop Hamline, "while the graces are immature, and the cleansing is a preparation for their unembarassed and rapid growth."

If maturity is a special blessing, to be sought and enjoyed subsequent to entire sanctification, then there are three blessings instead of two, viz., justification, entire sanctification and perfection. But who knows when maturity is gained, and what it is when secured? Are we to grow in grace until we can grow no more? Fruit, which is mature, has reached the end of its growth. Is it true that an attainment may be reached from which no further progress in grace can be made? This would seem to be the doctrine taught by these "maturity advocates."

But there is no attainment in grace, no growth in maturity, beyond which there is no progress. The end will never come when it shall be said, "Thus far shalt thou go and no farther."

3. Still another mistake is made in regard to the subject of Christian perfection, and it is widespread. It is, that our perfection is in Christ, and not in ourselves. That our perfection is not *of* ourselves is true, but to say it is not *in* ourselves is false. Antinomians boast that they are perfect only in Christ, their heavenly Representative, and imperfect in themselves. As He was possessed of perfect humility and love,

they need it not in themselves as they are perfect in His person.

"To avoid this error," says Mr. Fletcher, "be perfect in yourselves, and not in another. Let it fill your own heart and influence your own life; so shall you avoid the delusion of the virgins, who give you to understand that the oil of their perfection is all contained in the sacred vessel which formerly hung on the cross, therefore their salvation is finished; they have oil enough in that rich vessel; manna enough and to spare in that golden pot. Christ's heart was perfect, and therefore their's may safely remain imperfect; yea, full of indwelling sin, till death, the messenger of the bridegroom, come to cleanse them and fill with perfect love at the midnight cry. Delusive hope. Can anything be more absurd than for a sapless, dry branch to fancy that it has sap and moisture enough in the vine which it cumbers? When did Christ ever say, "Have salt in another?" Does He not say, "Take heed that ye be not deceived." "Have salt in yourselves!" Does He not impute the destruction of stony-ground hearers to their "not having root in themselves"? If it was the patient man's comfort that the root of the matter was found in him, is it not deplorable to hear modern believers say, without any explanatory cause, that they have nothing but sin in themselves?

"But," continues this marvelously clear and forceful writer, "while you endeavor to avoid the snare of the Antinomians, do not run into that of the Pharisee, who will have their perfection of themselves; therefore, by their own unevangelical efforts, self-concerted willings and self-described runnings, endeavor to 'raise sparks of their own kindlings, and warm themselves by their own painted fire and fruitless agitations.' Feel your impotence, own that 'no man has quickened' and perfected 'his own soul.' Be content to invite, receive and welcome the light of life, but never to form or engross it."

The Pharisee and the Antinomian are with us. The one class are trying to save themselves, and the other insisting that their salvation was finished on the cross, and they have nothing to do but to believe that fact, and take Christ as their substitute. He being possessed of all virtue and all perfection, while they are full of sin and must remain so till death. What fearful deception!

The gospel clearly teaches that we are made pure by Christ, whose blood is applied by faith, and "cleanseth" us from all unrighteousness."

Having considered the perfection of the text, we desire to call the reader's attention to a single word in the passage — a word over which there has been more or less division of sentiment. It is the preposition, "*unto*." "Let us go on *unto* perfection." We have have been told that the word has the sense of toward; that we are to go on toward perfection; we are to make laudable efforts to secure it, approach it as nearly as possible, but with no expectation of reaching it or enjoying its richness in this life. This would be less unreasonable if we were not commanded to "*be* perfect." "Ye shall therefore *be* perfect as your Father in heaven is perfect." This does not mean to make laudable efforts to be perfect; do the best you can. No, but we are to *be* such — actually possess the grace.

Then it is very clear that the word "*unto*," when properly understood, does not have this sense. It has the sense of starting for and reaching our destination, and abiding there.

Dr. Robinson, the American Greek lexicographer, who is good authority, defines this preposition thus; "It implies *motion upon, to, towards any place or object as a limit, aim, end, with subsequent rest thereupon.*" It means that we are to start for somewhere and get there and rest there when the object is gained.

It is true that in seeking Christian perfection there are approaches to it, and preparations for it, but there comes a time, and it need not be far in the future, when the point is gained and the rest secured. After conversion, then comes the necessity of "light on the pathway of holiness," conviction for the blessing; a full and complete consecration or devotement; simple artless trust in Jesus for the blessing desired. This requires time, but it need not be many days or weeks, for when the soul perceives its need, gives itself wholly to Christ and implicitly trusts Him for a clean heart, it is given in that moment.

When we say that heart purity or Christian perfection is an *instantaneous* blessing, the term instantaneous needs a word of explanation. It is not instantaneous in the sense that the wink of the eye is instantaneous, or a flash of lightning is instantaneous, or the explosion of gun-powder is instantaneous, or the tick of your watch is instantaneous. But it is instantaneous in the sense that a *marriage* is instantaneous. There are preparations for it, and approaches to it, but there comes a time when the officiating party says, "I pronounce you husband and wife." Then the contract is completed, which is done substantially in a moment.

It is instantaneous in the sense that a *death* is instantaneous. A person may be some time dying, but there comes a moment when he passes from life to death. There was a moment when he ceased to live, and the death may properly be called instantaneous. But surely people are not five, ten, or twenty years dying, as Christians profess to be dying to sin. This would be a sad fact in a person's life; and it is equally sad in the Christian life. But death to sin may be at any time when the soul chooses to trust God through Jesus Christ for the soul cleansing power of the blood which cleanseth us from all unrighteousness.

We have considered the doctrine of Christian perfection as held by that great body of Christian believers known as Wesleyan Methodists. This is the Arminian wing of the gospel army. And it is a matter of great joy that the Calvinistic wing is coming, slowly it is true, but coming to see eye to eye on this subject with their Arminian brethren.

Thousands of them have entered into the land of "perfect love," and are reaping the rich fruits in a sweet and joyous experience. They no longer sing —

> "'Tis a point I long to know,
> Oft it causes anxious thought,
> Do I love the Lord or no,
> Am I his or am I not?"

But with Wesley they sing,

> "'Tis done, Thou dost this moment save,
> With full salvation bless,
> Redemption through Thy blood I have
> And spotless life and peace."

For this the Church of God should shout,

> "All hail the power of Jesus' name,
> Let angels prostrate fall,
> Bring forth the royal diadem,
> And crown him Lord of all."

The reader will bear with us while we earnestly press one or two reflections.

1. Going on unto perfection is the only safeguard against backsliding.

We do not say that every person will backslide who does not seek definitely the experience of perfect holiness. Some have no special light upon the subject, their minds never having been called to it. They are making earnest efforts to serve God and get to heaven. They are living up to all the light they have. Others have been educated to believe that such an attainment is impossible in the present life. They have considered it more a visionary ideal, a fancy of a few extravagant persons, than a possible religious attainment. Many of these people are good, and are doing the best they know. They are loyal to God, as they understand it. But there are tens of thousands who have come, time and again, face to face with this subject. They have seen it from time to time to be their duty to love God with all their hearts. They have made special efforts at different times to seek entire sanctification. They are convinced that such an attainment is possible; that Jesus can save to the uttermost; that His blood can cleanse from all sin. They have finally decided, however, that they cannot pay the price; that a profession of holiness means ostracism and the entire abandonment of many things that professors of religion practice and which they themselves enjoy, and they have concluded to give up all special effort to seek heart purity, and move on with others at " the poor dying rate " common around them. These should, and might have entered into the Canaan of perfect love, but they have returned to the wilderness, and are spending their time in sinning and repenting, and more of their time in sinning than in repenting. Holiness has become more or less distasteful, if not repulsive to them, and they do not enjoy, as formerly, the fellowship of the holy. What a defeat they have sustained ; what a rich treasure has slipped away from them, and what a future awaits them!

It is said that when Hannibal had conquered the Romans on the plains of Italy, nothing seemed needed but a spirit of determined perseverance to have given him posession of Rome itself. But, flushed with their victory, the Carthaginians spent their time in rioting upon the spoils of their enemies instead of pushing their conquests. During these scenes of riot the hardy Roman gathered up his scattered forces and returned with greater power and swept the invaders from the field.

Many of these souls have at times gained some victories, but not employing them in "going on unto perfection," they have been defeated and swept from the position they formerly occupied. They are now on the retreat and conquered by the foe. How will these souls meet their final responsibility? The fearful charge will be heard, "Ye knew your duty, and did it not." The country is full and the church is swarming with this class of backsliders, for they can be nothing else.

Such persons should call a halt —

> "Their way is dark and leads to death,
> Why will they persevere?"

Can we say no word to arouse them? Let the sorrows of the garden, the buffetings at Pilate's bar, the agonies of the cross, the intercessions of Him who ever liveth, move such to return to their first love.

The church languishes because of such members, and the ways of Zion mourn because so few come to the feast of full salvation.

Then many, once walking in the pure light, are now in darkness. The pure gold has become dim. They have not the peace they once had. Some great evil has overtaken them — some sin in an evil hour has tripped them and they have fallen. They do not want to confess that they have lost the grace which was once their chief joy. If such remain where they are, the certainty is that they will drift further away and never return. Resolve, fallen one, to break with sin now and forever, and give your soul no rest until Christ is again enthroned in your heart and your life is again devoted to God. Renew your old-time efforts and you will find Jesus ready — more than ready — to receive you and make you all His own.

2. Going on unto perfection is the most efficient method of promoting the whole work of God. God has organized the Christian ministry for this end. "He gave some apostles, and some evangelists, and some teachers, and some pastors," for the special end of "perfecting the saints," and for the "work of the ministry." And when the ministry do not devote themselves to their special work there is little or no real success.

"Let all our preachers," says Mr. Wesley, "make a point to preach of perfection to believers, strongly, constantly, explicitly." "When Christian perfection is not strongly and explicitly preached, there is seldom any remarkable blessing from God, and consequently little addition to the society and little life in the members of it."

"Speak and spare not. Let not regard for any man induce you to betray the truth of God. Till you press believers to expect full salvation now, you must not look for any revival." "I see where this is not done the believers grow dead and cold."

These are the words of a wise and holy man — a man of vast experience and extensive observation. And facts everywhere confirm this testimony.

Let the command be heard all along the line, from all the ramparts of Zion, "Forward, march!" Let the pursuit of holiness become general, then shall the church become the light of the world, and we shall all come "in the unity of the faith — to the stature of the fullness of Christ, to a perfect man in Christ Jesus."

"Fly swifter round, ye wheels of time,
And bring the welcome day."

V.

SUFFERING AS CHRISTIANS.

G. W. BRINDELL, ELDORA, IA.

"If any man suffer as a Christian, let him not be ashamed; but let him glorify God on this behalf" (1 Peter 4:16).

Though the word *Christian* is found but three times in the sacred Scriptures, and notwithstanding the fact that in the first centuries of this era it was a term of special reproach, to-day it is a term of surpassing honor. To be entitled now to bear that name is a privilege beyond the highest titles of nobility known in this world — connecting us indeed with Him who is *King* of kings and *Lord* of lords.

And yet strange as it may seem, the term in the Scriptures as well as the character it portrays is identified with special sufferings.

It is remarkable how much is found in the first letter of the Apostle Peter on this subject. "For this is thankworthy [worthy of thanks], if a man for conscience toward God endure grief, suffering wrongfully" (2:19). "But and if ye suffer for righteousness' sake, happy are ye: and be not afraid of their terror, neither be troubled" (3:14). "Beloved, think it not strange concerning the fiery trial which is to try you as though some strange thing happened unto you: but rejoice, inasmuch as ye are partakers of Christ's sufferings; that, when His glory shall be revealed, ye may be glad also with exceeding joy. If ye be reproached for the name of Christ, happy are ye; for the spirit of glory and of God resteth upon you: on their part He is evil spoken of, but on your part He is glorified. But let none of you suffer as a murderer, or as a thief, or as an evil-doer, or as a busybody [meddler, R. V.] in other mens' matters. Yet if any man suffer as a Christian, let him not be ashamed; but let him glorify God on this behalf" (4 : 12–16).

Now assuming that this letter is inspired by the Holy Ghost, what instant relief and immense comfort will be experienced by the hosts of God's little ones who are "reproached," and "evil spoken of," and who suffer wrongfully not for "evil doing, but for righteousness' sake." For while it is true that Christians escape the pains and penalties of wrong doing, they are here taught to expect special sufferings and even fiery trials incident to and resultant from the Christian life and testimony in this world. And so far from grieving or fretting because of these sufferings, all these texts summon them to rejoice and to glorify God in the midst of the sufferings, assuring them of present happiness — "happy are ye" — together with gladness and exceeding joy when his glory shall be revealed.

Now in this text observe :

1. *Christians are admonished and forewarned.* The oft-repeated cautions already quoted imply that the church of that day was in danger of being misled into the belief that they had erred in espousing Christianity, seeing that so much opposition and so many trials were

so soon encountered. So far from it, he is admonished not to be ashamed, but rather to glorify God in this behalf.

These are empty words and meaningless caution and counsel to all who fall below the standard of "*Christian*." By this word the apostle evidently means much more than the generic term by which Christian nations or communities are distinguished from Jewish, Pagan or Mohammedan. All the texts quoted point to one now possessing the spirit of Christ, changed into the same image, truly converted and born of God; a man changed in character, in social and business life and habit, in his associates, in his themes and methods of conversation; one not of the world, chosen out of the world and one whom the world therefore hates. And such were Peter and his fellow-disciples whom our Lord forewarned, informing them that the time would come when those in authority would think they were doing God service by putting them to death. The true *animus* of the world toward real Christians is revealed in our Lord's wonderful sermon on the mount; *vide* Matt. 5. Here He pronounces beatitudes on the poor in spirit, on them that mourn, the meek, on those that hunger and thirst after righteousness, on the merciful, the pure in heart and the peace-makers.

Now the thoughtful listener or reader must be prepared for a great surprise. Will not the real Christian, or certainly the one thus advanced, being now "filled with righteousness" and "pure in heart" as well as peaceful in life — will he not discover that at last he at least has conquered a truce with the world and secured its favor and good-will? Nay verily! The eighth beatitude reveals his mistake, and the real spirit and true relation of this world to every genuine Christian. Evidently to emphasize this truth, we have here a double beatitude in a climax to this advanced experience. "Blessed are they which are persecuted for righteousness' sake: for their's is the kingdom of heaven. Blessed are ye, when men shall revile you, and persecute you, and shall say all manner of evil against you falsely for my sake. Rejoice, and be exceeding glad: for great is your reward in heaven: for so persecuted they the prophets which were before you."

From these teachings of our Lord we learn that there is no immunity from suffering, there is no escape from persecution — provided only we are real Christians; and the more pronounced and farther advanced we are in the Christian life, the more certain are we to draw the fire of our ever watchful and malignant foe. All church history may be cited in proof of this position. True, as our Lord foretold his immediate disciples, the authorities condemned them all to a violent death.

The disciple was not above his Master, nor the servant above his Lord. This apostle, Peter, was crucified, James and Paul were beheaded. Only John was known to live to old age and that only after banishment to Patmos and other fiery trials. Church history records ten general persecutions by the Roman emperors, and the catacombs of the imperial city remain to-day eloquent witnesses both of the virulence of the sufferings of the early church, and of the gracious possibility of being peaceful and triumphant in the fiercest fires. But

SUFFERING AS CHRISTIANS.   81

has not all this violent persecution ceased and passed away in this more enlightened period? Verily we have entered upon a wonderfully improved inheritance.

Still it must be admitted that our not remote ancestors were no strangers to persecution. It has not been very long since the martyr-fires of Smithfield were extinguished, since John Bunyan was confined twelve years in Bedford jail for preaching the gospel, since Puritans and Quakers were fined and imprisoned, Roger Williams banished, and Wesleyans stoned and otherwise abused for the same offense. So that we must admit the truth of the statement that we can hardly appreciate the goodly heritage into which we are born.

Nowhere in this country, scarcely anywhere in the civilized world, would any ruler or judge imagine, much less affirm, that he thought he would be doing God service by putting Christians to death. Few are now imprisoned, none are exiled (except by the Czar of Russia) and as a rule in all Protestant Christendom, all are permitted to worship God according to the dictates of their own conscience.

But do these improved conditions imply that the offense of the cross has ceased? Is a decided and thorough Christian an attractive and pleasing spectacle to the world of to-day? Is earnest Christianity the path now to popular favor?

Let the devout and consecrated pastors and people throughout the church of God answer these questions. Ay! all candid observers will have to answer them in the negative. The offence of the cross has not ceased, thorough Christian living is not popular, and that

Scripture is still true, "They that will live godly in Christ Jesus shall suffer persecution."

While the character of the sufferings is modified and none are scourged or crucified or beheaded now, still the same spirit of hate and heartless opposition to the spirit and image of Jesus obtains in and dominates the world that lieth in the wicked one to-day as it did in all the ages past. Hence the value of these Scriptures, and the importance of the admonitions, the warnings and encouragements of these texts from St. Peter's first epistle.

But it is time that we at least mention two distinctions in the sufferings of Christians and worldlings. Both alike, are called to suffer the common ills of life, and these should be differentiated from the sufferings as Christians mentioned in the text.

While it must be conceded that Christians escape the special penal consequences of individual wrong-doing which overtake the ungodly in this world, they have to endure more or less of suffering resulting from heredity, environment and constitutional infirmity. But these they suffer not because they are Christians but as members of the human family. If Christians violate the laws of health they must endure the penal consequences of such violation, even as others.

The second discrimination to be observed between Christians and worldlings is the conduct of each under the common ills that flesh is heir to. Whereas, as a rule, worldlings endure life's ills either stoically or ungraciously — with many out-cries and complaints — genuine Christians usually, like Paul, eke good out of them even here, and rejoice in anticipation of still greater advantage in the life beyond. The three texts which they feel authorized to employ and apply are found in Rom. 8 : 18, "For I reckon that the sufferings of the present time are not worthy to be compared with the glory which shall be revealed in us"; Rom. 8 : 28, "And we know that all things work together for good to them that love God"; and 2 Cor. 4 : 17, "For our light affliction, which is but for a moment, worketh for us a far more exceeding and eternal weight of glory." So instead of murmurs and complaints when any of life's ills befall them they bravely endure them as a necessary part of the discipline of life, and instead of arraigning the justice or goodness of God, reply to all such suggestions in the language of one of old, "Shall we receive good at the hand of the Lord and not evil? The Lord gave and the Lord hath taken away, blessed be the name of the Lord."

And at this point perhaps a word of caution will be timely. No one claims that a pure heart implies a faultless judgment. If then a thorough Christian may and does err in judgment, and by reason of that error he be overtaken with painful penal consequences, let them lead him to heart-searchings, genuine repentance and subsequent increased carefulness; but let him not further err by attributing the sufferings occasioned by his carelessness or his defective judgment to the fact of his being a Christian. His likeness to Jesus induces a suffering all its own and peculiar to itself, and this is the suffering referred to in this inspired and instructive letter.

Nor is it confined to this letter or to this apostle. The whole New Testament is freighted with the startling and impressive truth that there are sufferings peculiar to the Christian calling and inseparable from a genuine and thorough Christian experience. Recall the sayings of Jesus, a few of which have been already quoted, the double beautitude, drinking of His cup and being baptized with His baptism, being hated, delivered up and beaten (Mark 13). "Yea, the time cometh that whosoever killeth you will think that he doeth God service" (John 16:2).

Be reminded of Paul's admonitory experiences. At the threshold of his discipleship he tells us he was notified how great things he must suffer for the name of Christ. And all through his letters we meet such passages as, "I am crucified with Christ"; "the world is crucified to me and I unto the world"; "I count all things but loss"; "I count not my life dear unto myself"; "I die daily"; "I bear in my body the marks of the Lord Jesus"; "that I may know Him, and the power of His resurrection, and the fellowship of His sufferings, being made conformable unto His death." So John and Peter, when scourged by order of the council, rejoiced that they were counted worthy to suffer for His name's sake.

Now, in view of all the testimony from Scripture and church history, let all genuine and thorough Christians cease being surprised or nonplused or discouraged when their life or testimony is disputed or they are ostracized or snubbed or relegated to the rear — even though it be by those they love in their own church or family, seeing it is history repeating itself from our Lord's day to this hour.

By the texts here employed we are admonished and forewarned. In the white light of these Scriptures we find ourselves in the best of company, and discover that we sound a lower depth of blessedness than it were possible for us to reach were we less pronounced and thorough disciples of our glorious Lord — even the fellowship of His sufferings.

Now, with this background of admonition, we advance to consider briefly the second grand division of our theme, namely —

II. *Christians are encouraged, assured and inspired.* And well may this apostle who, when before the Sanhedrim, and publicly whipped, rejoiced that he was counted worthy to suffer *for His name*, advise the early church that, when they "suffered as Christians, they should not be ashamed but glorify God on this behalf."

And so far from withholding their testimony as they were commanded to do, they replied, "Whether it be right in the sight of God to hearken unto you more than unto God, judge ye. For we cannot but speak the things which we have seen and heard." And proceeding with John to the most public place in the city, they preached again in *this name* as before.

It was Peter, too, who after James was beheaded, was imprisoned and chained to four quarternions of soldiers, yet slept so soundly that the angel who came to deliver him had to arouse him and remind him to bind on his sandals, cast his garments about him and follow him. Scourged, imprisoned, chained and in imminent danger of death, he was not ashamed but rejoiced that he was counted worthy thus to suffer for Christ's name.

Well may his "beloved brother Paul" counsel us to glory in tribulation, seeing he encountered perils by land and sea, in the city, in the wilderness and among false brethren, declaring that none of these things moved him, neither did he count his life dear unto him; affirming that because as a preacher and teacher of the Gentiles he suffered these things he was not ashamed, yea, he was filled with comfort and exceeding joyful in all his tribulation.

Thus, Madame Guyon, the most saintly French woman in all history, when a prisoner for four long years in the infamous Bastile whose walls were twelve feet thick, could sing —

> "Strong are the walls around me,
> That hold me all the day;
> But they who thus have bound me
> Cannot keep God away:
> My very dungeon walls are dear,
> Because the God I love is here.
>
> Thy love, O God, restores me
> From sighs and tears to praise;
> And deep my soul adores Thee,
> Nor thinks of time or place;
> I ask no more in good or ill
> But union with Thy holy will."

Thus the martyrs John Huss, Jerome of Prague, and countless multitudes beside could and did rejoice even in the flames. "Courage, Bro. Ridley," exclaimed his fellow-martyr Latimer when the fagots began to burn around them. "Let us play the men to-day, and we shall kindle a light in England that shall never be put out."

Our sufferings for Christ are so mild in comparison with those of the martyrs that they are hardly worthy of mention, yet are they not real? Does not every genuine Christian need the encouragement, the assurance and inspiration of these texts?

Being ignored by those who formerly recognized us, contemned, neglected, at times reviled and abused because of our pronounced testimony, these texts teach us that all this, and much more of the same sort, is insufficient to bring the blush of shame to our cheek. If any man suffer as a Christian let him not be ashamed, but glorify God on this behalf.

Not until we testified definitely to our spiritual regeneration did the ungodly sinner or self-righteous moralist sneer at our Christianity. Not until we could and did testify definitely to our cleansing from all unrighteousness, did any in the church reveal their displeasure and contemn us.

Still we are not ashamed, but continue to testify to the truth of that Scripture: "If we confess our sins, He is faithful and just to forgive us our sins, and to cleanse us from all unrighteousness." Being reproached we are pronounced happy, and tried by fiery trials we are commanded to rejoice.

Many reasons may be given why genuine Christians may and should rejoice when suffering for Christ's sake. We mention just three:

1. Because our own conscience acquits us of guilt. We may and do err in judgment. We are not always

wise in utterance, correct in judgment, or without error in choice or action, but in our heart of hearts we are conscious of pure motives and intentions. We know that man judgeth by the outward appearance, but God readeth the heart. So that every Christian can say with Peter, "Lord, Thou knowest all things, Thou knowest that I love Thee." In the midst of the furnace of suffering we can look up, and smiling amid our tears softly say, "*Jesus, for Thee* I suffer this, not for wrong-doing, but because I follow Thee in the midst of a wicked and perverse generation to whom Thou makest my life a standing rebuke. Jesus, for Thee."

2. A second reason for this command to rejoice and glorify God on this behalf is found in the goodly fellowship into which we find ourselves introduced by these sufferings as Christians. We have already mentioned the sufferings of the disciples and apostles of our Lord, and hinted at the noble army of martyrs and confessors both in the early and modern church. But the great and inexpressible and well-nigh inconceivable honor is found announced in this letter (v. 13), "Ye are partakers of Christ's sufferings." Just how that can be we are not able to explain. We know He was in all points tempted as we are, that He suffered being tempted, is touched by the feeling our infirmities, and so is prepared to sympathize with us in our sufferings. And this may suggest that in some way which His infinite love has devised, these consecrated sufferers for His sake, are in some sense admitted as joint heirs and fellow-sharers, not only in His sufferings, but also in the glory and joy into which He has entered.

3. A third reason for this command is found in the joyous hopes for the future world which these texts inspire. Not only are all who suffer as Christians not to be ashamed, they are to glorify God on this behalf; not only is it said "Happy are ye," it is also emphatically declared that "when His glory shall be revealed, ye may be glad also with exceeding joy." That, you observe, is almost the precise language of the eighth beatitude, only that commands us to be exceeding glad *here* when persecuted and falsely accused because great should be our reward in heaven; whereas the joy and gladness of the text points to the exceeding joy of the heavenly world.

Now, as a rule, thorough Christians are not concerned about their enjoyments in heaven. Rarely do we sing of the "Home over there." In our earlier experiences, we indulged in that pleasing prospect much more than we do now, singing "Jerusalem my happy home" and the chorus

> "How I long to be there
> In its glory to share
> And to lean on Jesus' breast."

With a deeper experience we have the joy of fellowship not only of the sufferings of Christ, but also of His triumphs even here and now. "For the spirit of glory and of God resteth upon us." A section of heaven is let down into the very souls of those who suffer as Christians. With Paul, "We are sorrowful, yet always rejoicing," "Rejoicing in hope of the glory of God which shall be revealed in us." "Wherefore let us comfort one another with these words."

VI.

PERFECT IN GOD'S WILL.

E. I. D. PEPPER, PHILADELPHIA, PA.

"Ye may stand perfect and complete in all the will of God" (Col. 4 : 12).

To ATTEMPT to meet the wishes of others is ensnaring, unsatisfactory — impossible. We cannot please anybody in everything. We cannot please everybody in any one thing.

In insisting upon our own will, we shall soon find that selfishness in any or in all its forms — self-complacency, self-sufficiency, self-will, self-assertion are damaging, dangerous, destructive; now, henceforth, forevermore.

St. Paul, in our text, assures us that it is our privilege, and therefore, "meet, right, and our bounden duty," to stand perfect and complete in all the will of God.

I. "THE WILL OF GOD."

In its essence, the will of God is the sum of His divine attributes and the outcome of His absolute perfections. As revealed in Scripture, "the will of God is the transcript of the divine mind." As revealed in the redeeming Christ, the will of God is the incarnation of the divine nature, the embodiment of His

gracious purpose and the outbeaming of His infinite love. As revealed in providence, the will of God is the unfolding and enforcement of the divine administration. The will of God is infallibly wise, holy, just and good. It is impartial, universal and all-comprehensive. "God is no respecter of persons." "He maketh His sun to rise on the evil and on the good, and sendeth rain on the just and on the unjust." "Every good gift and every perfect gift is from above and cometh down from the Father of lights." The will of God is considerate and sympathetic. "Like as a father pitieth his children, so the Lord pitieth them that fear him." "Thy tender mercies and Thy loving-kindnesses . . . have been ever of old." The will of God is protective, providential, guiding, teaching, comforting, saving. It is the best every way for our highest, holiest and heavenliest interests. It is always "better than our hopes, better than our fears, better than our deservings."

II. WHAT SHOULD BE THE CONSTANT ATTITUDE OF OUR WILLS TO THE DIVINE WILL?

Shall we prefer our own will or the will of others to His? How absurd! Shall we antagonize in any way the divine will? By doing so we shall incur damage, danger, death, with unconditional submission to His mercy or justice at last. Shall we fret under His will? That is only adding the disquietude of a bad temper to our other discomforts. Shall we surrender to His will? A rebel does that. Shall we submit to His will? A disobedient child does that. Shall we be resigned to

His will? Resignation is only an apathetic and helpless attitude of the mind and heart. A child, resigning herself into a dentist's hands, graphically described this mental condition when she said, "Just as the tooth killed me it came out."

Shall we acquiesce in His will? There is no enthusiasm in acquiescence. The literal interpretation of "enthusiasm" is, "God in a man." A woman may say, "Yes," to her lover, without a particle of love or devotion or fervor. Shall we consecrate ourselves wholly to His will? We may do that — we ought to do that — as a matter of principle and duty. Dr. Durbin said, "Ought is the strongest word in the English language." Yet, after all, our entire consecration may be only a hard, stern, severe piece of force work. We consecrate ourselves to His will because we must. This is "wheelbarrow religion," which "moves only so far as it is shoved." This kind of consecration is like that of the blind horse in the treadmill, grinding out its master's corn.

Nay! The attitude of our wills toward the divine will must be all of this — and very much more. The Chinese "Amen!" means, "My *heart* wishes it to be exactly so." The primitive Christians, in pronouncing "Amen!" in their public assemblies, raised themselves on their tip-toes and shouted it out like thunder.

Our wills should be in perfect *harmony* with the divine will. What is harmony? "Harmony is the concourse of musical sounds — a succession of modulated and progressive chords." Our minds, and hearts, and wills are to *make music* with the divine will. Read these sublime words of Rev. Dr. Daniel Steele, "To some of my readers these words may seem not as a sober description of the real life of a soul still prisoned in the body, but rather as the flight of a poetic imagination. Well, call it poetry — you do not destroy its reality. Do you not know that God is composing a grand poem in human history, and that the saints are verses? 'Ye are his poem' (see the Greek of Eph. 2:10). My supreme ambition is to be a perfectly rhythmic and mellifluous line in the glorious epic of redemption. Many years I was a discord, full of redundant syllables and erroneous quantities. How quickly the great Poet brought me into harmony and rhythm when I fully submitted myself to Him! May the angels and archangels, the seraphim and cherubim, find no blemish in my verse, when with wonder they read the finished poem!"

Yes, it is true that, "Ye are his workmanship" (Eph. 2:10), in the Greek reads, "Ye are His *poiema*" (poems). "Wherefore be ye not unwise, but understanding what the will of the Lord is. . . . be filled with the Spirit; speaking to yourselves in psalms and hymns and spiritual songs, *singing and making melody* in your heart to the Lord."

Yes, harmonize all the chords, pull out all the stops, and make heart-melody to God — always, in all places, in all things, among all people, under all circumstances. "Sorrowful, yet alway rejoicing." In music the minor harmony sounds more sad and plaintive, but it is none the less beautiful and musical. Some of the sweetest harmonies were born out of the deepest human woe,

What amazing words of unity are these of Jesus, "As Thou, Father, art in me, and I in Thee, that they also may be one in us. . . . I in them, and Thou in me, that they may be made perfect in one." And, also, these, "He that is joined unto the Lord is one spirit." What union, communion, fellowship, are breathed out in such language! Therein is contained, with all other sorts of prayer, the prayer of meditation and adoration. Our worship is never interrupted by our work. Our most menial work becomes our highest and holiest worship.

Read the following words from Lady Maxwell:—

"I have, though deeply unworthy, been favored with such wonderful lettings into deity as no language can describe or explain; but the whole soul dilates itself in the exquisite enjoyment — so refined, so pure, so tempered with sacred awe, so guarded by heavenly solemnity, as effectually to prevent all irregularities of desires."

III. THIS HARMONY WITH ALL THE WILL OF GOD MAY BE PERFECT.

1. His will is indicated in His words and ways; in His plans and purposes and providences; in His active and permissive dispensations. In our case, that Scripture, "My thoughts are not your thoughts, neither are your ways my ways, saith the Lord," may be so changed as to amount to a complete reversal.

2. We may will *whatever* God wills. Whatever God wants us to be, or to do, or to suffer. "The baptism with the Holy Ghost" is not merely a baptism

PERFECT IN GOD'S WILL.

for "power" but also for purity; not merely for "service" but also for sanctity. We will observe and comply with the divine order that we must *be*, before we can either *do* or *suffer*. We will not be "choicy" or dainty in our work. We will have no mental reservations from any duty or sacrifice. We will have no artful substitutions of one duty for another that we happen to like better. We will be obedient in the minutest details — not with a sore scrupulosity, but with a tender conscientiousness. We will be faithful in the least and lowest as well as in the greatest and highest. He that is unfaithful in the lesser cannot be trusted in the larger.

Two plates of glass cannot come perfectly together while the tiniest grain of sand remains between them. A watch placed on its face, went on and kept good time; turned on its back, it instantly stopped, because an almost invisible piece of glass turned over as the watch was turned; and by being so turned over, either hindered the watch from going or made way for it to keep time again. We will always be *abounding* in the work of the Lord. As to suffering — our disappointments will be accepted as God's appointments.

A sister once remarked to me, "I am disappointed that I did not hear your sermon." I replied, "I will give you a sermon now — and that is, never be disappointed." Are you trodden down? Well, someone has well said, "The best wood is put in for door sills, over which everybody treads." God's "chosen vessels" will be shown sooner or later "how great things they must suffer for His name's sake."

3. We may will *however* God wills. We may agree with His will in *manner* as well as in *matter*, in the *way* as well as in the *what*. The *manner* is almost, if not quite, as important as the *matter*. " Manners make the man" either false or true — willing, without whining — fulfilling His will skilfully, not bunglingly, making all things after the pattern shown to us in the mount.

4. Willing *whenever* God wills. Prompt — without hesitancies, debates or delays. Neither too fast nor too slow — keeping step with God, marching shoulder to shoulder with God. Discerning "the divine moment." Living with the " I Am," moment by moment, in an ever-present now. "What are you doing here?" said someone to an old saint in a crowded street. The reply came quickly, "Walking and talking with God."

5. Willing *wherever* God wills, amid all associations — congenial or "crooked and perverse." Under all circumstances — no matter how adverse. Alike in pulpit or pew, in business or pleasure, in the sanctuary or in the slums, in garrets or in cellars, in highways and in hedges, in the parlor or in the kitchen, or when entirely alone. No preacher could live long to preach without a cook to provide him food; hence the cook may be as clearly in the line of God's will as the preacher whose food she provides.

IV. WE MAY HAVE THE FULL ASSURANCE THAT WE ARE PERFECT IN ALL THE WILL OF GOD.

The words "perfect" and "complete" in our English version are tautological; but the literal translation of the Greek word "complete" is "fully assured." The oldest manuscripts, the revised version, Dr. Adam Clarke, Dr. Whedon and others so translate it. It is the same Greek word that in Romans 4: 21 and 14: 5 is translated "fully persuaded."

The fact is, that the Holy Ghost satisfactorily attests every religious experience — conviction, conversion, entire sanctification, growth, maturity. "We have received the Spirit of God that we might know the things [not simply *one* thing] that are freely given to us of God." There are not three kinds of full assurance; but there may be full assurance in three directions — understanding, faith and hope. The full assurance of understanding concerns itself with the Bible and the teachings of the Holy Ghost and other competent instructors; the full assurance of faith concerns itself with the present; the full assurance of hope concerns itself with the future, to all eternity.

Some vainly assert that there is a witness of the Holy Spirit with our spirits to our pardon, to the fact that we are converted, but that there is no such witness of the Holy Spirit to our purity, to the fact that we are entirely sanctified. But this does not stand to reason. Is the light strongest at dawn or at meridian? Logically, reasoning beforehand, would we not naturally expect the witness to purity to be clearer than the witness to pardon? And is this not a fact of actual experience? Moreover, is it not Scriptural? "The path of the just is as the shining light that shineth more and more unto the perfect day." Reading Acts 15: 8 and 9 carefully, we find: (1) that the original

Pentecost, and all subsequent similar manifestations, purified hearts by faith; (2) that God bore witness to this Pentecostal purifying work by the gift of the Holy Ghost. So that the Spirit fully assures us in the very commencement of this experience that we are perfect in all God's will.

But we can be fully assured at every step of our progress in this experience. Enoch, in walking with God, had the testimony that he pleased Him. If we walk in the light, as God is in the light, two things occur: (1) the blood cleanses and (2) we have fellowship with God. The Spirit attests our prompt, continuous, momentary, universal, ever-increasing conformity to God's will, according to our light, ability, opportunity, readiness and holy habit of perfecting holiness in the fear of God. This testimony is life-long — down to the last conscious moment.

The Holy Ghost specially attests to this experience in emergencies. In trial, temptation, suffering, work; in activity as long as God wills; in suffering as long as God wills; in mental and spiritual distress; under great strains of responsibility; when we are not in spiritual darkness but in providential perplexity; when opposition, persecution, slander, and evil report are busy with us.

V. THIS PERFECT HARMONY WITH ALL GOD'S WILL AND THIS FULL ASSURANCE OF IT, MAY BE ABIDING.

"Ye may *stand* perfect and fully assured in all the will of God." *Standing* does not sound like *dying* as soon as we reach this state. Will God kill us just

PERFECT IN GOD'S WILL. 99

when He can make the very best use of us? Do men usually hasten to discharge their best trained workmen? Will God take us away when we are best qualified, most pliable, most useful? Is it not more likely that He will keep on hand a few specimens of what He can do for, and in, and through, and by one who is holy in heart and in life, one who stands perfect and fully assured in all His will? But why argue the question? Listen to a few out of many assuring Scriptures, "This is the true grace of God wherein ye stand"; "The God of all grace [will] make you perfect, stablish, strengthen, settle you." God tells us positively that our hearts can be kept from evil and established by grace in the truth and in every good word and work; that we can stand fast by faith in the liberty wherewith Christ has made us free; that whatever judgments may be passed by men on us as God's servants, He is able to hold us up and make us stand; that we can stand against the wiles of the devil; and having done all, we can still stand.

VI. THIS FULL ASSURANCE, THEN, THAT WE STAND PERFECT IN ALL GOD'S WILL IS POSSIBLE, PLEASURABLE AND PROFITABLE.

1. It is possible. "Ye *may* stand perfect and fully assured in all the will of God." It is our privilege if we fulfill the conditions. "That he may stablish your hearts unblameable in holiness. We have already remarked that Dr. Durbin said, "Ought is the strongest word in the English language"; but "ought" is not stronger than love, and not as strong, when it comes to

helping and cheering us on to be, and do, and suffer as we ought. Dr. Hodgson, in his famous speech at the Philadelphia convention, said, "I do not propose to stand at the gate of holiness as the watch dog of orthodoxy, but I propose to go in with the rest to enjoy my privilege." There may be times of providential perplexity when we cry, "We know not what to do, but our eyes are unto Thee." God quickly responds, "I will guide thee with Mine eye." Some are guided by words or by the whip, but others so well understand the look of the loved one's eye, and are so eager to anticipate his every wish, that they can be guided by a look.

2. It is pleasurable. Even in our most agonizing Gethsemanes, while pleading that any cup of suffering and sorrow, for ourselves or for others, may pass away from our lips, yet in sweetest harmony with the Father's will, we may stand ready to drink it to its very dregs. Christ said, "Lo! I come to do Thy will in the body that Thou hast prepared for me." He was ready to become incarnate that He might suffer death for man. In reference to this death, in the Psalms, He is represented as saying, "Lo! I delight to do Thy will, O God!" He delighted in His atoning death. Fenelon said, "I adore Thy will, O God, without knowing what it may be." The martyrs glorified God in the fires and shouted at the death-stake. Musical harmonies are beautiful in the major; they are more plaintive but quite as beautiful — sometimes more beautiful — in the minor. A crowd pressed upon Christ. Within that crowd was the inner circle of

the disciples; then came His own blood relations; but He rather claimed as His nearest and dearest relatives those who did the will of the heavenly Father.

3. It is profitable. Christ said, "My judgment is just, because I seek not mine own will, but the will of Him that sent me." The only perfect judgment is that which has an eye single to the glory of God. Anything else, or anything less, has in it the bias of self-interest. Again, Christ said, "My meat is to do the will of Him that sent me." So our meat, our sustenance, our health, our strength, our energy, our life, is in doing God's will.

VII. Would we be *perfect* in God's will? Would we be perfect in *all* His will? Would we be *fully assured* that we are perfect in all His will? Would we *stand* in the full assurance that we are perfect in all His will? If we would, we must consecrate ourselves wholly, unconditionally, forever to Him. We must sign our name to the bottom of the blank sheet and let Him fill the paper with His will. We must be like Abraham, ready to go out not knowing whither we are going. Are we wholly the Lord's? Has He accepted our entire consecration? Has He sanctified us wholly? If so, henceforth may we stand perfect and full assured in all His will!

VII.

SANCTIFY THEM.

C. J. FOWLER, HAVERHILL, MASS.

"Sanctify them through Thy truth: Thy word is truth" (Jno. 17:17).

THOSE who are familiar with the Scriptures, recognize these words as from our Lord's prayer — the prayer he offered for all believers. Not only for those who were about him, but for all, of all time. "Neither pray I for these alone, but for them, also, which shall believe on me through their word."

The prayer was for those about whom He speaks to the Father in these words, "I pray for them; I pray not for the world, but for them which Thou hast given me; for they are Thine. I have given them Thy Word; and the world hath hated them, because they are not of the world, even as I am not of the world."

That for which He prayed — the grace he sought for them — was something distinct from the experience they already had. It was an experience definitely and suddenly realized, as their subsequent history witnesses. That these disciples had grace — had real Christian experience — is exceedingly clear in this entire prayer.

"SANCTIFY THEM."

For what did He pray? What is that which this word is made to carry?

Sanctification is used in the Scriptures interchangeably with justification, regeneration, adoption, conversion and the like, but not in that sense alone. The Corinthians are addressed as "sanctified in Christ Jesus," and at the same time their entire sanctification is denied, for they are addressed as "yet carnal" and exhorted to perfect "holiness in the fear of God." In Paul's epistle to the Thessalonians, prayer is offered that they may be sanctified "wholly."

Sanctification is a *double* term — used for the *partial* work of salvation and for the *complete* work of salvation. This is a distinction that needs to be kept in mind if confusion of thought would be avoided. What is true of this term and doctrine in the Scriptures is not true of justification or of adoption. To say, "If one is justified or adopted, he is justified and adopted, and that is the end of it and all of it, might be exactly true; but it would not be true to say, "If one is sanctified, he is sanctified, and that is the end of it and all of it." *Because*, as we have said, sanctification is a double term, having a two-fold meaning, while the other terms are single, having one meaning.

It may be best, for the clearest understanding, to always use the qualifying word "entire" when one means complete sanctification, but it is not necessary to do so in the interest of exact statement. We use the term sanctification here in its completed sense.

Sanctification is not —

EXEMPTION FROM TEMPTATION.

Instead of the sanctified being placed, because of the experience, where they are no longer tempted (as certain persist in saying is taught), they are placed where they may be, and probably are tempted more severely than ever before. Since temptation is a process of discipline and development, larger tests may be placed on one, since the nature to be developed is stronger to bear it. An adult would need more rugged and violent exercise to strengthen his muscle than a mere child would. The difference between one sanctified and one not sanctified is the difference between an adult and a child.

Sanctification is not exemption from —

ALL LIABILITY OF FALLING.

Instead of teaching, as some affirm we do, that a sanctified soul has come to a place where he cannot fall, we instantly and constantly declare its opposite. The experience and grace of sanctification enhance one's probabilities of standing — make one more sure. Sanctification places one where he *may* not fall, not where he *cannot*. It is one thing *to be able not to fall*, and quite another *not to be able to fall*. We teach the former.

Sanctification is not exemption from

MISTAKES.

What are mistakes, primarily, but errors of judgment? No amount of grace changes one's essential nature. Man's essential nature is finite, limited, restricted. Such a nature not only *can* err, it *must* err in the very nature of things. No mind, save an infinite mind, can be free from errors of thinking.

Hence sanctification is not exemption from

WRONG PRACTICES.

Conduct cannot be better than conviction. No one will make his living better than what he sees it should be. If it be better, it would be a mistake, for it would be doing better than he intended. Judgment must graduate conduct. If judgment be astray, practice must be. Blessed is the man, if not happy, who brings his conduct into harmony with his convictions.

Since one does not always *know* just the exact right, so he will not always *do* just the exact right.

But, *such* wrong conduct is not condemnable, either by God or man. Because the *intention was right*. A loving father prepares a medicine for his sick child, but by mistake, he poisons it. Who condemns him? Neither God nor man. His *intention* saves him from the clutches of the law and from divine penalty.

Sanctification is not a better ethical or outward life than justification. Surely one must be true to his light to keep justified, and no one can be more than true to his light. Justification demands as correct outward deportment as sanctification does. It is a grave error to think because one is only justified, and makes no profession of holiness, he may be indifferent as to his conduct. "Whosoever is born of God doth not commit sin."

Sanctification may clarify the vision — may cause one to see the divine requirement more fully, and in that way change the outward conduct; but it does not have to do with outward conduct, primarily, in contradistinction to justification.

Sanctification is not alone

SALVATION.

That is, there is a salvation apart from sanctification; we mean to say, one who is not sanctified has *a* salvation.

The Scriptures call attention to the *places* of ultimate human destiny — heaven and hell. None go there by any sovereign decree. God does not say to one, "You shall go to heaven," and to another, "You shall go to hell." Character — *what one is* — graduates destiny. What one is, is determined by his relation to Jesus Christ; He is the touch-stone of character. One goes to heaven because he is *fitted* for heaven; there is no other place for him in the universe of God; he is heavenly and must go to his own place. So, one goes to hell because he is *fitted* for hell; there is no other place for him, he goes to his own place. As a falling body strikes the earth by natural law, so a sinful, sinning soul drops into hell, under a law of its nature. As a live bird, freed from confinement, flies away and up, so a holy, heavenly soul, goes to God and heaven by the law of its nature.

A salvation may exist without fitness for heaven. A sinning soul comes to the altar for prayer. He is converted, hopefully, soundly converted. We say he is saved, and we say well, for so he is. He is justified freely — treated by God as though he had never sinned; he is regenerated graciously, new life imparted to him; he is adopted fully, made "an heir of God and a joint heir with Jesus Christ." He is saved, saved from the guilt, dominion and choice of sin. But is he *fully* saved? Is he delivered from "all sin," and thus fitted for the inheritance of the saints in light? Experience, theology and the Scriptures say, "No." What say the theologians? Says the eminent Dr. Hodge of Princeton, "According to the Scriptures and the undeniable evidence of history, regeneration does not remove all sin." The renowned preacher, Frederick W. Robertson, remarks on the fifty-first Psalm, "Two sides of our mysterious two-fold being here. Something in us near to hell; something strangely near to God. Half diabolical — half divine: half demon — half God. In our best estate and in our purest moments, there is a something of the devil in us, which, if it could be known, would make men shrink from us. The germs of the worst crimes are in us all." The senior Dr. Tyng says to young communicants, "Be watchful, your Christian course is to be maintained in the midst of temptations. Though truly a child of God, you still carry with you a heart far from sanctified, a remaining sinfulness of nature in its appetites and propensities, which demand unceasing vigilance. You cannot afford to relax your vigilance over these outgoings of your own sinful nature." John Wesley says, "That believers [regenerate persons] are delivered from the *guilt* and *power* of sin we allow; that they are delivered from the *being* of sin we deny." The Holy Spirit declares, "The flesh lusteth against the Spirit, and the Spirit against the flesh."

Here is an unlikeness to heaven in those who are really Christians; here is a salvation, and yet that with it, which heaven has nothing of. "There shall in nowise enter into it anything that defileth."

Just here, *experience is indisputable — all know there is a condition of wrongness within them after regeneration.*

In the gospel, provision is made for its removal, "The blood of Jesus Christ, His Son, cleanseth us from all sin."

The method of recovery is by

CO-OPERATION.

The same as in regeneration. The truth is preached to a sinner. He sees his need, accepts the gospel and is saved. Thus he has *co-operated* with the truth unto his salvation. Just so is one recovered from all sin. He hears the truth, sees his need, apprehends his privilege, and, accepting the proffer, enters into full redemption — is sanctified.

But there is another class of people, Christians, to whom the truth has not thus specifically come. They, though seeing their need of holiness, do not understand it to be their privilege to possess it; and they go on through life without it, and so far as we know, die with no added light upon the question. A most frequent and obstinate objection to the doctrine of holiness is voiced in these words, "What becomes of these good people who know nothing of this truth. They are Christians, and good Christians; they are not, manifestly, entirely sanctified; now, if this experience is absolutely needful in order to enter heaven, and they know nothing about it, what of them? Are they lost?"

This leads to our saying: There is another feature of the process of recovery from all sin, which is, *the ministry of the Holy Spirit upon a passive or non-resisting agent.* What is meant by a "passive or non-resisting agent?" Here, for instance, is a child one year old. Is that child a responsible moral agent? No, it has not yet come to the time of responsibility. Is the child in a saved state? *i. e.*, if it were to die at that time of life, would it be saved? We all, unhesitatingly, say "Yes." But let us stop for a moment. While the child is innocent from any actual and voluntary transgression, is it free from all sinfulness? Has it no moral taint, no indwelling sin-principle? As this precious babe lies in its mother's lap, you are interested, not only in its gentle cooing and sweet smiling, but you are struck by the presence of something beside gentleness and sweetness. See its little body straighten and its feet fly; hear its yell and squall while the face reddens, indicating, unmistakably, what in an adult would properly be called *rage*.

Parents speak of it as "spunk," "naughtiness," "temper" and the like. *It is sin — real, inner badness.* Not voluntary and responsible wrong-doing, but real and lamentable *wrong being*. We cannot hesitate to declare that the child has in its little selfhood, something they do not have in heaven. That exhibition of spirit and temper is impossible there. No question is raised here as to the probability of its being taken to heaven in the case of death, but that it would not be taken there *without change*. Certainly, that something we recognize present in the child must be absent in order unto its admission there.

Paul states the actual, gracious condition and standing of such children, "Therefore as by the offence of one *judgment came* upon all men to condemnation; even so by the righteousness of one *the free gift came* upon all men unto justification of life." "Life," "justification of life," is the inheritance of this child by virtue of the atonement. He farther says, "Whom He justified, them He also glorified." Justification secures glorification; but, in the nature of things, not without farther change. "Holiness, without which no man shall see the Lord," applies to irresponsible children as to men.

Now, since this life is the period of probation and recovery from sin must be here; since the child has sinfulness of nature; since no such element of character is admitted to heaven; since this child is in irresponsibility; we conclude the Holy Spirit applies to the child the merit of Christ's sacrifice, sanctifying and cleansing it from all sin. The child is a *passive, non-resisting agent*, and its salvation is the salvation of one who is not a voluntary, active agent, but of an involuntary, passive one. This is our meaning of the "ministry of the Holy Spirit upon a passive, non-resisting agent."

The eminent Dr. Hovey, in "Biblical Eschatology," teaches, "From the fact that no account of the last judgment refers to the case of infants or idiots, we think it rational to infer that, from the beginning of time, the effect of the fall upon their moral nature has been removed by the Saviour, through the work of the Spirit, before they enter the life to come. No other hypothesis agrees so well with the assuring silence of Scripture in regard to their destiny; for we are unable to find within the lids of the Bible any hint of their being lost forever, or any faintest suggestion of prayer for their renewal after death. It is, therefore, safe to trust that, in the case of those who are thus removed from the only hopeful state of probation, the second Adam has, by His perfect grace, destroyed the work of the first Adam."

What now is true of infants, we apprehend is true of adults, about whom question is raised. What becomes of these good people? If they are Christians, as is claimed for them, they are justified; if justified, they are entitled to glorification; nothing but a forfeiture of their justification can defeat their glorification. If they had no light on farther privilege and duty they did not *reject* light; not rejecting light, but walking in all they had, kept them continually in the Lord's hands, and the Lord can and will care for all souls who trust

We have no fear about irresponsible children, idiots and the heathen, "who do by nature the things contained in the law." We have no concern about good people who love God and seek to keep His commandments, but who are so circumstanced as they have limited light on Christian attainment. Our concern is for those who have light, that they may improve it and not fall into condemnation by its rejection.

All justified people are "heirs of God, and joint heirs with Christ." Nothing but a refusal to comply with whatever conditions God places upon one, brings condemnation and causes forfeiture of the child-relation and experience. This condemnation perils the soul, and if not recovered from, causes its loss forever. The secret of its being lost is not so much that sanctification was not experienced as that justification was not maintained, and *justification was lost by refusing the farther light of sanctification.* The eminent Mr. Fletcher taught that the grace of the Holy Spirit, sanctifies all *who do not resist His influences.*

Our answer, then, to the question as to what becomes of good people who knew nothing about sanctification as such, is, God takes them to heaven; but *not without sanctifying them.* They are saved on exactly the same principle that irresponsible children, idots and the heathen, who do not reject what light they have, are saved, as passive, non-resisting agents. He who is justified is sure of heaven; *but, if farther light is given to Christian privilege and duty, he must most certainly accept and walk in it to maintain his justication.*

Says Bishop William Taylor, who has had no little observation of Christian experience and who is no mean theologian, "What, do you mean to say that a justified soul is in danger of being lost? Nay, justification by faith secures to us a title to heaven, holiness, the fitness for it, but the justified soul is in the immediate care of the Holy Sanctifier, who holds the keys of the gates of death and will perfect His work before He opens the gates; but the man or woman who dares to ignore a positive command of God and neglect a palpable duty, will hereby disjoint their justified relation, grieve the Holy Spirit of God and fall into the snare of Satan."

Many souls, then, are lost, not primarily because they were not sanctified, but because they were not justified; and many such *lost their justification by refusing sanctification.*

Sanctification is entire and perpetual dedication of the whole self-hood to God.

> "Take my soul and body's powers;
> Take my memory, mind and will;
> All my goods and all my hours;
> All I know and all I feel;
> All I think, or speak, or do;
> Take my heart, but make it new."

Sanctification is the utter expulsion of the sin-principle. It is the fullness of what, before, one has had in part. Sanctification is "an *instantaneous deliverance* from all sin." It is "the *pure* love of God and man shed abroad in a faithful believer's heart by the Holy Ghost given unto him to *cleanse* him and to *keep him clean* from all the *filthiness* of the *flesh and spirit*, and to enable him to fulfill the law of Christ, according to the talents he is intrusted with, and the circumstances in which he is placed in this world." "The degree of *original sin* which *remains in some believers*, though not a transgression of a known law, is nevertheless sin, and must be removed before one goes to heaven, and *the removal of this evil is what we mean by full sanctification.*" "Regeneration is the beginning of purification. Entire sanctification is finishing that work."

"They came to the gates of Canaan,
　　But they never entered in;
　They came to the very threshold,
　　But they perished in their sin.

"On the morrow they would have entered,
　　But God had shut the gate;
　They wept, they rashly ventured,—
　　But, alas! it was too late.

"And so we are ever coming
　　To the place where two ways part;
　One leads to the land of promise,
　　And one to a hardened heart.

"Oh, brother, give heed to the warning,
　　And obey His voice to-day;
　The Spirit to thee is calling,
　　Oh, do not grieve Him away.

"Oh, come in complete surrender,
　　Oh, turn from thy doubt and sin;
　Pass on from Kadesh to Canaan,
　　And a crown and kingdom win."

VIII.

HOLINESS.

C. S. NUSBAUM, KINGMAN, KAN.

"Follow peace with all men, and holiness, without which no man shall see the Lord" (Heb. 12: 14).

THIS text presents to us our duty to our fellow-men, and to our God. It needs no interpretation in order to take away from its full meaning. Peace with man and holiness unto the Lord, is God's idea of the Christian life. Peace and holiness live in harmony together in the same place. In the eleventh chapter, the apostle presents to the church of his day, and of the future, a picture containing characters of wonderful achievement in Christian life, giving the secret of their victories. Faith stands out prominently as the conqueror, crowned with glory and honor. In the presence of this great galaxy of soldiers in the army of God, he draws up in line a class of Christians of his day, who were lacking in faith and courage; and calling their attention to the possibilities of Christian character when all the requirements and conditions are met, he urges them forward by telling them to lay aside the garments of worldiness, "the weight" and the unrighteousness of heart, "the besetting sin" and prepare themselves fully for "the race" with their eyes fixed on Jesus, "the author and finisher of their faith," and thereby become better acquainted with God and His providences. At the same time He explains very carefully and plainly the divine object of corrections and chastisements. Evidently a large number of the church had mistaken ideas of God's dealings with them, and concluded that their chastisements were the result of His *anger*, instead of His *love*, and consequently became discouraged and careless in the service of God, and I believe, in a state of heart backsliding, which is certainly indicated by the exhortation contained in verses 12 and 13. Now, after a brief rehearsal of their real condition, and the reasons for it, he lovingly and tenderly exhorts them to "lift up the hands which hang down and the feeble knees," which certainly indicates weakness, discouragement, inactivity and faithlessness. Gestures appeal to the eye, speech addresses itself to the ear, and both are used to express the thoughts and interests, feelings and purposes of the heart.

I infer from this exhortation that this people were like a great many of the people who belong to the church to-day, out of the "strait and narrow way," making "crooked paths," and yet hoping "to hold out faithful" (?) "and finally meet you all in heaven." What a heaven that would be! Paul would awaken them to their true situation and condition, and urge them to make straight paths for their feet, like Jeremiah. "Thus saith the Lord, *stand* ye in the ways and *see*, and *ask* for the old *paths*, where is the good *way*, and *walk* therein, and ye shall find *rest* for your souls."

Paths of obedience to God. Then we are ready for

HOLINESS. 117

the experience of holiness. Every Christian experience is a holy experience, but not every Christian experience is the experience of holiness. The soul that is walking "in the light, as He is in the light" will enjoy fellowship and communion, and be conscious of the cleansing power of the blood. "Straight paths" will lead us to the fountain of cleansing, where we can present the living offering, and prove that the good and perfect will of God is even our sanctification. Then let us notice :

I. Conditions necessary to receive the experience of holiness.

Only those whose hands are employed in the service of the Master, whose feet are running on the King's errands of mercy, and whose path is heavenward, have the call "unto holiness."

(a) The first essential requisite is, to be a child of God, born of His Spirit, adopted into His family, begotten unto a lively hope, at "peace with God through our Lord Jesus Christ" "freely justified," "a new creature in Christ Jesus."

(b) A deep conscious sense of need, and the knowledge of its provision. "Woe is me! for *I* am undone," (Is. 6: 5). "Behold, I was shapen in iniquity ; and in sin did my mother conceive me," (Ps. 51 ; 5) "Create in me a clean heart, O God; and renew a right spirit within me . . . Take not Thy Holy Spirit from me " (Ps. 51:10). "Restore unto me the joy of Thy salvation" All these indicate a deep sense of need. As seekers for holiness of heart, we must settle once for all, these two things, viz: God has provided it for *me*, and I can no longer please Him without it. When these are settled thoroughly the soul will soon receive its inheritance.

(*c*) Then consecration and faith. The presenting of our *bodies* (Rom. 12 : 1). Committing our *way* (Ps. 37 : 5). Consecrating our *service* (1 Chron. 29 : 5) and our *wealth* (Mal. 3 : 10). Even *ourselves* (Ex. 32 : 29), all of which informs us as to *who, what, to whom,* and the *why* of consecration. Then the exercise of faith in Him, of whom it is said "Faithful is He that calleth you, who also will do it." Let us notice the reasonableness of this doctrine, as John Fletcher states it: "If the light of a candle brought into a dark room can instantly expel the darkness, and if upon opening the shutters at noon, the room that is filled with gloom can instantly be filled with meridian light, then why absurd to believe that the instantaneous rending of the veil of unbelief, or the sudden and full opening of the eye of faith, can fill the soul with the light of divine truth and the fire of love? May not the Sanctifier descend upon your waiting soul as quickly as the Spirit descended upon your Lord at His baptism? If the sun can instantly kindle a mote, if a burning glass can in a moment calcine a bone, and turn a stone to lime, and the flame of a candle in the twinkling of an eye can destroy the flying insect, how un-Scriptural and irrational is it to suppose, that, when God fully baptizes a soul with His sanctifying Spirit, and with the celestial fire of His love, He can not, in an instant, destroy the man of sin, burn up the chaff of corruption, and fill the believing soul with pure seraphic love!"

HOLINESS. 119

Ah, yes, the child of God, conscious of his need, and with a free-will offering of all he is, and has, in the exercise of faith, will, in an instant, feel the thrill of joy, and the perfect peace, love and rest that God gives to His own children. Hallelujah!

II. What is the experience of holiness? I answer in human language, a pure heart filled with God's love.

Purity, peace and power. To be *saved* from all uncleannesses, *cleansed* from all filthiness and idols (Ezek. 36: 25-29), also from all filthiness of the flesh and spirit (2 Cor. 7:1) and from all sin (1 John 1: 7).

Purged. "Thine iniquity is taken away, and thy sin purged" (Is. 6: 7). "Every branch that beareth fruit, He purgeth it that it may bring forth more fruit, (John 15: 25).

Purified. "Who gave Himself for us, that He might redeem us from all iniquity, and purify unto Himself a peculiar people" (Titus 2: 14).

Saved, cleansed, purged, purified. These are terms familiar only to the child of God. This is the negative work of God's grace. The positive is giving to the cleansed heart perfect *peace*. "Thou wilt keep him in perfect peace, whose mind is *stayed* on Thee: because he trusteth in Thee" (Is. 26: 3). As peace is the result of justifying faith, perfect peace is the result of sanctifying faith. Perfect *love*— "If we love one another, God dwelleth in us, and His love is perfected in us;" "Perfect love casteth out fear" (1 John 4: 12, 18).

Rest of soul. "Take my yoke upon you, and learn of me; for I am meek and lowly in heart: and ye shall find rest unto your souls" (Matt. 11 : 29). And fullness of *joy*. "These things have I spoken unto you, that *my joy* might remain in you, and that your joy, might be full" (John 15 : 11). *Perfect peace, perfect love, rest and fullness of joy*. All this, and more, is the Christian's inheritance.

III. Reasons for seeking and obtaining the experience of holiness.

1. Because God has provided it for us, and demands it of us.

"And the Lord spake unto Moses, saying, Speak unto all the congregation of the children of Israel, and say unto them, Ye shall be holy: for I the Lord your God am holy" (Lev. 19 : 1, 2).

"But as He which hath called you is holy, so be ye holy in all manner of conversation; because it is written, Be ye holy; for I am holy" (1 Peter 1: 15, 16).

(*a*) At a fearful cost. We are ready to believe that Christ died for the world, but do we know that He gave Himself for the church that He might sanctify it and make it a holy church without blame before Him? "For *their* sakes I sanctify myself, that they also might be [truly] sanctified through the truth" (John 17 : 19). Husbands, love your wives, even as Christ also loved the church, and gave Himself for *it ;* that He might sanctify and cleanse it with the washing of water by the Word, That He might present *it* to Himself a glorious church, not having spot, or wrinkle, or any such thing; but that it should be holy and without blemish" (Eph. 5 : 25–27). "Wherefore, Jesus also, that He might sanctify the people, . . . suffered without the gate" (Heb. 13:12). If it be true that Christ gave His life that we might be made holy, how can we, in the face of such a price and in our great need, remain at peace with Him without it. Let us look up and ask and receive it now.

2. We cannot meet God's idea of salvation in its completeness without it.

God said to Abram, "Walk before Me, and be thou perfect." And God changed his name to Abraham, making him "the father of many nations" and "exceeding fruitful," establishing His covenant with him and giving him the "land of Canaan" "for an everlasting possession" (Gen. 17:1–8). Jesus said to His followers, "Be ye therefore perfect, even as your father which is in heaven is perfect" (Matt. 5:48). "Wherefore He is able also to save them to the uttermost that come unto God by Him, seeing He ever liveth to make intercession for them" (Heb. 7:25).

God's idea of salvation is in keeping with His omniscience and omnipotence. Nothing short of full and complete salvation can satisfy God. The salvation of our God is as great as Himself. Certainly, He who is able to do exceeding abundantly above all that we can ask or think, can save a soul from all sin and fill it with His own presence. A perfect Christian is God's greatest work. If it be true that man is best satisfied in the presence of his greatest achievement, and is delighted most in the production of his highest ideal, then God is most delighted in the presence of a soul, body and spirit, preserved by His grace blameless unto His coming. We can honor God most by what we have Him do for us here in this life. Let us all test His power to the uttermost in the salvation of our souls.

3. It completely satisfies the soul.

(*a*) As to our experience. "That He would grant unto us, that we being delivered out of the hand of our enemies might serve Him without fear, in holiness and righteousness before Him, all the days of our life" (Luke 1:74, 75). "They shall be abundantly satisfied with the fatness of thy house; and thou shalt make them drink of the river of thy pleasures" (Ps. 36:8). "As for me, I will behold Thy face in righteousness: I shall be satisfied, when I awake, with Thy likeness" (Ps. 17:15).

The soul of man was never created for sin to have any room in it. It was created for the holiness of God. Every demand of the soul is a struggle for purity, and every struggle is an effort for liberty and freedom. Sin makes slaves and brings bondage and death, but holiness brings purity and freedom, peace and power.

(*b*) Then it satisfies the soul as to *service* for God. Holiness of life causes the soul to cry out, "Here am I, send me." It takes the *can't* out, and says, "I can do all things through Christ which strengtheneth me," and trusts the loving Christ who says, "My grace is sufficient for thee," and who is "able to make all grace abound toward you; that ye, always having all sufficiency in all things, may abound to every good work," and in the midst of the greatest difficulties be made to proclaim in the face of the enemy, "With God all things are possible." Oh, how the various callings and professions are burdened with men never intended to follow them. The ministry to-day is loaded with men never called of God to preach; the laity of the church, with many who have never lived near enough to God to hear *the call*, or too far away from Him to see the possibility of undertaking it, who ought to be in preparation now for their life's work, or preaching the gospel of Christ. When God has full possession of the heart He has no trouble in carrying out His plans. There is talent and wealth enough to-day in the possession of the church, if in the hands of God, to bring the world to Christ in the next quarter of a century. Oh, brethren, give yourselves to God.

Dr. Boardman tells us of a Quaker lady of wealth, position and culture, who was happily converted to God. All doubt and fear in regard to her acceptance with God was driven away, and for a time she was exceedingly happy. But her besetting sins troubled her. She could suppress them, but could not exterminate them. Her service was very unsatisfactory. It was more from duty than love. She wanted to have the wellspring of life in her as a fountain whence should flow forth rivers of living water. To attain this, she made many vigorous efforts, only to fail. At last, in a meeting, she heard of the better way of faith in Jesus, and left herself, burden and all, in his hands. Joy in its fullness flooded her soul and she was free and happy as happy could be. When asked how it came about, she said, "Oh, I just shifted the responsibility over on Jesus." What an ocean of meaning in that statement. The only responsibility God ever gave us was to "reckon ourselves dead indeed unto sin and alive unto Him," and "walk in the light, as He is in the light." He is abundantly able to take care of our experience and work. "Seek ye first the kingdom of God, and His righteousness, and all these things shall be added unto you."

4. It gives us power with God and man. "In *that day* [the day of Penetcost] ye shall ask me nothing. Verily, verily, I say unto you, Whatsoever ye shall ask the Father in my name, He will give it you" (John 16: 23).

"If ye abide in Me, and My words abide in you, ye shall ask what ye will, and it shall be done unto you" (John 15: 7).

Now the burden of the message contained in the fourteenth, fifteenth, sixteenth, and the prayer of the seventeenth chapters of John, were to make plain "the promise of the Father," viz.: "The gift of the Holy Spirit," and the results of His coming, which were purity and power, just what the church needs today. Every Christian, in order to enjoy the greatest privileges of the gospel, must have his own personal Pentecost.

Power over temptation. "There hath no temptation taken you but such as is common to man: but God is faithful, who will not suffer you to be tempted above that ye are able; but will with the temptation also make a way to escape, that ye may be able to bear it," (1 Cor. 10: 13). "The Lord knoweth how to deliver the godly out of temptations," (2 Pet, 2: 9).

"Temptations come and trials too,
  While hellish darts are hurled,
But Jesus saves me through and through
  In spite of all the world."

Oh, how temptation loses its power when the heart is free from every thing that would sympathize with it, and filled with love and peace, and singing the songs of Zion, a true picture of which is found in Is. 35: 10, "And the ransomed of the Lord shall return, and come to Zion with songs and everlasting joy upon their heads; they shall obtain joy and gladness, and sorrow and sighing shall flee away." Such a soul, in tune with heavenly harps, with God as a wall of fire about him, and the angel of the Lord encamped around him, and abiding under the shadow of the Almighty; I would like for some one to tell us what chance the devil has at him. There is a safe place for the child of God here in this life where he can be delivered out of the hand of his enemies and go forth to conquer the world, the flesh, and the devil, overcoming the enemy at every step, and having "right to the tree of life," and "hidden manna"; being "clothed in white raiment," "a pillar in the temple of God," "inheriting all things," and at last having the honor of sitting "with Christ in His throne."

Holiness is the natural life of the purified. You might as well attempt to check an earthquake as to stop the stream of holiness from the life of the individual, or church, that has been washed in the blood of the Lamb and baptized with fire and the Holy Ghost. Oh, the power and influence of a holy life in a community; somehow it is joined to the Omnipotent. Argument can be resisted, logic can be met, eloquence can be overcome, and persuasion and invitations scorned, and appeals and warnings evaded and disregarded. But the silent force and power of a holy life, and the presence of a devoted and consecrated soul melts the hard heart, turns the stubborn will and leads the sinner to Christ. Holiness is truth embodied, it is the gospel on fire burning on the altar of the heart, beaming from the eyes, breathing from the lips, and preaching from the life, until the world is compelled to believe.

Holiness takes hold of God with one hand, and the sinner with the other, and brings them together. But lastly :

5. It prepares us for life and heaven. Paul would urge us on to holiness "lest any root of bitterness springing up trouble you," implying that the preventative — holiness — exterminates these roots of bitterness, which cause many to fall from the grace of God. How much better is the soul that is free from these roots of bitterness, prepared for life and its realities. God brought us salvation for this life first. We need it to live with, and death will have no power over us, and heaven will be the natural result of a faithful life. But there can be no heaven to come without holiness here. The one depends wholly upon the other. "Without holiness no man shall see the Lord." It seems to me this ought to alarm many who are seemingly so indifferent as to the demands of God upon them in this life. "Who shall ascend into the hill of the Lord? or who

shall stand in His holy place? He that hath clean hands, and a pure heart" (Ps. 24: 3-4).

Without holiness there can be no such heaven as the New Testament describes, or the heart longs and craves for. Scenery and grandeur the most beautiful, mountains, woods, rivers and skies the most charming, palaces and temples the most costly; the streets of gold, the sea of glass, the walls of precious stones, health and ease, luxury and pleasure, education, poetry, art and literature in their perfection — all this, without holiness of life and character, would never be a heaven to the soul. Hear Chrysostom in his dying hour asking for clean white robes. He threw aside his soiled garments, and arrayed himself in pure white, and calmly waited the coming of his Lord, and when He came he shouted "Glory be to God for all things that happen."

I have taken great comfort in reading the rich experience of the late Mrs. Bishop Castle. For years she was an earnest seeker of holiness but not until 1878, Nov. 22d, in the last year of her life, did the ever memorable day come. She was alone when "the lamp of the Lord descended." When her daughter came in she found mother's face "shining," as she said, "like the face of an angel." After a moment of silence she broke forth "I have found this full salvation." She was soon afterward stricken down and for months was kept in her room to tell the story of how Jesus was "able to save to the uttermost." Her expressions of gratitude were constantly coming from her pure heart. " The Lord has washed my heart so clean! Oh, this sweet peace, it flows as a river to my soul. This room is full of glory." All her clothes must be perfectly free from any signs of dirt. She said, "Since Jesus has washed me so clean I want everything clean around me." The white clothes on the stand and bed were regarded as "emblems of purity."

One morning she exclaimed, "Oh, that I had found this years ago, how much good I might have done. Oh, how bright the cross, how beautiful the crown. Oh, it is nothing for a Christian to die. When I am gone clothe me in white; have my coffin covered with white; have it plain, not expensive, and save the money for the missionary cause."

In her last moments her spirit was quiet, and occasionally she would remark, "I am waiting, just waiting. The Saviour is still at my side and the angels are waiting to take me home."

Oh, what a victory through Christ! It was holiness of heart that gave strength and courage, and led Cranmer, Hooper, Bradford, Noyes and Latimer and millions of others to covet a martyr's death and crown. It was the sweet and precious experience of holiness that led George Shadford to cry out in his dying hour, "Victory! Victory! through the blood of the Lamb!" and John Wesley to exclaim, "The best of all is, God is with us," and Charles Wesley to calmly remark, with his last breath, "I shall be satisfied with Thy likeness — satisfied, satisfied!"

Dr. Preston said, when about to step over, "I have walked with God while living, and now I go to rest with Him."

Dr. Goodwin, when facing death, said, "How an enemy is turned to a smiling friend."

Abbott, "Glory to God, I see heaven sweetly opening before me!" Oh, my friends, holiness will do to live by and bring the greatest victory in death. Remember, "Without holiness no man shall see the Lord."

IX.

UNITY WITH GOD.

M. D. COLLINS, D. D., OCEAN GROVE, N. J.

"Neither pray I for these alone, but for them also which shall believe on Me through their word; that they all may be one; as Thou, Father, art in Me, and I in Thee, that they also may be one in us: that the world may believe that Thou hast sent Me. And the glory which Thou gavest Me I have given them; that they may be one, even as we are one: I in them, and Thou in Me, that they may be made perfect in one; and that the world may know that Thou hast sent Me, and hast loved them, as Thou hast loved Me" (John 17 : 20-23).

IN this prayer the breath of Jesus' intercession is on every believer, in every age, and in every place. Time and events do not deflect the prayers of Jesus. We are as individually in this prayer as were the twelve. It is easy to see it is a prayer for unity, but how diverse have been the interpretations as to the nature of that unity. Some have thought it a theological, some an ecclesiastical and some a social unity. It seems strange there should be diversity of opinion concerning language so concise and compact.

I. *See the pattern of the unity for which He prayed*, "As Thou, Father, art in Me and I in Thee, that they also may be one in us."

There are two sides to this unity, "As Thou, Father,

art in Me," is one side; "and I in Thee," is the other side. Let us, then, devoutly inquire, "How does God, the Father, dwell in Jesus Christ the Son?" I do not desire to arouse curious queries as to the Trinity, but how does God, the Father, dwell in Jesus, the Son of Mary, and the Saviour of men? I think the reply must obviously be, "*God dwells in Jesus by the glad, free and full bestowment of every beatitude of His nature upon Him.* "For it pleased the Father that in Him should all fullness dwell" (Col. 1: 19). "For God giveth not the Spirit by measure unto Him" (John 3: 34). "God also hath highly exalted Him, and given Him a name which is above every name: that at the name of Jesus every knee should bow, of things in heaven, and things in earth, and things under the earth; and that every tongue should confess that Jesus Christ is Lord, to the glory of God the Father" (Phil. 2: 9-11).

This is precisely the state He desires we should enjoy. It is remarkable that just the language, with no abatement of its sweep or comprehensiveness, is used in the promises to and prayers for disciples of Jesus, "And of His fullness have all we received, and grace for grace" (John 1: 16). "And I am sure that, when I come unto you, I shall come in the fullness of the blessing of the gospel of Christ" (Rom. 15: 29). "And to know the love of Christ, which passeth knowledge, that ye might be filled with all the fullness of God" (Eph. 3: 19). "Till we all come in the unity of the faith, and of the knowledge of the Son of God, unto a perfect man, unto the measure of the stature of the fullness of Christ" (Eph. 4:13). "For in Him dwelleth all the fullness of the Godhead bodily. And ye are complete in Him, which is the head of all principality and power" (Col. 2:9,10). "And what agreement hath the temple of God with idols? for ye are the temple of the living God; as God hath said, I will dwell in them, and walk in them; and I will be their God, and they shall be My people" (2 Cor. 6:16).

You may say, "I cannot see how one can be 'filled with all the fullness of God.'" But God has not restricted Himself in the communications of His blessings, to the limitations of our comprehension. I am not deprived of all the nourishing results of food by my inability to comprehend the laws of assimilation in the human digestive process. I do not understand how pure air oxygenates the blood through the lungs, or even that it does that thing, and yet, if I can get pure air into my lungs, it will invigorate my body through my blood some way. I may be equally in the dark as to the *how* of "being filled with the fullness of God," but I may be so filled nevertheless. I once came across a beautiful little flower on the eastern slope of the Rocky Mountains. I paused beside it to rest. The sun was shining, as he can shine, through a cloudless Colorado sky. I said to this little beauty, "Why, you seem to have the whole sun to yourself; you take him in in all his brilliance to the very borders of his wide face — every ray, all his heat — all, all are yours; and yet you do not rob any other flower, thousands of which carpet the mountain-side below you."

Somehow, so, I do not care so much to know how

I have a whole Christ to myself, "who loved me and gave Himself for me," just as though I were the only sinner who had gone astray into dark rebellion against God, and for me He laid aside the robes of His glory, came to Bethlehem, took on Him my nature, descended to Calvary, and there died in my stead; then down the steeps of death to the bottom of Joseph's tomb; then up to life, up to prefatory resurrection power, and up to the throne, there "ever living to intercede for me," as though I were the only one needing His prayer. All the seeming *general* promises of God have an *individual* focal point. Christ did not die for the masses; He died for the individual. "Whosoever will, let *him* come."

So we conclude God dwells in Jesus by the glad, free, full bestowment of every beatitude of His being upon Him.

The other side of this unity, "and I in Thee," elicits the query: "How does Jesus dwell in the Father?" I judge that it is *by the glad, free, and full yielding of every activity of His being to the will of God.* It is not thinkable that He should maintain the unity of the Father's presence, love, and power, a moment, with any question in His will as to the performance of His Father's will. And yet, it is not an automatic union. He voluntarily does the will of Him that sent Him. How constantly He pursued the will of God during the whole period of His earthly pilgrimage! In the darkest hour in Gethsemane and on Calvary, "I come (in the volume of the book it is written of Me,) I delight to do Thy will, O God!"

And this is the pathway of our unity with God. Every hindrance to the ongoing tide of spiritual life and power, every shadow and haze on the question of salvation, has been directly or indirectly associated with the question of our obedience to Christ our head. Faith, the one essential prerequisite of salvation, obtained and retained, is, in its essence, obedience to God. Oh, if we will but make the will of God the end of all query as to life and duty, we shall find heaven's joy everywhere we go. So Jesus "dwells in the Father" by the glad, free, and full offering of every activity of His nature and life to the will of God. Here, then, is the two-fold unity He desires we should have. Dwelling in God, by the glad, free, and full yielding of every activity of our being to His will; and He, dwelling in us by the glad, free, and full bestowment of every beatitude of His being upon us.

II. *Out of this unity flows the glory which Christ received from God, and gave as the heritage of the disciples.* You observe that there are two glories spoken of in this prayer. In the fifth verse He prays, "And now, O Father, glorify Thou Me with Thine own self, with the glory I had with Thee before the world was." That was His glory, as a member of the Trinity, of which He emptied Himself at the incarnation. But here He speaks of a communicated glory — " The glory which Thou *gavest* me." What was this glory? Two Scriptures will give us the key. Peter says, "For he received from God the Father honor and glory, when there came such a voice to Him from the excellent glory, This is my beloved Son, in whom I am well pleased," (2 Pet. 1:17), and Jesus, speaking of the power by which He performed the miracles of His earthly life, said, "But if I cast out devils by the Spirit of God, then the kingdom of God is come unto you," (Matt. 12: 28). By these Scriptures you see that the glory Jesus received was the glory of the Divine sanction and co-operation.

Jesus, as the Saviour, subordinated His life to the principles of obedience, "learning obedience by the things which He suffered"; and yet, as an obedient Son, He moved so harmoniously along the lines of the divine will that God the Father could, and did approve of Him, and God the Holy Ghost, as executive of the Godhead, furnished the power which moved with such miracle marvels in the supernatural of His earthly life. Jesus was in such unity with God, that every activity of His life was borne upon, buttressed, and filled with the Holy Spirit. He said to the inanimate form borne on the bier and followed by the widowed mother, "Young man, I say unto thee arise" and immediately the Holy Spirit gave life to the body and he arose, and greeted his wonder-gladdened mother.

O, brethren, this is the glory that Jesus has prayed we may have — the glory of such unity with and in the Holy Ghost as that he can, and he will if he can, approve, buttress and co-operate in and with our lives, so that men shall glorify God in us. Who knows the sweep of possibilities here? Surely, we have but touched their borders. To have the bright cloud of God's mantle overshadow us, and a voice out of the cloud say to our deepest consciousness, "This is my beloved Son, hear ye Him," is to be energized in the mightiest way for the contests of earth, and to be buttressed against the strongest onslaught of the enemies of righteousness. To be able to speak, move, act, in such unity with the Holy Ghost as that He will supplement and empower the utterance and action with divine results, this it is to feel the hidings of power and to enjoy the unity Jesus prayed believers might have.

Truth, to save men, must be incarnated. We should have known little of God had He not come to us in the bosom of our Elder Brother, Jesus Christ. Abstract truth will not reach men to-day. The Bible, alone, will not. Its truths must be planted in human lives in order to reach human beings. And so Jesus prays for this, that our lives may be the unhindered field where these truths may root, grow, bud, bloom and bring forth fruit, and so reproduce Jesus among men. This is the awful grandeur to which the provisions of grace and the prayers of Jesus would elevate Christian living — to reproduce Jesus among men. Oh, to what simplicity of method, to what sincerity of purpose and to what holiness of life should we give ourselves in the execution of this trust!

III. *Three things Jesus desires to have effected through this unity.*

1. The perfection of the disciples: "That they may be made perfect in one." The great need of our Christianity to-day, for its propagation among men, is *better samples of its saving power*. The unity here prayed for is a blessed incorporation of perfection as taught elsewhere by Jesus. It lies in two things: (*a*) *Com-*

plete abandonment to the will of God. This He taught clearly to the rich ruler, "If thou wilt be perfect, go and sell that thou hast, and give to the poor, and thou shalt have treasure in heaven: and come and follow Me" (Matt. 19 : 21). And (*b*) *full inhabitation by His Spirit.* His promise of the Spirit at Pentecost included this, "For He dwelleth with you, and shall be in you" (John 14 : 17). We have not so much further to do with the elaboration of perfection now, as we have to point your attention to its relation to the propagation of the gospel in the world. Jesus evidently saw, in the perfection of His disciples in every age, the shortest and surest route to the salvation of the race.

2. The second thing Jesus desired effected through this unity was that the world might know that He is a Saviour, "That the world may know that thou hast sent Me." Twice He speaks of this, in the twenty-first verse, "That the world may *believe* that Thou hast sent Me," and in the twenty-third verse, "That the world may *know* that Thou hast sent Me." This shows that Jesus desires that Christian life may be both an inspiration to faith in Jesus as a Saviour, and then that it should be an unmistakable evidence that Jesus is a Saviour. God has some incontrovertable arguments for salvation in Christian living. I once met a blatant infidel, who said the "whole thing of Christianity was a fraud and hypocrisy." But when pressed as to its wholesale nature as an assertion, he acknowledged he did not mean "all," for, said he, "My mother was a Christian." Ah, many a true Christian mother has been instrumental in planting a conviction of the

reality of Christianity in the heart of her boy who, though he fell into all the blinding power of the world and the devil, could never get away from the indelible mark made in his soul by his mother's life — *it is so!* This, which is possible in some cases, Jesus desires shall be universal in the ranks of believers, and every disciple be an unanswerable argument that *Jesus is a Saviour*. Surely, this will not permit that " we say we have fellowship with Him, and walk in darkness," and thus contradict the very truth we seek to propagate.

3. The third thing Jesus sought to effect through this unity is that "the world may know . . . that Thou hast loved them, as Thou hast loved Me." This is the most difficult part of this wonderful prayer to grasp. Who can tell us how God loved His only Son, who voluntarily went to Calvary, and died for the sins of the world, to show God's love for the world? I doubt if Gabriel could tell us what reciprocities of love played between the heart of the Father and His Son who had obeyed unto death. But that untellable and almost unthinkable thing is the very thing God has for the world. And this is that which He wants us to show the world. Oh, what transparency, simplicity and devotion is needed to execute such a trust! How the pursuit of human ambitions, selfish aims, and earthly honors pales before such a God-honored trust! May the prayer of Jesus be answered in our lives and we go forth in this unity that is so high a definition of perfection, that incites faith in Jesus as a Saviour and that exhibits the love which God hath for his Son and for the world!

X.

SUPREME LOVE TO GOD.

REV. J. A. WOOD, SOUTH PASADENA, CAL.

"Thou shalt love the Lord thy God with all thy heart, and with all thy soul, and with all thy mind" (Matt. 22:37).

THIS passage is an epitome of Christian duty, and comprehends all that God requires of man, including all the duties enjoined in the Decalogue, — love to God and man, comprising the whole of experimental and practical Christianity. "On these two commandments hang all the law and the prophets." They are iterated again and again in both Testaments. Three of the evangelists — Matthew, Mark and Luke, give us the text.

To recover fallen man from his alienation and corruption, and secure his observance of this commandment, was the great design of Moses and the prophets in the earlier dispensation and of Christ and the apostles in our dispensation.

"This is the first and great commandment." It is first in importance, for it comprehends all others. It is first and greatest, not only in comprehension, but in dignity, excellence and duration. It is the statute law in the moral universe, binding equally on all created moral beings from the highest celestial intelligences to the lowest of the human race.

In this great, first commandment, our whole duty is made a *love service*. How different this from the common error that Christian duty is tedious and burdensome! In the experience of the devoted heart, it is more of a delightful charm than a reluctant constraint. Our Lord declared His "yoke" to be "easy" and His "burden" to be "light." John says, "His commandments are not grievous."

Christian duty may appear hard and intolerable to *corrupt* human nature, but it is easy and delightful to the *renewed* heart. How could it be otherwise, as God's service is a good service, a useful service and a profitable service! It is not merely tolerable, but delightful. It is an assisted service, hence an easy service. It is a rational, spiritual, love service.

The divine requirements are never malevolent, capricious, selfish or arbitrary. They are necessary, being based in the nature and relation of things, and originate in, and harmonize with, infinite wisdom and love. They accord with our highest interests and happiness, and never conflict with them. They involve the highest liberty and freedom of which our nature is capable. Evangelical love to God is the antithesis of legal bondage. A complete Christian life is the perfection of liberty — the soul's loving recreation. "Whom the Son maketh free shall be free indeed."

To the devoted soul nothing is more agreeable than that which God requires. Faber expressed it thus;

> "I worship Thee, sweet will of God,
> And all Thy ways adore,
> And every day I live I seem
> To love Thee more and more."

I. *Consider the object of supreme devotion.*

"Thou shalt love the Lord thy God" — Father, Son and Holy Ghost — the Triune God — our Creator, our Preserver and our Redeemer! As God is the fountain-head of all beings, He is to be loved by all with supreme devotion. His nature and perfections, moral and natural, command the homage and superlative love of all responsible creatures. The depraved and rebellious condition of humanity, with blinded minds and guilty consciences, is a very unfortunate state in which to form correct views of the infinitely holy God.

The reasonableness and obligation of this duty to God is seen in His adorable perfections, in our relations to Him, and in His benefactions and purposes which flow from His infinite generosity.

The glorious character of God is revealed in the declarations, "God is love" and "Love is of God." In these two short sentences we have a beautiful portraiture of the lovely character of the incomprehensible God. Never was there more meaning in so few words. Here we see love to be the essence of the divine nature. His love, like His nature, is unchangeable and eternal, "the same yesterday, to-day and forever." His adorable character deserves, as it commands, universal confidence and worship. His requirements do not exceed the demands of His supreme benevolence and worthiness, and they never go beyond our honest convictions of duty. If God is infinite love, He ought to be supremely loved by every creature He has made.

"Love is of God." He is the original fountain of all love — the origin of all that is loving or lovable in creation — and all love is originated, sustained and animated by Him, whether it be in men or angels, in the highest or lowest of His creatures, responsible or irresponsible.

Christ was God's love incarnated, and the atonement eclipses all other manifestations of love in the universe. "God so loved the world, that He gave His only begotten Son, that whosoever believeth in Him, should not perish, but have everlasting life."

God's love, as manifested in creation, providence, and especially in redemption, will constitute the chief element in the bliss and glory of heaven. It will be seen as a boundless, fathomless ocean of glory that never can be measured or fully comprehended.

"God is glorious in holiness." His purity, majesty and loveliness beggar all description. All the virtue, purity, beauty, excellence, loveliness, generosity and love in the created universe combined, outside of God Himself, is only as a speck of dust compared with the sun, when contrasted with the perfections of God. They are only the streams or trickling drops, from the infinite fountain of divine perfections.

The obligation to love God is seen in our relations to Him. "The Lord *thy* God." He is our Creator, Preserver and Redeemer. As such (I say it reverently), He is our nearest relative — our heavenly Father! our constant Preserver! our glorious Redeemer! He is nearer to us than the mother who bore us, or the earthly father who fondled us in childhood. God is as near to us as we are to ourselves. Preservation is equivalent to a constant creation. It takes the same power to sustain creation as it did to cause creation, and hence the same power to sustain our being as to create our being. All power is from God. The power to see, to hear, to feel, to think, to know, to will and to love, is all from God. "For in Him, we live, and move, and have our being." We cannot stir a hand, or a foot, or a tongue, but by Him. We had our being from Him not only at the first, but have it from Him still. Without His constant care and preservation we would sink at once into nonentity. We are God's offspring; He is our Father that begat us, and preserves us, and all life, motion and being is from Him. We should ever remember that our continued existence, is by His present, all-pervading and supporting energy.

Look at His generosity and benefactions. These exceed all our apprehension or comprehension. We cannot number them, one of a thousand. They have swarmed about us every hour of our existence. They come from above and beneath us, and from every point of compass around us. They never cease day or night. They are so associated as to augment each other a thousand-fold. They constitute innumerable millions of items, and embody every blessing we ever had, or now have, or can ever hope to have. We are absolutely shut up to God for every blessing of this life, and will be for all eternity. While we are absolutely dependent, and will be eternally, all our resources are in God, the author of infinite benefactions.

God, the object of supreme worship, has given humanity every expression of tenderness and sympathy, care and grace, and has the highest purposes conceivable in regard to them. Any man who will refuse to love and who wickedly insults and disobeys God, ought to suffer, and will suffer the natural and penal results of his sins.

II. *Consider the nature of the love God requires.*

It is not natural in fallen man, but gracious, and exists only in renewed natures. Love to God dwells in no unregenerate heart, hence the necessity of the new birth, which is the beginning of love to God. "He that loveth is born of God, and knoweth God." Every regenerate man has "the love of God shed abroad in his heart by the Holy Ghost, which is given unto him."

This love divinely implanted in the heart, is consonant with the nature and relation of things, and it has a *filial* aspect. God is our heavenly Father. All Christians are "sons and daughters of the Lord Almighty." The promise is, "I will receive you, and ye shall be my sons and daughters, saith the Lord Almighty." Here is the filial relation, and love answers to it.

God is infinitely trustworthy, and this love has a confiding aspect. Love always confides, and "faith [confidence], works by love," and love makes faith natural and easy. God, in His boundless benevolence, is the Great Giver, and this love correspondingly flows out in gratitude to Him and holds the soul in a delightful responsive attitude to the reception of His bounties.

"The sweetest bliss of moral beings is in loving, and this love has an inspiring aspect of delight in God. It rejoices in Him, adores Him, and is charmed and delighted with Him. Inspired by this love, the soul cries out; " This God is my God forever and ever." and " Whom have I in heaven but Thee? and there is none upon earth that I desire beside Thee." This love is the temper and the moulding force in the Christian life. It breathes itself through the whole spirit, pervading the activities, and giving character to the exterior life.

III. *Notice the extent of this love.* "Thou shalt love the Lord thy God with *all* thy heart, with *all* thy soul, and with *all* thy mind." This love is to be bounded or limited only by our knowledge and capacity, "with all our heart." Richard Watson, in his exposition, says, " The terms heart, soul, mind, to which St. Luke adds strength, are not intended so much to convey distinct ideas as to give force to the precept by the accumulation of words of nearly the same import."

Mr. Wesley, in his notes, says, " *With all thy soul*, with the warmest affection; *with all thy strength*, the most vigorous efforts of thy will; *with all thy mind* or understanding, in the most wise and reasonable manner thou canst, thy understanding guiding thy will and affections."

These words must mean that God is to be loved with the entire affection of the soul, so that all its powers and faculties are devoted to His service. This is perfect love, and in order to it, the whole soul must be under the reign of grace and cleansed from all impurity. No man can love God with all his "heart," "soul," "mind," and "strength," until the blood of Christ has cleansed him from all sin, so that no antagonisms to the love of God remain in the heart.

The provisions and promises of God cover our necessities, and are co-related to His commands. "The Lord thy God will circumcise [purify] thine heart, and the heart of thy seed, to love the Lord thy God with all thine heart, and with all thy soul, that thou mayest live." The apostle asserts, that "circumcision is that of the heart, in the putting off of the body of the sins of the flesh, by the circumcision of Christ," No man should complain of inability to love God with all his heart, or to the extent of His capacity or ability, as God has promised; "I will put my Spirit within you and cause you to keep My commandments, and ye shall keep My judgments and do them."

This first and great commandment enjoins evangelical, or Christian perfection. Perfect love, or Christian perfection is simply the observance of this command — *loving God with all the heart*. "Pure love," said Wesley, "reigning alone in the heart, this is the whole of Christian perfection." The Methodist catechism defines Christian perfection as — "The state of being entirely cleansed from all sin, so as to love God with all our heart and mind, and soul, and strength." This catechism was revised by Bishop Hedding, and Drs. Olin, Bangs and Holdich, and endorsed by the general conference.

St. Paul says: — "The end of the commandment is charity [love] out of a pure heart."

The holy Fletcher defines Christian perfection as follows,—"It is the pure love of God and man shed abroad in a faithful believer's heart by the Holy Ghost given unto him, to cleanse him, and to keep him clean, 'from all filthiness of the flesh and spirit,' and to enable him to 'fulfill the law of Christ,' according to the talents he is intrusted with, and the circumstances in which he is placed in this world."

All who are cleansed from all sin, love God with all their heart; and all who love God with all their heart, will obey Him with all their power.

REMARKS.

This love, experimentally and practically, constitutes true evangelical obedience. "Love is the fulfilling of the law,"—the substance and fulfillment of the law. "On these two commandments hang all the law and the prophets."

Love to God, is the main feature of moral likeness to Christ. "As He is, so are we in this world." To be godly is to be godlike, and in the possession of this love, "we are made partakers of the divine nature." "He that dwelleth in love, dwelleth in God, and God in him." In this divine union is our "love made perfect." "Herein," says John, "is our love made perfect."

This love in its incipiency is a distinguishing mark of the new birth:—"Every one that loveth is born of God, and knoweth God." This imparted love is the chief element in regenerate nature, and is the breath and temper of all true piety. Being a special fruit of the Spirit, it is a mark and badge of Christian discipleship. "By this shall all men know that ye are My disciples if ye have love one for the other."

This dispositional, abiding force dwelling in pure hearts, controls and directs the life and extends its influence through the whole soul, and is the bond of unity in the moral universe. It is the highest and grandest element in moral beings, full of sympathy, kindness and tenderness. It is only through a heart full of this love, that mankind can know the true meaning of peace, of rest, and of joy and fellowship with God.

XI.

CHRISTIAN PERFECTION.

G. W. WILSON, DES MOINES, IA.

"Be ye therefore perfect" (Matt. 5:48).

No THEME has aroused more discussion in the church for the last one hundred years than that of Christian perfection. It has been represented and misrepresented. Many erroneous views have been taught, and yet in spite of friends making mistakes in teaching, and foes misrepresenting what is taught, thousands have sought and obtained this experience, and are living in this blessed spiritual state, and the doctrine and experience are spreading throughout the whole church of God.

We are commanded to be perfect as our Father which is in heaven is perfect. This clearly implies that some perfection is not only to be aimed at but reached, and that it is to be a character of perfection, like what our Father which is in heaven possesses. Certainly not in degree, but why not in kind, if we possess the same nature?

Perfection in God is the absolute rectitude of His nature, and to command us to be perfect is but to express the ground of spiritual unity and fellowship between God, men and angels. Though a command, it is not so much an expression of authority — setting up a standard — as a statement of unchanging and unchangeable principle. Anything contrary to love is contrary to God. He being absolute, and we finite, we cannot comprehend the measure of His love, but we can taste its quality, and be as utterly free from anything contrary to His Spirit of love as He is Himself. It is *His* blood that "cleanseth us," "even as *He* is pure," and if we become "partakers of the divine nature," we have the same quality of *moral* rectitude.

That which is imperfect cannot embrace the perfect, and no man without the blessing of perfect love, though he have an open Bible and much intelligence, has ever been in perfect accord with the love nature of God, or been in spiritual harmony with the rectitude of His nature and the rightfulness of His authority and commands. "If any man love Me he will keep My words," etc. Not age, growth, intelligence, size, development or evolution make heaven a place of security, but perfection, or its synonyms — *oneness, purity.*

God created man perfect in the only sense in which he ever can be so in nature. He was undeveloped, certainly could not have had his growth, and yet some of our leading teachers to-day talk of a perfection of *maturity*, which would be a higher standard than Eden, and is an impossible thing. *A perfection of maturity in spirits of eternal progression is a contradiction of terms.*

By virtue of their subordinate relation, body, soul and spirit — the whole man — is fallen by sin, and by the introduction of sin his whole nature is depraved and perverse. The spirit is unclean; the nature is depraved. Now, in adjusting nature, we must discover its laws and purposes, to learn the remedies. God begins at the fountain. A perfect spirit is absolutely essential to any other kind of ultimate perfection, and God's revealed method is to perfect our spirits by an immediate and divine process, and this is possible and demonstrated by glorious experience and because of the spirit nature of man. You will at once discover that a perfection of growth is impossible by virtue of what spirit nature is, as also a perfection of maturity; but a perfection of quality and character is compatible with its nature and the revealed methods of Scripture.

Spirit may be pure, though never mature. It may be love, and love only, though infantile. *Sin does not destroy anything essential to true human nature, it only depraves it.* Now, if that which depraves it is removed, and the effects of the depravity corrected, then spirit nature will normally conform to the laws that govern it, and it will perfectly fulfill the purpose of its Creator.

Dr. Adam Clarke says, "We count those things perfect that answer the end whereto they were instituted." The Spirit of God is love, the spirit of a perfect man is love, this is the bond of fellowship between the two; therefore, he who is filled with the spirit of love, is a perfect man, according to the Scriptural standard of perfection, and his moral nature is in perfect accord with the moral nature of God. He does not grasp the absoluteness of the infinite — but infinite and finite are one, for they are both of the "one Spirit." "That they all may be one; as Thou, *Father*, art in Me, and I in Thee, that they also may be one in us" (John 17 : 21).

Our experience, and the words of Scripture ought to agree, for those words can only be made real to our consciousness by experience. Now, does any one seeking (not theorizing about), Scriptural perfection, ever conceive that the lack in his case is quantity, or bigness? If the heart were allowed to talk, it would speak of uncleanness, impurity, sin, for the existence of which there is no harmonious adjustment. It is not so much the consciousness of the lack of love, as the positive fact of something contrary to it, that we wish removed, that we may be perfect in faith, obedience and love. *When sin is not manifest, and we consciously love, we are never disturbed about our relation to God, but like any other soul, according to the law of our spirit-nature, we desire unceasingly an increase of love.* But when sin manifests itself within, and its character is revealed, and we discover it as our sin, the output of our nature, we desire its extirpation, and its existence causes fear, loathing, and a sense of uncleanness of spirit, that makes us cry out for its removal. Because sin does not manifest itself at once after conversion, many young converts in their first love say, " I know I desired nothing but God, and I felt nothing but love at my conversion ; was I not pure then ?"

Now, another consciousness asserts itself, the absence of all impurity, and the soul wholly under the law of love, hungering, thirsting, eating, growing and realizing that " perfect love casteth out fear." The consciousness of sin is the ground of our conviction that our nature is not in harmony with God's. No amount of ignorance, mistakes, inefficiency, intellectual dulness, or lack of ability to serve or do, can produce this, for we know that "He remembereth that we are dust," and is "touched with the feeling of our infirmities."

The degree of our love is determined by our capacity; the intensity of sin by the type imparted. The one may be cleansed away, until spotless and pure, we love with a pure heart fervently; the other may increase and abound according to the law of our spirit nature through endless eternity. Sin is not governed by the law of growth; its type changes, its virus becomes more intense, but it never grows — it is a state, but not a personality. Growth does not diminish it, however much you grow; but glory be to God, it can be cleansed away by a divine act instantly, and the soul or spirit nature be made pure, and the perverted powers be adjusted by the filling the nature with love, its normal condition. *The spirit is then perfect in the only sense it ever can be in nature, or, natural.*

It is now subject to the law of growth and development and all this is conditioned on different grounds than that of purification. Cleansing, making pure, is conditioned upon our "putting away all filthiness of the flesh and spirit" and trusting the cleansing blood to purify *us* from all inbred sin — love filling the nature that is now purified; but this nature now must grow normally, and consequently the soul must feed on spirit food. Overlooking this, many are purified and made white, who make little progress *in* holiness.

This spiritual perfection rightly relates a man to God. It makes the spirit natures one in unity, not personality, and gives God his rightful place on the throne of the heart of man. Before sin entered man, God was in him, and there was no ground for a mediator, or grace, or any of the conditions of the redemptive plan. Sin has disturbed his rightly adjusted powers, and now he needs checks, inspirations, revelations, motives, etc., involving faith, prayer, illumination, strong motives toward righteousness, all of which were not necessary before sin came; and the adjusting these things to our triune nature, in teaching the way of salvation, has caused much misunderstanding.

Before sin entered, man's intellect and sensibilities needed no especial inspiration outside of the indwelling God, working Himself out through the exterior man; and all the gracious motivities now used to counteract the fall, had no ground for existence; his freedom was natural. Now he is just as free, but it is the result of supernatural help — this is essential to holy character.

When man is rightly related to God and himself by perfect love, he is rightly related to any other right self and holds the attitude of rightness toward every other self in the universe of God. Heaven has in it " the spirits of just men made perfect." When man's entire being is perfected, and God perfects the entire man, there will be no temple but his heart, no mediation, no grace; the original plan will be restored.

Sin has not only perverted the spirit nature, and

tainted the fountain, but it has perverted the intellect and defiled the body.

To speak of bodily perfection in this life is to contradict Scripture. It has promised that the resurrection will "change our vile body, that it may be fashioned like unto his glorious body, according to the working whereby He is able even to subdue all things unto Himself." The closing scene of redemption will be the elimination from our physical nature of all that sin has introduced, restoring it to its normal relation to mind and spirit, and who can tell the possibilities of a glorified body?

Because of these physical disabilities, no teacher of Scriptural perfection, who is intelligent, teaches that perfection of conduct or action is possible in this life. But while we do not teach any possible perfection of the body in this life, we do teach that a perfect heart will exalt the physical type, and by abstaining from all filthiness of the flesh and spirit, and by yielding our members "servants to righteousness unto holiness," we may develop a higher type of physical manhood, and impart an intenser vitality to the oncoming generations, and our progeny may possess a much richer physical and mental inheritance. Occasionally, God, by faith, performs physical cures, but never eradicates the seeds of disease, so that one never dies, and wholeness by healing is not to be expected in this life. We gladly admit this much, that many die from diseases of the body that have their origin directly in a depraved heart or a diseased mind, that if made pure in heart, would live long and useful lives here.

Nor do we teach that mental perfection is possible in this life. Imperfect apprehension and comprehension result in false reasoning, which ultimates in wrong actions, which have no moral character because the moral nature is not involved. If a man could reason correctly on all questions he would never err, but this is not possible, unaided by the Spirit, even in questions of morals. Sin has impaired our mental powers, and error, ignorance, misjudgment, false reasoning, mental obtuseness, idiosyncracies, doubt, (which is not the same as unbelief) all these must be treated from a mental standpoint. Error must be met with truth, ignorance with knowledge, false premises with sound ones, mental obtuseness with mental clearness, perversity with teachableness. Our thoughts however independent must yield to Him who says, "My thoughts are not your thoughts." Doubt must yield to clearer vision, and all this means time, knowledge, growth, etc. A man could have a perfect heart, and believe the world is flat. It would impair his usefulness but in no sense his moral character. His spiritual vision may be perfect, while his mental blindness needs an apology. Many good and perfect Christians do many foolish things, the folly of which a more intelligent unholy person would not for a moment tolerate, and for want of proper discrimination, they are declared unholy, because unwise. After Pentecost, Peter was still the victim of a false education, and had to be convinced of the broadness of the gospel he was commissioned to preach, by a vision from heaven. He was no more spiritually perfect, after his housetop vision, but a wiser man.

Barnabas and Paul, both full of the Holy Spirit, could not agree about John Mark. In after years Mark accompanied Paul. On questions of eschatology men perfect in love may differ, and love each other none the less. Much that we know now will soon be useless, and can only fill a niche in memory's chamber. The larger vision, the deeper knowledge, dispenses with it, as the noonday dispenses with the cheerless gray of day dawn.

We do teach perfection in the realm of our affections and intentions.

We know what an imperfect affection is; its insufficiency, its fitfulness, its clamorings for a somewhat to fill the aching void, lust for the world struggling to supplant love to God, and fitful visits from the heavenly Guest; seasons of fervor, followed by seasons of declension, sometimes regretting our pledge of love, that we may court the world; repentings, relentings and renewals, with a feeling that we are not entitled to a love to which we have been untrue; confidence mixed with fear, longingly but shamefully looking into the face of Him whom we have grieved, and wondering if He loves us still. Whatever else we do, or do not see, we feel —

> "It is worse than death, my God, to love,
> And not my God alone."

And we cry for —

> "A heart in every thought renewed,
> And full of love divine;
> Perfect, and right, and pure, and good,
> A copy, Lord, of Thine."

We have not only a feeling that we ought, but that we can, love God perfectly, that we can be perfect in our devotion to Him, and be His — His only — forever. Nothing lacking in my consecration. Nothing lacking in my faith. Nothing lacking in my love — I thus fulfill all law, and am perfect, spiritually.

Sin is selfishness. Perfect love destroys selfishness. God made our hearts to love Him, and one another. He commands us to do so with all our hearts. He that does so is perfect in love, and enjoys Christian perfection. *Love never matures — it is not a growth — nor does it grow.* *You* may grow, and in a comparative sense mature, and so be called a mature Christian, have a mature judgment, etc. *But love never matures*, it increaseth and aboundeth more and more; but every increase is a gift from the divine Giver, and not a growth. You may grow *in* love, the tree may grow *in* the soil; but love does not grow; it is "shed abroad in our hearts by the Holy Ghost, which is given unto us."

It is a gift, and may now be imparted by the Giver, on the conditions upon which it is bestowed. If the heart is all love, there can be no sin — a heart without sin is a perfect heart. A pure heart is a gift. The only perfection in spiritual things is perfection in love, therefore Christian perfection is a divine gift, and all Christians may enjoy this glorious state.

As our volitions determine our character, our wills may ever say, "Thy will be done," and hand over all into God's hands, for that will to be fulfilled — even so. Amen!

XII.

THE CHILDREN OF GOD.

G. A. McLAUGHLIN, EVANSTON, ILL.

"Whosoever is born of God doth not commit sin" (1 John 3:9).

Two truths are plainly apparent in this text: first, the doctrine and experience of the new birth — "born of God." Second, the life of the new birth — "doth not commit sin." A class of people attempt to deny the first, but they do so in opposition to the plain statements of the Holy Scriptures. Another class admit the first and deny the second. While on the one hand they assert the doctrine of regeneration, they declare that to live without committing sin is an impossibility.

Their denial is also in opposition to the plain statements of the Holy Scriptures. Both truths are in the text. If the former be true, so also is the latter. If the latter be false, then the former is also false. They must stand or fall together. People who deny the possibility of living without committing sin usually obtain their religious ideas from public opinion instead of the Word of God. Many modern professors of religion are like old-fashioned New England mariners who sailed by landmarks and never dared put to sea because they were unacquainted with the rules of navigation. The landmarks, that many in the church go by, are the lives and opinions of others instead of the teachings of the Word of God. I expect no one to accept what I say in this sermon only so far as it is substantiated by the Word of God. "To the law and to the testimony; if they speak not according to this Word there is no light in them."

It is to be lamented that so many who profess to believe the Word of God, are not more particular to have an experience in harmony with the Word of God. How few are particular to enquire as to the Scriptural definition of sin. Instead of doing that, they protest that they can not live without committing sin, notwithstanding the assertions of Scripture to the contrary. In the Scriptural sense, errors of judgment or mistakes, are not sinful actions. The quality of an action — good or bad — is determined by the motive that prompts the action. Two men may perform the same act and in the one case it may be a sin; in the other a virtuous act. For instance: A gives a sum of money to feed the hungry, out of the generosity of his heart. B also gives an equal amount for the same purpose, but gives it because he is running for office and wishes to be thought a benevolent man. The same act in the one case is virtuous, in the other it is the sin of hypocrisy. "As a man thinketh in his heart so is he."

Dr. Lyman Abbott says of the Greek verb which is here translated "Doth not commit sin," "It signifies in the New Testament always moral wrong, never a mere error in judgment." If mistakes be sins then the case is hopeless for all the children of God. For St. John says in the previous verse, "Whosoever committeth sin is of the devil." David like a good shepherd did not perplex his flock but rightly divided the Word, discriminating between errors, faults, sins and the great transgression. In the 19th Psalm he says, "Who can understand his errors? cleanse thou me from secret faults. Keep back thy servant also from presumptuous sins; let them not have dominion over me: then shall I be upright, and I shall be innocent from the great transgression." Our degree of light in every case determines our responsibility. God does not require of us more than the degree of light we have, or might have.

Like a kind parent He does not punish our innocent ignorance. Paul says, "Where no law is, there is no transgression," and again, "Sin is not imputed when there is no law." The first sin of our first parents was not a mere error of judgment, but wilful disobedience to revealed light, and all other sinful acts are the same disobedience. Jesus said to the Pharisees, "If ye were blind, ye should have no sin: but now ye say, We see; therefore your sin remaineth." If we were to paraphrase our text we would say, "Whosoever is born of God does as well as he knows." He who cannot accept this standard of Christian living, must discard it for one of two reasons: either because it is too high or too low a standard. If it is too high, then he wants a religion below doing as well as we know, which is a religion that amounts to nothing. On the other hand if this be too low a standard, then he wants an impossible religion, for a religion that requires us to do better than we can know, is absurd. Note a few reasons why Christians live without committing sin.

I. *God requires as much of us after regeneration, as he required in order to be regenerated.* No sane man, it seems to me, who has read the Bible, will deny that repentance is a necessary condition in order to conversion. And what is repentance? It is not merely a copious flood of tears wrung forth at the thought of past sins. It is more. It is abandonment of sin. This may be either with or without the tears. "Let the wicked forsake his way and the unrighteous man his thoughts; and let him return unto the Lord, and He will have mercy upon him: and to our God, for He will abundantly pardon." Here the condition of pardon is ceasing to commit sin. The command to Nebuchadnezzar, "Break off thy sins by righteousness" applies to all men. It does not mean, leave off your sins a little at a time, but break them short off.

Since God requires this as the condition of spiritual life, he can require no less than this after we are possessed of spiritual life. A man who sins after conversion is therefore a backslider as truly as were Adam and Eve. It was only one sin that made them backsliders and forfeited eternal life to them. "For whosoever shall keep the whole law and yet offend in one point, he is guilty of all." In the light of this truth it seems to me that the cry that we can not live without committing sin comes from those who spend their lives in sinning and repenting, and who do not remain obedient to God long enough to know that this is the normal life of the believer.

II. *No person was ever yet compelled to commit sin.* I appeal to experience. Let the reader refer back to the most heinous sin he ever committed and he must confess that he had the power to have chosen the opposite. Whoever declares sin to be necessary, makes man a mere machine, without the freedom of will which we all know that we possess. The logical sequences are even worse. For if we cannot avoid sinning then it follows that God creates us to be sinners. This makes God the author of sin — a blasphemous doctrine! With the freedom of the will stands or falls both the justice and mercy of God.

For it is unjust and unmerciful to hold us guilty for sin if we cannot avoid it. But the objector may say " Our circumstances or sinful nature may overcome our wills and thus compel us to sin." We affirm that this can never be. Divine grace is promised for every emergency, no matter how great. God has declared in His Word, " God is faithful, who will not suffer you to be tempted above that ye are able; but will with the temptation also make a way to escape, that ye may be able to bear it."

In the light of this truth let no man say it is necessary to sin. In so doing he impeaches the faithfulness of God who has promised deliverance, if we seek His grace.

III. *The common sense of humanity rejects a*

religion that will not keep from sinning as of no present or future value. It is a common objection to religion that there are so many who do not exemplify it in their lives. The world endeavor many times to show by the lives of mere professors that religion is a sham. The idea is that if religion be divine it should make people do the things they ought to do and leave undone the things they ought not to do, and if it does not it is not worth having, and if lost such a religion would not be missed. So it has passed into a proverb, that "Prayer will make a man leave off sinning, or sin will make a man leave off praying." And a religion that does not furnish power to save a man from his sins now, can not furnish any surety of saving that man from future penalty of those same sins. If such a religion is powerless to save in this life there is no surety of the future life. Present weakness hinders faith for the future, while present salvation is a pledge of future salvation.

IV. *A religion that will not enable us to do what we ought, is below ancient heathen philosophy.* Many of the ancient heathen lived up to their light, reformed from their sins and were noted for good outward lives.

Adam Clarke, the prince of commentators, says very aptly in his comments upon our text, "We have the most indubitable evidence that many of the heathen philosophers had acquired, by mental discipline and cultivation, an entire ascendancy over all their wonted vicious habits. Perhaps my reader will recollect the story of the physiognomist, who came into the place where Socrates was delivering a lecture. His pupils, wishing to put the principles of the man's science to proof, desired him to examine the face of their master, and say what his moral character was. After a full contemplation of the philosopher's visage, he pronounced him the most gluttonous, drunken, brutal and libidinous old man that he had ever met.' As the character of Socrates was the reverse of this, his disciples began to insult the physiognomist. Socrates interfered, and said, 'The principles of this science may be very correct, for such I was, but I have conquered it by my philosophy.' O ye Christian divines, ye real or pretended gospel ministers, will ye allow the influence of the grace of Christ a sway not even so extensive as the philosophy of the heathen, who never heard of the true God!"

V. *A Christian loves to do God's will.* This is a test of his love and no man is a Christian who does not love Jesus. But he can not love Jesus, if he breaks his commandments. "If ye love me, ye will keep my commandments." We know there is a current sentiment that it is difficult to keep the commandments and that this is the reason that we can not avoid sinning. But this view makes God a taskmaster and Christians slaves. This makes religion a service of terror instead of love. But this too is contrary to the Word of God which declares, "And this is the love of God that we keep His commandments, and His commandments are not grievous." The man who called his lord a hard master in the parable was in turn, called by his lord, a wicked and slothful servant.

It is the class of lazy nominal Christians who complain of the way. Jesus says, "My yoke is easy and My burden is light." But it is objected sometimes that our text means that whosoever is born of God does not sin habitually, but only occasionally. There is nothing in the text to warrant this. But surely the grace that can keep us habitually, can keep us from sinning occasionally. Who can doubt this?

VI. *We have examples of those who lived thus in a darker age than ours.* There was, for instance, a good man, by name Zacharias, and his wife Elizabeth under the old dispensation. It is said of them by the pen of inspiration, "And they were both righteous before God, walking in all the commandments and ordinances of the Lord blameless." If two persons could thus live under the old dispensation, it is certain that any one can so live under the dispensation of the Holy Ghost.

And that is just the way we are now expected to live. Paul says, "That ye may be blameless and harmless, the sons of God, without rebuke, in the midst of a crooked and perverse nation, among whom ye shine as lights in the world."

Some endeavor to evade the force of this truth by vainly supposing that a bed-time prayer will atone for the sins of the day, with the expectation of committing the same sins to-morrow. Because the Lord is merciful, they think He will continue to forgive even when we do not propose to abandon sin. The apostle found such in his day, to whom he said, "Shall we continue in sin that grace may abound? God forbid.

How shall we who are dead to sin, live any longer therein?" We, as Protestants, pity and condemn the papal indulgences or licenses permitting men to sin. But do not many Protestants who use the goodness and mercy of God as a license to continue in sin do about the same as Catholics, thinking that we can have stated seasons of atonement and forgiveness?

VII. *Jesus declared that children of God would do the works of God.* Vice versa he declared that it was the children of the devil who did evil works. He said, "Ye do the deeds of your father," referring to the devil; while on the other hand He said of believers, "Verily, verily I say unto you, he that believeth on Me, the works that I do shall he do also." The works of the devil are sins. Let the devil's own do his works, but not the child of God, for he does the works that Jesus does. The apostle John says this is the characteristic distinction between the children of God and of the devil. "In this the children of God are manifest, and the children of the devil."

VIII. *What is the relation of this experience — regeneration — to entire sanctification?* We introduce this point here because so many have supposed that to live without sinning is entire sanctification, when in fact it is only the initial experience of the Christian life. Every one born of God thus lives, according to our text. I ask my readers right here to examine their own experience and note what is the great hindrance to such a life as we have been considering. It will be found in every case to be — not the devil, nor circumstances, but self. Inbred sin is the secret enemy within the soul that begets our besetting sin. Evil tempers and dispositions are the expression of inbred sin and hinder us in our endeavors to keep the commandments. Hence to a regenerated soul, entire sanctification that destroys the self-life becomes a necessity. It is hard enough to be fighting the devil and the world without having to contend against our own evil hearts. That work of divine grace that removes the inward foe is a help to our Christian activity. Hence entire sanctification is a work wrought in us to complete what was done in us at regeneration, and to make regeneration easy in its outward life of not committing sin.

XIII.

EZEKIEL'S VISION OF THE HOLY WATERS.

B. CARRADINE, D.D., ST. LOUIS, MO.

Ezekel 47: 1-12.

THE prophet Ezekiel was granted a number of visions concerning the church of the future. Among them none is more impressive or richer in blessed suggestions, or clearer in the description of the coming holiness of the church than that granted him of the waters bursting out of the holy sanctuary and streaming out over the world. No one can read the first twelve verses of the forty-seventh chapter of the prophecy without realizing the following three facts: One is, that a great blessing is to come to the world; another is that the blessing is to come out of the church. God has been pleased to bless mankind through His people in the past, and will do so to the end. Let every one tempted to Come-out-ism remember that the great approaching grace is to come out of Zion. A third fact taught is that the blessing that is to do much for the race is holiness. The very caption of the chapter reads: "The Vision of the Holy Waters." Moreover, as the waters came out of God's blessed sanctuary, where nothing unclean could enter, how could they be anything else but holy?

Some deeply interesting truths in regard to the holy waters appear in this passage. One is that it starts humbly. It is first seen issuing from under the threshold of the door of the temple. It does not pour down as a cascade beautiful and imposing from the pinnacle of God's house, but is first seen near the floor and ground.

Truly holiness has never originated among the dignitaries and hierarchies, civil or ecclesiastical. Invariably it makes its first appearance among the poor and obscure. When holiness first gushed forth as a distinct blessing for the church in the New Testament times, it appeared among a band of humble disciples. When it flowed again with marvelous power in the Wesleyan revival, the curious fact of its being confined to the poor was again noticed. It is equally remarkable to-day that the present holiness revival is seen in the Salvation Army, despised by many, and is also sweeping among the humbler members of the various churches, while the heads and functionaries of the church, in company with the wealthier classes, look on amazed, disapprovingly and skeptically, at the whole movement. Paul states a solemn truth in the words: "Ye see your calling, brethren, that not many wise men after the flesh, not many mighty, not many noble, are called," while another inspired writer declares that God hath chosen the poor of this world to be rich in faith. The holy water appears under the threshold.

Another fact stated is that the waters came down at the south side of the altar. We are brought at once into the presence and upon the spot itself of sacrifice. Holiness is of God, but cannot flow out to the world except through the sacrifice of the Son of God. The south side of the altar is mentioned. This is the warm, sunny side. There are religious experiences and moralities and ecclesiastical formalities that produce rigidity and coldness. We have known Christian people who, when in their coffins, will scarcely be colder and stiffer than they are now. But holiness touches the south side of our nature, pours sunshine in the soul, and produces the tropical spiritual life. It makes a summer land. Frostiness of manner and chilling speeches are at an end. Fragrance of spirit, melody in the heart, brightness of countenance, and the burning heat of love declare a religious southland. How the writer wishes that God's people who are cold, if not freezing, on the north side of the altar would come around on the south side and get thawed out and be spiritually warm thereafter for evermore.

The holy waters soon became visible. Who supposes that a fountain gushing up in the church and flowing down the aisles and under the door and out upon the street and down the street could be hidden? If this be the case, who can doubt that when the experience and life of holiness arises in the church, pours out at the door in the person of the people enjoying it, and streams in every direction toward home, street, and avenue, it will be equally manifest? It could not be concealed on the day of Pentecost, nor in Wesley's time nor in our time. The strange news is now on every lip, some wondering, some doubting, some believing, but all in the land cognizant of the fact that a peculiar religious experience has arisen in the church and is sweeping through the land in every direction.

The holy waters could not be stopped; neither can that which it typifies be arrested. The blessed flow of holiness cannot be prevented. A man can divert it from his own heart and life, but he cannot keep it from the world. What folly it would be for one standing down a stream to endeavor to dam it up when it has back of it a fountain, and back of that an inexhaustible subterranean river? Yet what consummate folly is it in one to think that he can arrest the flow of a blessing whose source is in God, and that has a Niagara drop from a world above the stars, and the weight of God's hand and God's will upon it in addition. Did the reader ever try to stop a spring by throwing stones into it, and notice that the water gushed up still, and trickling through the rocks, went on its musical, laughing, triumphant way down the valley? How much less able is one to check that fountain opened up for sin and uncleanness! And yet there are men foolish enough to try it. It would certainly be a poor fountain if the satire, laughter, and denunciation of a man could dry it up. We notice that in spite of everything in this line it flows on. We have seen what was regarded as a skilful and powerful hand, wielded by a high functionary in the church, or by one commissioned by that functionary, attempt to seal the fountain and thus stop its flow, when just as they thought the work was done, puff, gush, and lo! the ecclesiastical cement was blown out of sight, and the holy water was gushing again. Think of a man trying to bail the Mississippi River dry with a dipper! Yet have we seen men attempt a far more insane and impossible thing in endeavoring with a dipper of human authority, conferred on them for a few years, to empty the channel of grace of the wonderful stream of holiness flowing out of the very throne and heart of God. With careful hand and calculating eye the dipper is placed in the stream, then suddenly elevated, and its contents flung as far as the authority can throw, when lo! it appears that simply a minnow swimming in the experience has been flung away, while the holy water still flows on.

The water increased. This is taught beautifully. First it reached the ankles, then the knees, then the loins, and finally went over the head. This holds good in the individual case. It is a mistake to think there is no growth or improvement after the blessing of sanctification. Holiness people never say that, but their testimony is that it gets better, deeper, sweeter, every day. And so the time comes when the man is fairly swallowed up in the life, and self is lost to sight.

The figure is true also in a world-wide sense. Many to-day are smiling and sneering at this movement of God. It seems so shallow in its sweep, is confined to such a few camp meetings, has been received by so few of the wealthy and prominent, that no one dreams of being overtaken by it, or its overflowing the land. But the passage teaches that it is an increasing tide, and will steadily rise higher until no one can stand before it. The very pots in the house of the Lord will be holy, the bells on the horses will bear the name, and all will be righteous from the least unto the greatest in those days.

We have only to glance about to see how rapidly the heavenly flood is rising and spreading. In one state alone there are two hundred holiness preachers. Look at the increasing holiness literature, the one hundred holiness periodicals, the sanctified evangelists now covering the country, and the people everywhere who are sweeping into the blessing.

The holy water is to redeem the desert. The writer once saw the Great African Desert. Parched, desolate, and vast as it is, it could be reclaimed by means of the Mediterranean Sea. A greater desert is human life, and greater than man and man's wants is the abundant and never failing grace of God. The vision of the holy waters is but a stream from the sea of the divine fullness. And this ever widening and deepening stream is to redeem and reclaim the spiritual deserts of the world. It seems to have a peculiar bent or tendency in that direction. It moves toward the forsaken and desolate. It rises up to the garrets of a city, descends to the cellars, and goes with its sweet, loving flow to morally abandoned places and lives. Its object is to reclaim the waste and make it bloom like a garden of the Lord.

The holy waters bring life. The remarkable statement made by the prophet is that everything that liveth and moveth shall live where the waters come. Holiness brings life; and, mysterious as it may at first appear, brings it not only to the dead, but to everything that liveth and moveth. It is the regenerated and truly growing Christian who is the first to obtain the blessing.

Here is life added to life. And this is the very experience of this great grace. It is another blessing, containing a deeper and fuller measure of life. Christ spoke of this when he said he came that we might have life, and that we might have it more abundantly. This was what took place at Pentecost; not life, but a more abundant life.

It certainly as a blessing brings life. A man receiving it begins to live indeed in a way worthy of the name. There is life to prayer, to praise, to testimony, to Christian activity, and all this in turn touches and arouses the sinner, and so he obtains life.

The holy waters produce food. They seemed to have the power of making trees spring up of a fruit-bearing character. And this is just what takes place where holiness is received. There spring up under its influence devoted men and women of God, and from them come sermons, testimonies, prayers, songs, and lives that are soul food for the people. Holiness brings food for the soul, rich, strengthening, and satisfying. Millions to-day are perishing for the lack of that food, and are mocked in pulpit and in so-called religious papers by what is termed spiritual provision, that is no more nourishing to the spirit than sawdust to the body.

The holy waters beautified. Look at the picture

drawn by the prophet, of a river lined with trees. We know of nothing lovelier in nature than the graceful bendings of a river whose flowery shores are lined with lofty and spreading trees. Grassy banks, shadowy nooks and dells, with singing birds, are all concomitant with this scene.

God takes this attractive spectacle in nature to describe the beauty of holiness and the beautifying power of holiness. There is nothing that makes the face and life more attractive and lovely. There comes a beauty of expression, a holy charm in manner evident even to the careless observer. When the church obtains this grace, she is going to draw and win the world for God.

The holy waters called forth a host of workers. This thought is suggested by the words, "The fishers shall stand upon it from Engedi even unto En-eglaim." Holiness creates fishermen for souls. This has been and is the invariable result from the day of Pentecost until this day. Let this blessing enter the heart, and workers for God or soul fishermen spring up at once. They want to fish for souls and they know how. Some go out with a line; they seek for and obtain individuals. Others go forth with nets; they have greater gifts or possess more of the Spirit, and so bring in great companies for God. But all are fishermen of souls. The passion for the work is thoroughly aroused. In place after place, and church after church, the writer has noticed it. When holiness comes to the people of God, they are transformed into burning, tireless workers for Him.

They reach from Engedi to En-eglaim. Oh, how we need them from one end of the land to the other; from Boston to San Francisco, form London to Pekin!

A final discovery in regard to holiness, taught by the holy waters, is that it produces a religious experience and life that is unchanging and full of blessedness to others. The remarkable characteristics pertaining to the trees growing by the holy waters bring out this fact.

"Their leaf shall not fade." That is, the religious profession and the corresponding outward appearance of the life are always the same. There are no spells of gloom, fits of dumbness, and bewailings over departed joy and power. The testimony and life are ever bright, strong, and attractive. The leaf, green and fresh, rustles in the wind all the year round.

" The leaf thereof for medicine." Everywhere that the experience of holiness shall be told it shall heal some heart, cure doubt, and do good. To speak of what we possess in this beautiful and blessed life is to throw a leaf full of healing on some sin-sick soul. Truly, these are some of the leaves that are to bring healing to the nations. Once the writer was relating his experience to a large audience where there was considerable skepticism in regard to the blessing of sanctification. Months afterward he found that the leaf of that open testimony had fallen upon the listening ear of one woman and had brought healing to her soul.

" The fruit thereof shall be for meat." A holy life is moral nourishment. Even people who deny holiness will admit that the lives of godly individuals have stimulated and strengthened them. Truly, we feed upon each other, and there is nothing that so nourishes and invigorates the soul as holy teaching and holy living.

"Neither shall the fruit thereof be consumed." This looks like a contradiction to the other statement, but it is only one of the paradoxes of the Bible. It means that, in the giving forth of the life to others, the person himself suffers no waste. As in the miracle of the loaves and fishes, the bread, in spite of constant breaking and distribution, remained unwasted; so this life, in spite of constant demands as well as assaults made upon it, will abide the same. The fruit is not consumed. To the person's delight he finds an unwasting fullness in his experience that lasts not only from day to day and from year to year, but through all the lifetime.

"It shall bring forth new fruit." There will be fresh experiences every day, new works and enterprises for God and man. Men may stone off and pluck away and partake of the fruit of that life continually, but new fruit, new fruit, new fruit will be seen abounding just as constantly throughout all the days, months and years of that life.

All this mentioned above takes place, says the prophet, "because their waters they issued out of the sanctuary." Without the waters of holiness, none of these things would or could possibly occur. The vital and unbroken connection with God and the spiritual world is the only explanation of the perennial experience. The constant inflowing of the divine life into our lives will always produce religious activity, moral beauty, unfading freshness of spirit, blessedness to self, and a life abounding in comfort and relief to the spiritually sick, sad and sinful of the world.

Oh, that the holy waters would begin to flow in every church, appear at the threshold, stream over the land, and fill every heart and the whole world with the knowledge and love and glory and saving power of our God!

XIV.

GROWTH IN GRACE.

H. N. BROWN, NORWICH, CONN.

"But grow in grace" (2 Pet. 3:18).

THE idea is somewhat prevalent that the world has outgrown evangelical Christianity — that the Bible is antiquated, and the gospel of our Lord Jesus Christ is not adapted to this smart age, having failed to make sufficient allowance for human progress. Much is said and written about growth and development, based upon the false assumption that a conflict exists between "salvation by grace through faith," and the law of growth; hence the text is sometimes quoted in opposition to the doctrine and experience of instantaneous regeneration and entire sanctification, imparted by the Holy Ghost to the individual meeting the requisite conditions. We are free to admit that the Bible fails to sanction, and evangelical Christianity repudiates as false and absurd, those unphilosophical theories of growth that teach in the scientific world that man is but the development of the lower order of animal creation, and in the religious world that Christian character is but the development of unregenerate nature; but on the other hand, we unhesitatingly affirm that growth, progress, development, are the

universal order of God's kingdom, both in nature and grace. Where there is life, growth and development follow, or dissolution, decay and death will ensue.

We now invite attention to the law of growth and its conditions.

Entering the vegetable kingdom, we behold the farmer, after a proper preparation of the soil, deposit the seed-corn; whence it germinates, takes root, springs up, and develops, first the blade, then the ear, and then the full corn in the ear — provided the conditions of growth are observed; for there are certain conditions of growth which must be observed in order to secure the development and maturity of the good seed.

In the first place, as before stated, a proper preparation of the soil is necessary for the reception of the seed; but this is not all that is required. Ever since the decree of God went forth, in consequence of man's sin, "Cursed is the ground for thy sake: in sorrow shalt thou eat of it all the days of thy life: thorns also, and thistles, shall it bring forth," — constant care and labor have been found necessary to meet and overcome the several obstructions of growth. The noxious weeds must be uprooted and destroyed, and the soil kept in a mellow condition for the reception of the refreshing and nourishing showers, and the light and warmth of the sun, or the growth of the plant will be arrested, and the crop never mature.

Passing from the vegetable to the animal kingdom, we behold the same law of growth in operation here. All animals are comparatively small and weak at birth, but gradually develop in size, strength, beauty and symmetry, until they reach the perfection of animal life. Man himself, as a physical being, commences life the most helpless and dependent of all in the animal kingdom; but if the conditions of growth are observed, we behold him passing successively through the stages of infancy, childhood, youth, up to the maturity of perfect manhood.

As we enter the realm of mind, we discover this same law of progression, or development; but with this important distinction, namely: There is a time and point in the vegetable and animal kingdoms beyond which growth is impossible. The corn is mature and must be harvested, or it becomes worthless. The animal reaches its maturity or perfection of development, after which deterioration and finally death, will ensue. Not so in the realm of mind. We know of no time or point beyond which the mind of man is incapable of expansion and progression.

Having thus briefly considered the law of growth in its relation to the realm of mind and matter, we are now led to the question of its relation to the kingdom of grace.

Before a proper answer to this question can be given, a definition of grace is required, and this directs our attention at once to God as the *Author*, and man as the subject, of grace. 1 Peter 5:10: "But the God of all grace, who hath called us unto His eternal glory by Christ Jesus."

Man was originally created upright, intelligent and free, in the image of the triune God; which image consists of "righteousness and true holiness." By the

GROWTH IN GRACE.

abuse of his free-will man fell from his first estate — lost the moral image of God — incurred the penalty of violated law, and entailed upon his posterity a corrupt or depraved nature. We are now prepared for a definition of grace.

Grace is the divine favor, or mercy, manifest in the wonderful scheme of human redemption, making provision by the atonement of our Lord Jesus Christ for the complete deliverance of man from all sin, and his full restoration to the lost favor and image of God, in perfect harmony with the claims of holy law and divine justice. This is grace in provision, and in this sense it is universal. "For the grace of God, that bringeth salvation, hath appeared unto *all* men" (Titus 2:11); "But we see Jesus . . . that He by the grace of God should taste death for *every* man" (Heb. 2:9).

Again: Grace is the application of the benefits of the atonement to him who hath repentance toward God and faith in the Lord Jesus Christ. "By grace are ye *saved* through *faith*" (Eph. 2:8). This is grace applied.

It must be obvious to any intelligent mind, that we must first become a partaker of the grace of God before we can grow therein. And right at this point we perceive the grievous error of those who teach that all that is necessary to make a man pleasing to God and fit for heaven, is simply to develop his natural powers and abilities. Reason and experience unite with divine revelation in delaring the depravity of the human heart, or moral nature of mankind. The prophet Jeremiah declares, "The heart is deceitful above all things, and desperately wicked" (Jere. 17 : 9). Jesus Christ declares, "Out of the heart proceed evil thoughts, murders, adulteries, fornication, thefts, false witness, blasphemies" (Matt. 15 : 19). Paul also states that "The carnal mind is enmity against God" (Rom. 8 : 7).

Apply the law of growth to such a nature, and what is the result? It must inevitably be a development in sin. Culture and education have no power to change the moral nature of man. Sin cannot develop holiness. "Can the Ethiopian change his skin or the leopard his spots? then may ye also do good who are accustomed to do evil" (Jere. 13 : 23).

Our Saviour utters this emphatic language, which has direct application here, "For every tree is known by his own fruit. For of thorns men do not gather figs, nor of a bramble-bush gather they grapes" (Luke 6: 44); and again, "Do men gather grapes of thorns, or figs of thistles? Even so, every good tree bringeth forth good fruit, but a corrupt tree evil fruit. A good tree cannot bring forth evil fruit, neither can a corrupt tree bring forth good fruit" (Matt. 7 : 16-18).

The province of growth is not to change the essential nature of either plant, animal, or moral nature of man, but rather to develop the inherent qualities of that upon which it operates; hence the effort to produce a Christian character by developing an unregenerate nature, will prove as fruitless as the endeavor to grow grapes from thorns, and figs from thistles.

We assume, then, that in order to grow in grace we **must first be made** a partaker of grace; and now we ask what is man's first need — what grace is first required? and the reply is at once anticipated. Man is in darkness, and needs the grace of enlightenment or conviction. It is the office and work of the Holy Ghost to convince man of his ruin and to reveal the remedy: "To reprove the world of sin and of righteousness and of judgment." This work He faithfully performs; for "This is the true light that lighteth every man that cometh into the world." We may grow or increase in this grace of enlightenment; if instead of resisting the Spirit, we prayerfully heed and obediently follow the light imparted, our convictions will intensify until, an humble penitent, we sue for mercy, and are prepared for the reception of the grace of justification. "And unto you that hear shall more be given" (Mark 4: 24).

Man is a trangressor against holy law; justly condemned; waiting only the execution of the sentence against him. His great need is pardon, or the remittal of the penalty he has incurred. Again: He is weak and depraved in his moral nature — "dead in trespasses and sins"; and though his past guilt is removed by a free pardon from the throne of God, his next step would be into sin, involving him again in guilt and condemnation. He needs a radical change in his moral nature — the impartation of divine life into his dead soul, freeing him from the dominion of sin and Satan. He is an outcast from the family of God, and needs adoption into the heavenly family. So to the truly penitent sinner who believes in Jesus Christ as his atoning Saviour, is imparted the grace of justification in its broad sense, including the free and full pardon of all sins that are past, the impartation of spiritual life and power — freeing the soul from the dominion of sin — and the spirit of adoption whereby he cries Abba, Father. This work of the Spirit, for and in man, is usually denominated *conversion*.

He has now fairly crossed the threshold, and is within the kingdom of God's grace; and under the warming and life-giving rays of the Sun of Righteousness, should grow and thrive. The graces of the Spirit, complete in number, are implanted in the regenerate heart — love, joy, peace, long-suffering, gentleness, goodness, faith, meekness, temperance; and in these he is to grow and increase.

But, as in the kingdom of nature, so we find in the kingdom of grace: the growth of the graces of the Spirit is frequently arrested by the uprising of roots of bitterness which still exist in the soul, and endeavor to gain ascendency over the graces of the Spirit. "The flesh lusteth against the spirit" (Gal. 5 17). "Looking diligently lest any man fail of the grace of God, lest any root of bitterness, springing up, trouble you, and thereby many be defiled" (Heb. 12:15).

The existence of these antagonistic elements in the soul after conversion, is a fact taught in Scripture, and sadly attested by universal experience; and the discovery of the same is a source of both surprise and grief to the true believer, and prompts the question: "Has provision been made for my deliverance from these unwelcome intruders?" Thank God, the Scriptures respond to this anxious inquiry with a clear, ringing and emphatic affirmative: "Behold the Lamb of God which taketh away the sin of the world" (John 1 : 29); "Who gave Himself for us, that He might redeem us from *all iniquity*, and purify unto Himself a peculiar people, zealous of good works" (Titus 2 : 14); "Our old man is crucified with Him, that the body of sin might be *destroyed*" (Rom. 6 : 6); "Who His own self bare our sins in His own body on the tree, that we, being *dead* to sins, should live unto righteousness : by whose stripes ye were healed" (1 Peter 2 : 24); "Being made free from sin and become servants of God, ye have your fruit unto holiness, and the end everlasting life" (Rom. 6 : 22).

Right at this point many stumble, becoming conscious of inward existing evils, and without Scripture warrant, are taught by both pulpit and pew that there is no deliverance from this inward conflict this side of the grave; become discouraged, and cease to "fight the good fight of faith," and return to the beggarly elements of the world; while others, still pursuing the way of life, expend most of their spiritual force and energy in keeping these inward foes in subjection. Oh, what need there is that the pulpit give no uncertain sound here, but should clearly, frequently and emphatically declare the privilege of God's children to be "delivered out of the hand of our enemies," and "serve Him without fear in holiness and righteousness before Him, all the days of our life" (Luke 1 : 74, 75).

There are yet others, who, admitting the existence of inherited depravity after conversion, teach and profess to believe that deliverance from the same is accomplished by the law of growth. They will argue logically and Scripturally that initial salvation — that is, pardon, life and adoption — is by grace, through faith, and then very illogically conclude that complete salvation, or purity, is by growth.

As before stated, it is not the province of growth to uproot weeds in the kingdom of nature, or expel sin in that of grace. The farmer who should undertake to free his field from weeds by leaving them to be grown out by his corn, would be charged with folly, and become a subject of ridicule, and yet it is just as reasonable as to expect growth in grace to expel sin from the heart. The confusion which exists in many minds on this subject, comes from confounding the terms "*purity*" and "*maturity*." The first is a perfection (or unmixed state) of character, resulting from the elimination of all sin from the moral nature; the second is a perfection of development, and can only be used in relation to Christian experience in a comparative degree.

Purity is the result of a process of subtraction, or removal of dross or moral defilement. Maturity results from addition, increase. The one is instantaneous, the other gradual. We are *made* pure; we *grow* mature. Purity bears the relation to the growth and development of the graces of the Spirit in us, that health does to the growth of the physical being. As life and health are essential to normal physical growth and development, so spiritual life and health are necessary to normal spiritual growth and development.

GROWTH IN GRACE. 189

Both are *clearly* taught in the Scriptures. "Ye must be born again" (John 3: 7); "And you hath he quickened who were dead in trespasses and sins" (Eph. 2: 1). The words of Jesus and Paul most clearly teach the impartation of spiritual life, and in language equally forcible they both teach the bestowment of perfect health by the elimination of all moral disease. "Every branch in me that beareth fruit, he *cleanseth* it, that it may bring forth more fruit" (John 15: 2 — R. V.); "Having therefore *these promises*, dearly beloved, let us cleanse ourselves from all filthiness of the flesh and spirit" (2 Cor. 7: 1); "And the very God of peace sanctify you wholly," etc. (1 Thess. 5: 23). This spiritual life and health is communicated to us and maintained, nourished, and continued, by several gracious agencies, clearly revealed in God's Word. We will briefly notice some of the gracious helps to growth.

1. The prayerful study of God's Word. The Bible reveals to us our duties and privileges, our needs, and God's gracious supplies; our legacy, with its conditions. "The words that I speak unto you, they are spirit and they are life," (John 6: 63); "Search the Scriptures, for they are they which testify of me" (John 5: 39); "Thy word have I hid in my *heart*, that I might not sin against thee" (Ps. 119: 11).

2. Prayer. By prayer we communicate our wants to God, and receive His supplies. "Ask and it shall be given you" (Matt. 7: 7); "Pray without ceasing" (1 Thess. 5: 17). Healthy spiritual life thrives and develops only in the atmosphere of prayer.

3. Praise. Next in importance, if not of equal value, is praise. "Whoso offereth praise glorifieth me" (Psalm 50: 23); "Rejoice evermore," "in every thing give thanks" (1 Thess. 5: 16-18). It is related of the sainted Dr. Palmer, that when asked if he had no trials, as he always appeared cheerful, he replied: "I have my share of trials and temptations, but when Satan tempts me, I say, 'Glory to Jesus!' and he does not like to hear his Conquerer *praised*, and he leaves."

4. The faithful attendance upon the means of grace, such as the preaching of the Word, the sacrament, prayer and conference and class-meetings. "Not forsaking the assembling of ourselves together, as the manner of some is, but exhorting one another, and so much the more as ye see the day approaching" (Heb. 10: 25).

And lastly: earnest-work for others. "Freely ye have received, freely give" (Matt. 10: 8). Life and health are preserved by the reception and assimilation of wholesome food, the keen appetite and relish for which is stimulated by proper exercise. Active, earnest work for the Master, serves a double purpose, in instrumentally saving souls for whom Christ died, and producing in the worker a keen spiritual relish for God and divine things. "Give and it shall be given you, good measure, pressed down and shaken together and running over" (Luke 6: 38).

And "now may the God of peace" "make you perfect in every good work to do his will, working in you that which is well pleasing in his sight, through

GROWTH IN GRACE.

Jesus Christ" (Heb. 13: 20–21); "That we henceforth be no more children, tossed to and fro and carried about with every wind of doctrine, by the sleight of men and cunning craftiness whereby they lie in wait to deceive, but speaking the truth in love, may grow up into him in all things which is the head, even Christ, from whom the whole body fitly joined together and compacted by that which every joint supplieth, according to the effectual working in the measure of every part, maketh increase of the body unto the edifying of itself in love."

> "Awake, my soul, stretch every nerve,
> And press with vigor on;
> A heavenly race demands thy zeal,
> And an immortal crown."

XV.

LIGHT, THE BASIS AND MEASURE OF RESPONSIBILITY.

J. N. SHORT, CAMBRIDGE, MASS.

"And this is the condemnation, that light is come into the world, and men loved darkness rather than light, because their deeds were evil. For every one that doeth evil hateth the light, neither cometh to the light, lest his deeds should be reproved. But he that doeth truth cometh to the light, that his deeds may be made manifest, that they are wrought in God" (John 3 : 19-21).

LIGHT comes to us, as we have it in the gospel, and the question is, What will we do with it? Upon our action turns our weal or woe forever. The apostle tells us we are to be judged for the deeds done in the body. But, if judgment had no reference to the state and motives of the heart, no one could stand. Sometimes men with right motives do that which is wrong. But, other things being equal, such a man would be innocent.

The apostle said, "I had not known sin, but by the law." Hence, he says, "Sin is not imputed when there is no law." Our responsibility and judgment must be according to our light. Our faith must accord with our light, and our state and life must accord with our faith. So Jesus said, "And if any

man hear My words, and believe not, I judge him not: for I came not to judge the world, but to save the world. He that rejecteth Me, and receiveth not My words, hath one that judgeth him: the word that I have spoken, the same shall judge him in the last day."

ON THE GOSPEL WE STAND OR FALL.

Man was created to this end. There is a perfect correspondence between man's nature and the truth. According to the attitude he assumes, his conscience approves or disapproves. Light implies a moral nature to which such light is applicable. Hence, under the provisions of grace, all men under the gospel can obey in love all the will of God. Light reveals to man what he is, what his wonderful powers are for, and how much he is out of line with God. The moment light comes it places man in directly responsible relations to God.

LIGHT IS THE MEASURE OF RESPONSIBILITY.

If a man could not harmonize with the light of the gospel till death, as some teach, it would be to no good purpose to have the light, unless to torture man. God can as easily save all men at death as he can save a professed believer who has not been true to his light. But, if he had been true, he would have been saved from sin before death, unless salvation from sin is an arbitrary act of God. But Jesus said, "This is the condemnation, that light is come into the world, and men loved darkness rather than light."

PERSONAL RESPONSIBILITY.

We are responsible to harmonize with the light God has given us, which is the complete revelation of his will through Jesus Christ. If we are true we will harmonize with that light through grace. If not true, we are condemned for disobedience. But to harmonize with that light is present, full salvation; for that is to be in harmony with God, of whom the light is the expression. This is true, because a man can come fully to the light, or he cannot. If he can, that settles the question of his present salvation from all sin, when he comes. But the responsibility must ever rest upon him as a moral being, to come. On the principle that he can conform in part, he can conform fully to the light given.

THE BEARING OF INFLUENCE UPON PERSONAL RESPONSIBILITY.

Men outside the church make the wrong teaching and influence of others an excuse for rejecting the gospel; the same is true of some inside the nominal church. But when a man has the light of the gospel to the contrary, and is not true, he is as guilty before God as a sinning angel.

The attitude of the heart and the course pursued settles every man's state under the economy of mercy and justice. A true man will do as he believes God requires without respect to what his neighbors do. Peter was solicitous as to what John was to do, but Jesus said to him, "What is that to thee? Follow thou me." The reply of a military officer to one who was hesitating as to his action was significant, "Sir, what are your orders?" The answer of a friend to one in an emergency is to the point, "Do right, and risk it." All who obey God without respect to what men think, say or do always have the witness of the Spirit that they please God.

REVELATION IS FULL AND CLEAR.

God's will concerning the entire purity of the heart, and the holiness of the life, and the provision of grace to that end, is revealed as clear as light. Why do not all men see, understand and obey? Under the influence of the carnal mind they turn away from the speaking voice of God, and make their own ideas or the opinions of men the grand umpire in the case. "Measuring themselves by themselves, and comparing themselves among themselves, they are not wise." The ground of their condemnation is, "He that knoweth to do good, and doeth it not, to him it is sin."

TRUE MEN DESIRE TO BE RIGHT, AND KNOW IT.

Jesus tell us, that he that is of the truth comes to the light, that he may be right, and know that he is right. While a man is guilty for not improving his present light, he is equally guilty for not using his powers to discover truth, and thus bring his nature into full conformity with it. This applies to all without the church, but more especially to those within.

LIGHT AT THE DISPOSAL OF MORAL BEINGS BRINGS PRESENT OBLIGATION TO CONFORM TO IT.

If it be true that many about us do not know the full truth and their duty, if the means for their full enlightenment are at their disposal, the sole responsibility rests with themselves. A just God and the nature of the truth must hold them responsible as moral beings. Having the light of the gospel, ignorance is no excuse; for the Spirit convinces every man of sin, and of righteousness, and of judgment. The nobler instincts of man's nature point to the truth. Then if we do not seek to discover and possess what Jesus came to give, Jesus says it is because we do not desire to know the truth, that we may be right. Hence, a man has to cherish a spirit of opposition to the truth not to come to the light. Especially is this true of professed believers in the church.

So Jesus says, "Every one that doeth evil hateth the light, neither cometh to the light, lest his deeds should be reproved." As well as to all others, this applies to all in the church who do not come intelligently and fully to the light. Hence all in the nominal church who do not come to the light and become fully saved, do not love the truth. And there is no virtue in loving some truths, and not all truth; for it is the state of the heart that God looks at, and the truth is a unit. It is not truths, but truth. Then the opposite follows, showing that we are responsible for the entire conformity of our nature with the truth, and thus our entire sanctification.

Jesus says, "He that doeth truth cometh to the light that his deeds may be made manifest, that they are wrought in God." He who is disposed to be right, knows that by coming to the light he will discover where he is, and just how much he is out of line with God. When he makes this discovery, how long will it take him to get right, through grace, if he is honest before God? Not long with an open Bible.

Then every man under light is responsible for his unholy state: especially is this true of them professing to believe. Why? Because men can come to the light, they can submit to God; they can commit all, and trust fully. And this the sole and perfect condition of salvation through Christ now. But the man that doeth truth will do this, Jesus says. Only perfectly honest souls come fully to the light: and such souls come, and as a consequent become wholly conformed to the will of God. This is the necessary outcome.

THE WHY OF MAN'S PRESENT STATE.

The text then clearly explains why men are not justified and then sanctified wholly by the Spirit through belief of the truth; for the principle is one and the same. Possessing perfect organs of sight, the light being given, we are to blame if we walk in darkness. The man struggling in the billows, and will not lay hold upon the life line, is responsible if he sinks. We cannot devise means to save ourselves, but when God provides infinite grace, and places it clearly at our disposal, as he has in the gospel, we must, under the economy of grace, appropriate it or perish. Because this is so, nowhere do men live such guilty lives, and die such unholy deaths as under the gospel.

DEPRAVITY CONTROLS BY OUR CONSENT.

It follows, then, that the man professing truth consents to be blinded and controlled by his depravity when he does not advance by faith, and become conformed fully to the whole will of God. The gospel means perfect purity to the man who intelligently receives it: that is what God meant by it.

Christ said to some, "Ye will not come unto me that ye might have life." This is because man is not a machine; he holds his destiny in his own hands. It is a searching question: am I practically more interested in seeking truth and saving my soul than in anything else? In answering this question, God forbid that I should lie to my own soul, and purposely deceive myself.

THE STATE OF THE AFFECTIONS.

Then what is the subtile reason professed believers do not come to the light, and possess the gospel experience of complete salvation from sin now? Many, if they were to go to the judgment to-day would have to confess that, with their light and the interests at stake, they never made an honest, adequate effort for full deliverance from the sin of their heart.

If we seek the reason for this estrangement, it will

be found in the affections; "they love darkness rather than light." This is the depraved state. This is the reason man needs to be wholly sanctified by the Spirit through belief of the truth, after being justified, that he may be saved from the love of sin as well as from the guilt of sin.

Then it follows that the professed believer is not saved from the dominating power of temptation when he does not advance with a true heart into the full light of the gospel. Men in their natural state are led captive in this respect. But many professed Christians are as certainly bound by their unsanctified affections as the inebriate is by his appetite. It may be on finer lines. You might say then, "That is not so bad." But if a man is bound, is he not a prisoner? Jesus said, "He that committeth sin is the slave of sin." It does not make any difference what kind of sin it is. How can I be bound to or by any thing consciously, and stand the test of the judgment any more than the inebriate? He has as much right to gratify his appetite on his particular line, contrary to truth and righteousness, from his low standpoint, as I have, from my higher standpoint, my tastes on finer lines, contrary to the gospel. He has his way of sinning, and I have mine: and he has as much right to his way as I have to mine.

JUSTIFICATION RELATES TO ENTIRE SANCTIFICATION.

Hence the mass of professed believers have more reason to anxiously inquire, "Am I justified?" than "Am I wholly sanctified?" On the principle of the text, no man can be true and stop anywhere under light until he has reached the goal of a perfected faith and love. But how is this? Every man needs light to know himself, and thus the relation he should hold to God as a moral being. When he apprehends the truth, it is for him, then, through faith by the Spirit, to deny himself and put himself in line with the truth. This means self-denial and consecration always up to one's conception of truth. No man is justified whose present consecration is less than this.

But when a man takes this position he receives forgiveness and the quickening of the Spirit. Then, if he does not draw back, through an evil heart of unbelief, he must advance fully into the light by an intelligent exercise of faith, being led by the Spirit, to where his will becomes intelligently one with the will of God. Then his heart will be pure, and his love will be perfect. Then his development in the divine life will be normal.

TRUTH IS TO BE THE LAW OF HIS BEING.

It is not hard for the thoroughly wicked man to serve himself, for that is the law of his being. Whatever such a man does he serves the devil, because he ignores God and the truth. But when he becomes fully saved, he will do right as easily and gladly as he ever did wrong; for "where sin abounded, grace did much more abound." The ruling principle is perfect love. This makes Christ's yoke easy, and His burden light.

THE SUPREME POINT OF RESPONSIBILITY.

Where is the supreme point of responsibility? It is not that I am depraved, or have inherited sinful tendencies. I am not to blame for this. I am not to blame for coming into the world under adverse circumstances, if I did. But Christ's atonement offsets this in the case of every man, and there is no injustice done any. But these things are not our condemnation. If condemned now or finally, it is and will be because the full light came to us through the gospel, for the perfect, present cure of the malady of the heart, and we loved something contrary to the truth, and would not deny ourselves, and take the truth at the expense of the thing loved.

A man is wholly sanctified when his heart is intelligently in full, loving agreement with God. As professed believers, are we there? If not, why not? A mysterious, subtile something possesses our hearts, so that we do not seek Him with all the heart.

TRIED AND PROVED BY THE TEXT.

What application has the text to us for complete salvation in the present? There never can be more perfect light than we have to day. Christ says, "The light has come." The apostle John says, "The darkness is past, and the true light now shineth." We have then a perfect Saviour, a perfect atonement, full and forever finished. We have the Holy Spirit in all His fullness now given. We have the perfect, revealed will of God in His Word, given in commands and promises, principles and plain statements, so full and clear that we can never have more, for the Word of God can never be supplemented or improved. Jesus meant this when He said, "Light has come into the world."

If this infinite supply is not perfectly adapted to our need in the present, infinite wisdom has made a mistake — a grand blunder. If it does not save me now from sin, I cannot trust it for the future. But to think this, not say it, would be blasphemy. Hence, we say, it is perfectly adapted to the present needs of the heart. If it is, when intelligently received, its full benefit will be realized.

WHAT PREVENTS OUR PERFECT RECEPTION OF IT?

As we are not heathen, according to the words of Jesus, it is not ignorance, but a refusal to come to the light with a full heart; it is a refusal to perfectly choose the will of God. Such intelligent action would bring us into oneness of relation with God and truth. Then the Spirit of all truth would fill us, and, purifying the heart, cause us to love God with all our being.

But having the gospel, in our natural state, it is because of open rebellion. And then, as justified believers, if we do not advance into the full light to become wholly sanctified, condemnation rests upon us, because there is a subtile spirit of disobedience lurking in our heart, which remains and controls with our consent.

But when we come fully to the light, reaching the

point of full, intelligent heart agreement with God, then, as never before, God can unite Himself with us in the fullness of the Spirit. Then we are as saved as an angel. I do not say we are as strong or fully developed. We have a body still — marred and weakened by sin, and not to be redeemed until the resurrection. Also, our circumstances are not to be compared with those of angels. But, glory be to God, we can be as saved, and do the will of God on earth as they do it in heaven. Jesus made all the provision for this, and then taught us to pray that God's will might be done by us on earth as it is done in heaven. While I am not reponsible for that prayer being answered in all others, I am responsible for it being answered in my own heart.

Jesus indicates this when he says, "If ye keep My commandments, ye shall abide in My love; even as I have kept My Father's commandments, and abide in His love." So it is written, "And every man that hath this hope in him purifieth himself, even as He is pure." Hence it is written, "He that dwelleth in love dwelleth in God, and God in him. Herein is our love made perfect, that we may have boldness in the day of judgment: because as He is, so are we in this world." I prefer to be like Jesus in this world than like an angel in heaven.

DO WE QUESTION THIS TRUTH IN THE TEXT?

If we question that such intelligent submission and devotement, after pardon, would give us full salvation now, let us ask, "Having a perfect Saviour, with His work all finished, and the Holy Spirit forever given, and the many commands, which demand full salvation at our hands now, and the many promises, which assure us of present infinite provision of grace, why is it that we are not saved, fully sanctified through belief of the truth?"

There is but one answer. Either God is not true, or we do not meet the conditions. And I would as soon say that God was not true as to say that He had imposed conditions which I could not meet. Then, if we do not meet the conditions, this is our condemnation, if we do not belong to the school of the feeble-minded; for "the light has come into the world," and "the true light now shineth." We give place to unbelief.

This explains why the unconverted do not come to Christ, and why professed believers do not advance and become wholly sanctified, and in consequence lose their justification. It is heart rebellion in the case of each. In the case of the believer it may be more refined, but it is rebellion just the same. The heart is in love with darkness of some kind.

THIS STATEMENT TRIED BY THE TEXT.

"Every one that doeth evil hateth the light, neither cometh to the light, lest his deeds should be reproved." Your heart can hate light while your judgment respects it. Not recognizing this, many are deceived. But God does not look at the judgment, but at the heart.

"But he that doeth truth cometh to the light, that

his deeds may be made manifest, that they are wrought in God." Such a man is determined to be right, and know that he is right. Not wishing to be in doubt, he proves all things, and holds fast that which is good. Unless deceived by ignorant or false teachers, an honest believer must advance from the first principles of Christ to perfection; the perfecting of his faith and love.

THE TEXT AND THE NATURE OF THE TRUTH MAKE HOLINESS A NECESSITY TO ALL TRUE BELIEVERS.

Then the logic of the text proves that we cannot retain vital connection with Christ if we draw back, and do not seek and find deliverance from the impurity of our hearts. To retain our integrity and the witness of the Spirit, we must, in the nature of the case, obey the command, "Keep and seek for all the commandments of the Lord your God." That professed believers have not done this, is their condemnation. Is there any light revealed in Jesus Christ for complete deliverance from the sin of your heart, to which you do not come? Then did Jesus speak the truth when He said, "It is because you love darkness rather than light"? But it is true, "To him that knoweth to do good, and doeth it not, to him it is sin."

The text is a remarkable revelation of human nature. It tells us just what every man will do under the light of the gospel, and the reason why he will do it. Every one that does evil, or is disposed to do evil, will not come to the light — to the death of self. But every man that does the truth, or is disposed to do the truth, comes fully to the light. He will not stop and rest until it becomes a demonstrated fact that his life is all wrought in God. As professed believers, we belong to one of these two classes.

XVI.

BE YE HOLY.

I. SIMMONS, DANBURY, CT.

"Be ye holy, for I am holy" (1 Peter 1 : 16).

THE Bible uses superlative terms to express Christian experience. "Be ye therefore perfect, even as your Father which is in heaven is perfect." "That ye might be filled with all the fullness of God." "The blood of Jesus Christ His Son cleanseth us from all sin." "The very God of peace sanctify you wholly." "Be ye filled with the spirit."

"Be ye holy; for I am holy," is a command with a reason. God is holy. Through the atonement of Christ, by the Holy Spirit, man must be re-created into the same nature. The term holy is a complete term. The vessels of the sanctuary were holy because set apart to only sacred uses. "Holiness to the Lord" was to be upon the bells of the horses, to show that even the animals and the instruments of service were to be sacredly consecrated to God. "Be ye holy" means a sacred setting apart of the whole being, — spirit, soul and body — to holiness and holy uses. It compasses every act, thought and possession. It leaves no apartment of the nature for convenient, or less notorious violations of righteousness. It cannot be substituted by the imputation of Christ's righteousness as a covering. It is holiness, pure God-like holiness, consciously realized by its possessor as the gift of God, by the cleansing blood of Jesus Christ and the fire of the Holy Ghost, through genuine renunciation, complete consecration and present appropriating faith.

The need of a distinct and definite work to this end is apparent in the command itself.

1. First, as a command to unawakened sinners it can create no response. It appeals to nothing in common with itself. It is as a shout to a paralytic. The alarm bells of danger near would be far more arousing. The initial steps of pardon and reconciliation to God must first be taken. Repentance is an absorbing operation of the mind. When it is deep and thorough, and is accompanied by a forsaking that is equivalent to the amputation of a right hand, and by a consecration that to the extent of a babe's limited knowledge of life includes everything, and by a faith as simple and prompt as the dying thief's, then regeneration and justification become living facts of experience that give the command "Be ye holy" an authoritative emphasis never before realized. There are conversions in early childhood, also exceptional cases of maturer years, through religious training, in which these preceding mental operations are less powerful, but the same result is reached.

2. It is the clearness and definiteness of justification that incites to the experience of holiness. To be holy has a sweet significance and is an attractive pos-

sibility, illumined with the glories of the destruction of inbred sin, and fellowship with the Holy Trinity, to a truly justified soul. If some have misrepresented holiness in its fullness, by being powerfully converted from a backslidden or formal religion, while seeking it, and afterwards have expressed unbelief in it because carnal natives of the soul appeared to contest the perfect occupancy of the King, it only proves the imperative necessity of the experience. If, as in a few cases mentioned by Mr. Wesley, some have entered the perfect-love life almost simultaneously with conversion, their experience but confirms the doctrine, and should arouse the faith of all to reach quickly the commanded blessedness.

Does the command to be holy involve a special work of divine grace, dependent upon a special act of faith and attitude of the soul subsequent to justification? If not, then thirty-seven of Charles Wesley's hymns should be expunged from the hymnal of the church; for he sings,

> "Speak the second time 'Be clean,'
> Take away my inbred sin."

> "Fill us with Thy glorious power,
> Rooting out the seeds of sin."

> "Let us all in Thee inherit,
> Let us find that second rest."

> "Break off the yoke of inbred sin,
> And fully set my spirit free."

> "Lord, I believe a rest remains
> . . .
> Where fear and sin and grief expire,
> Cast out by perfect love."

> "But is it possible that I
> Should live and sin no more?
> Lord, if on Thee I dare rely,
> The faith shall bring the power."

These longings of the holy singer harmonize with the creed of every evangelical church, and with the experiences of a great company of saints living and dead. These are too numerous to be explained as exceptional in anything but their faith and consecration. They were of like passions with other men, and were tempted to live on the same common-place levels with the average multitudes, but they chose the higher path. It was rugged and steep, self-denying and radically disciplinary, but Jesus went that way, and walks there with His own, and makes it bright summer time all the year round. It was not temperament, nor education, but faith, mighty faith which opened their hearts to perfect love, and made their lives both peculiar and powerful.

The command to be holy, like the command to love God with all the heart, soul, mind and strength, is not accompanied with any explanation as to the method of obeying it. Experiences differ widely. There are circumstances in each case that make it unique. "There are diversities of operations" but the same Spirit. Let no man imitate another, or covet the details of his experience. Therein lie snares and a defeat. Inbred sin is a conscious fact to every soul. How to get it out is the question. The humble seeker must diligently study the Word, putting himself at the focal point of every command and promise, on the keen stretch to be holy because God is holy, and the method of becoming so will open up before him as the sun of the morning opens up the day.

1. Such a sincerity of search will reveal that God is able and willing, in superabundance to furnish the essential grace. Following his prayer for his Ephesian brethren for their inward spiritual mightiness, an indwelling Christ, a penetration and comprehension of the love of Christ beyond all knowledge, and a fullness as unto "all the fullness of God," St. Paul adds with an inspired insight into the resources at their disposal, "Now unto Him who is able to do exceeding abundantly above all that we ask or think . . . be glory . . . world without end." In his prayer for his Thessalonian brethren that their "whole spirit, soul and body be preserved blameless unto the coming of our Lord Jesus Christ," he cheers them with, "Faithful is He that calleth you who also will do it." How a soul justified by faith, saved from the old life, a witness to the love and power of God, can doubt His ability to make and keep him holy through and through is a problem. Such a doubt is more unpardonable than the unbelief of an unconverted man. The reverent familiarity with Jesus wrought by the Holy Spirit in the Christian life, should dissipate all questionings, for it was for His own He prayed, "Sanctify them through Thy truth." "Keep them from the evil." Ye who know your sins forgiven, know that the residue of the Spirit is with Him who is mighty "to save to the uttermost," and

is "able to keep you from falling and to present you faultless before the presence of His glory with exceeding joy."

2. There is a mental state that often clogs the feet, blinds the eye of faith and palsies the purpose. Nothing vitiates sincere searching for light like prejudice. Alas, that so many professors of the religion of Christ set themselves against holiness with violent opposition, because those professing it are "inconsistent," or are "fault-finding, captious and censorious." Alas that intelligent Christians should make their deductions from these defaulters, and overlook the upright who walk in the ways of the Lord. Whatever the failures, it stands true that Christ died "to purify unto Himself a peculiar people," "a glorious church," "holy and without blemish." There are many in the church, whose characters stand unchallenged for fidelity to the ten commandments, and for loyalty to the conventional requirements of church life, who seem strangely reluctant to believe holiness to be either their privilege or duty. Their prejudice must have a cause. The Scriptures plainly declare that "this is the will of God, even your sanctification," and that to "present your bodies a living sacrifice, holy, acceptable to God" is your reasonable service. What but the carnal mind which certainly manifests itself even in the regenerate nature, can explain the prejudice against the whole drift and tenor of God's Word. It is noticeable that the antagonism against the doctrine is never heard from those who are desirous that their lives should conform to the precept, "Whether there-

fore ye eat, or drink, or whatsoever ye do, do all to the glory of God." It is often in the mists of worldly compromise, of pleasant indulgencies or doubtful associations and amusements, that oppositions arise to holiness as apologetic defences for not coming out from among them and being separate. If there are sincere Christians who are living up to the light of their convictions, unbiased as to holiness, yet doubting its possibilty for them, as surely as the conscientious, but mistaken, Saul of Tarsus came to the "light from heaven, above the brightness of the sun," so surely will they come to see their inheritance by faith in the fullness of the atonement. But wherever there is prejudice, it is an impassable barrier to progress. It is a self-evident truth that growth in grace and prejudice against "perfecting holiness in the fear of the Lord" cannot exist in the same experience. Oh, if the disciples of Jesus would be unreservedly willing to let Him have full possession of them, and by His Spirit lead them into all truth, they would find the way short and sure from pardon to perfect love and purity.

3. The command to be holy, thoroughly and constantly set apart for God, in all times, circumstances and conditions, would indeed be impossible if it simply meant obedience to a code of laws. It would be a tremendous strain upon the strongest will, if holiness had not been ordained by the nature of God, to be a passion as well as a service. Hence the "Thou shalt nots" of the law, while maintaining their awful hold upon the soul to the last iota, are changed to "Thou shalt love the Lord thy God with all thy heart, and

with all thy soul, and with all thy mind, and with all thy strength." The emotional nature, when loyal to the will, is controlled in sweet exercise by its regnant authority, while in turn its volitions are made easy by the obedience of the desires, appetites and affections, and righteousness comes to be a most delectable taste. The laws, statutes and judgments of God are "more to be desired than gold, yea, than much fine gold; sweeter also than honey and the honey-comb." It is easy to understand how Christ would from the first teach, "Blessed are they that do hunger and thirst after righteousness, for they shall be filled." These appetites are all-controlling. They affect the whole man. When at their intensest strength, and fired by the Holy Ghost, they will subordinate the whole being to the object of their longing. Herein lies a vast difference between the moralist and the saint. The moralist does not hunger and thirst to be moral. Whatever his motives for morality might be, these terms would misapply. In the soul that is a "partaker of the divine nature," there is or ought to be, an intense hunger and thirst for the fullness of God. It may be pacified by factitious sustenance but never satisfied. If fed as the Scriptures direct, the fullness is near. These soul-longings for righteousness cut a straight path for "Pentecost" if not obstructed. There is no trouble about the "second blessing" or "perfect love," when the eye is single to be filled with God. The trouble with many Christians is not with their theology, nor their remarkable sensitiveness over holiness professors' failures, but with their appetites for spiritual things. When they thirst as a parched land for water, when they cry "As the hart panteth after the water brooks, so panteth my soul after Thee, oh God; my soul thirsteth for God, for the living God," they will hear Him say, "Ye are blessed, for your sufficiency is of God." "Be ye filled."

The lack of these spiritual appetites arises from the neglect of a spiritual study of the Word. Reasoning about religion is made to take the place of God's voice in His own revelation. His counsels are disregarded and His sharp distinctions in the Christian life are obscured. The Bible is a radical book. It discloses a difference between "babes in Christ" who "have need of milk" and are "unskilful in the word of righteousness," and stalwart saints to whom "belongeth strong meat" being "of full age." (Margin, *perfect*.) It furnishes no apology for "crooked paths." It gives no encouragement that growth in grace means growth into grace. It relates a radical difference in the disciples' spiritual nature before and after Pentecost. Its apostolic experiences illustrate and enforce entire sanctification in every case. Its ethics are possible only to souls complete in Christ Jesus. James says to the tempted and tried, "Count it all joy when ye fall into divers temptations." "Let patience have her perfect work, that ye may be perfect and entire, wanting nothing." Peter calls upon the "elect according to the foreknowledge of God the Father through sanctification of the Spirit," that they "be holy in all manner of conversation." John states plainly that "If we walk in the light, as He is in the light, we have fellowship one with another, and the blood of Jesus Christ His Son cleanseth us from all sin." And Paul declares " I have been crucified with Christ." These experiences express a state, which by comparing Scripture with Scripture is found to be urged upon all saints in such hortatory terms, as imply that not all have yet attained thereto. To whom does Paul speak when he urges upon the " dearly beloved," " Let us cleanse ourselves from all filthiness of the flesh and spirit, perfecting holiness in the fear of God"? It is "to the church of God which is at Corinth, with all the saints which are in all Achaia." His epistles are all the most affectionate appeals and fervent prayers for the churches, whom he addresses as " Beloved brethren," as " saints," as " faithful brethren," as the "sanctified in Christ Jesus," that they might be sanctified " wholly," "be filled with all the fullness of God" and put on love " which is the bond of perfectness." The devotional study of the Bible as Wesley, President Finney, Dr. Upham, Mahan and Dempster and hosts of men and women have studied it, will reveal three facts. First, that the new birth is a glorious work in the soul by the Holy Spirit, by which he is made a child of God and "hath everlasting life;" second, that after this new birth, and without any intentional sin or purposed departure from the covenant of obedience, he is conscious of an inward contest of opposing forces, spoken of as the *flesh* and the *spirit ;* and third, that many promises, appeals and commands are made concerning the privilege and duty of being cleansed from all pollutions of the carnal nature, emptied of sin, and filled with a perfect peace "that passeth all understanding" and a perfect love "that casteth out all fear." This threefold truth is the glad tidings of the gospel, and the substance of the epistles. It explains the mystery of the atonement and the salvation by faith in the blood of Christ. It interprets the meaning of the terms employed in the ages of type and sacrifice.

4. A devout and unprejudiced Christian, conscious of inbred sin, and hungry to be holy, after the standard of the text, is not far from the kingdom of perfect love, and may be helped by a few suggestions:

1. Make a full and searching consecration with a perfect abandon of possible results. You may be called to a foreign mission in a pestilential land. Sufferings and great trials may await you. An unknown quantity lies out there beyond sight or ken, but take it all in. Make the consecration without exception or mental reservation. Make over body, mind and spirit to God, deliberately, completely. But "Did I not do this at conversion?" You did and you did not. There is a sense in which the consecrations are similar, and a sense in which they differ. They are alike in that you act in both cases up to your knowledge and light. Rev. Alfred Cookman described the difference in four particulars: First, as a sinner your consecration was the offering of powers that are Scripturally stated to be dead in trespasses and sins; as a Christian you consecrate yourself as a "living sacrifice." Again, as a sinner your consecration was the offering of yourself as a whole, not having had

the light of the Spirit in detail upon your physical and mental faculties, hence you said as best you could,

> "Here Lord I give myself away,
> 'Tis all that I can do."

But as a child of God in the full light of justifying grace, you now see the force of entire consecration as never before, and you sing,

> "Take my soul and body's powers;
> Take my memory, mind, and will;
> All my goods and all my hours;
> All I know, and all I feel;
> All I think, or speak, or do;
> Take my heart, but make it new."

Again the tests presented by the Spirit are quite different in the consecrations. As a sinner, the loving Father imposes upon you only such tests as you can bear, but when as His obedient child you come for the fullness of the Spirit, the tests of sacrifice and service presented, touching the minute details of indulgence, separation, taste and association, are as much more exacting as the light is greater to reveal the delicate differences that fringe the borders between evil and good, and to give impulse to the choice between things "lawful" and things "not expedient."

This is clearly seen in the conditions of conversion. The absorbing thought of an awakened soul is, "God be merciful to me a sinner." To firmly resolve to leave off all sin, and to be obedient to God, are the chief considerations. The struggle is severest at these points. These settled, faith lays hold of Christ as the Saviour, and the mighty work is wrought. But as a son of God you come not for pardon in the consecration now under discussion. You are free from condemnation, being no longer under the law but under grace. Now begins a new thought of God with the new life. If you are true to the teachings of the Spirit through the Word, that thought will grow to be all-prevailing. It will grow with every prayer, and intensify with every devotional hour. Accompanying this thought will be a vivid realization of inward tendencies and conditions that disturb and perplex you. The Holy Spirit is leading you to eagerly seek for perfect communion with God, for perfect submission to all His will, and for the possession and fruits of heart purity. Your consecration will be far-reaching and deep-reaching. It will be entire.

2. Ask definitely to be made holy *now*. Fix the mind on that. "A deeper work of grace" is indefinite. You cannot imagine what it means. Better ask for the deepest work of grace. When you are on the threshold of eternal power and promise you need not reason about anything that God asks of you. "Be ye holy" is a command to you, and a pledge from Him. Holiness is its own explanation, and the best way to understand it is to plunge into it.

3. "Lay aside every weight." Right things may become wrong by the spirit and excess of their indulgence. John Wesley was an acute church statesman, and wisely made no attempt to distinguish between forbidden and permitted recreations, but drew the line at "the taking of such diversions as cannot be used in

the name of the Lord Jesus." The pleasures, the reading, the associates, may be weights or wings. The guide-boards on the highway of holiness read, " Be not conformed to this world," " Come out from among them and be ye separate," " Be ye followers of that which is good," " Do all to the glory of God."

4. " Walk in the light." It is a deadly theory that wrongs are tolerated in a justified life which are denied to a fully sanctified life. If every child of God were careful to depart from evil, his wings would grow for full salvation almost unconsciously. The distinct grace of entire sanctification ought not to be the rebuke to the commonly accepted grades of Christian living that it is. Many evade the light, and then console themselves that, not professing holiness, they are not bound to be scrupulous concerning doubtful things. What a mistake! It is a privilege to be holy — a privilege purchased with the blood of Jesus Christ — but woe to the Christian who chooses to postpone the duty. It is an obligation as imperative that " ye be holy " as that " ye must be born again."

5. Remember that every step of Christian attainment, from conversion to glorification, is *by faith*. Lay down no plan of His coming who has promised. Sometimes in the rushing wind, sometimes in the still, small voice, the fullness of God will roll over and through your being. You may burst into uncontrollable shouts of praise, or be enveloped in a holy hush. But hold to the Word which sanctifies, and believe that He comes. Neither consecration, nor feeling, nor vociferous crying and praying have any meritorious-

ness. Whenever a soul is fully saved it receives the blessed boon at the resting point of ceasing from self, and taking Christ in all His fullness. There may be agonies undergone in bringing one's self to the surrender and consecration, but the distress, however intense or prolonged, furnishes no purchase-price for "the unspeakable gift." When the consecration is complete it is faith's prerogative to believe He *doeth* it. He cleanseth. The faith and the fact are co-instantaneous. Why do so many of God's loved ones delay to consecrate, believe and obey? It is nigh thee! Meet the conditions, and lift up the heart to the Giver of Himself and of all blessing! Express your earnest desire in some such words as these suggested by John Fletcher, "I do believe that Thou canst and wilt baptize me with the Holy Ghost and with fire: help my unbelief: confirm and increase my faith with regard to this important baptism. Lord, I have need to be thus baptized of Thee, and I am straitened till this baptism is accomplished. Give me Thine abiding Spirit, that He may continually shed abroad Thy love in my soul. Come, O Lord, with that blessed Spirit! Come, Thou and Thy Father, in that Holy Comforter! Come to make your abode with me; or I shall go meekly mourning to my grave! Blessed mourning! Lord, increase it! I would rather wait in tears for Thy fullness than wantonly waste the fragments of spiritual bounties, or feed with Laodicean contentment upon the tainted manna of my former experiences. Righteous Father, I hunger and thirst after Thy righteousness! Send Thy Holy Spirit of promise to fill me therewith, to sanctify me throughout, and to seal me to the day of eternal redemption and finished salvation. Not for works of righteousness which I have done, but of Thy mercy, for Christ's sake, save Thou me by the complete washing of regeneration, and the full renewing of the Holy Ghost. And, in order to this, pour out of Thy Spirit: shed it abundantly on me, till the fountain of living water abundantly spring up in my soul and I can say, in the full sense of the words, that Thou livest in me, that my life is hid with Thee in God, and that my spirit is returned to Him that gave it — to Thee, the First and the Last, my Author and my End, my God and my all."

Oh, that all God's people knew of His fullness in Jesus Christ, ready to be poured out by the adorable Holy Ghost just now while we believe! To the blessed Trinity be glory evermore. Amen!

XVII.

GOD NEAR IN THE VALLEY OF DECISION.

ALEXANDER MCLEAN, NEW YORK, N. Y.

"Multitudes, multitudes in the valley of decision: for the day of the Lord is near in the valley of decision" (Joel 3: 14).

THE day of the Lord is near in the valley of decision. The primary meaning of this passage is generally supposed to refer to a controversy which the Lord had with His enemies, and that in the valley referred to He would cut them off; hence this place was called the valley of decision, or excision. It is clear, however, that positive and far-reaching results were there to be realized. This Scripture will here be used to throw light on *the destruction by the Holy Spirit of the Lord's enemies in the hearts of believers.*

I. *Decision is imperatively necessary to success.* Every day's experience, in the ordinary affairs of life, demonstrates its necessity. A decided character is sure to make an impression either for good or bad, according as the decision may have been wise or unwise. The persuasiveness of the platform, press, bar and pulpit have been employed through all ages to secure decision. Many of the friends of Jesus, who are favorably inclined to holiness, suppose they are right in taking time to think, or read, or listen to the experience of those who are in its possession. All this generally results in the loss of time, and possibly, in never coming into the grace of full salvation. Most Christians in these days have heard enough and read sufficiently about Jesus of Nazareth, to take His Word unquestioningly as law and gospel. He says, " Bessed are the pure in heart, for they shall see God." Of what possible benefit can it be to an honest inquirer to go back of the Lord Jesus Christ to reason about the verity of entire sanctification? Does He command it? Then it is true! Does He require us to enter upon it now? Then the path of duty to us lies only in an acceptance of this grace at once. To all those who admit the supreme authority of our divine Redeemer, the only question which can arise is, " Does Jesus plainly insist on entire sanctification, and do the inspired Scriptures warrant the believer in seeking this grace as attainable now?" What else can we understand our Lord to mean when He says, " Blessed are the pure in heart, for they shall see God "? This is one of the beatitudes, and they all have reference to the present life. What else could Jesus have had in mind but this grace, when He said, " Thou shalt love the Lord thy God with all thy heart, and with all thy soul, and with all thy mind. This is the first and great commandment. And the second is like unto it, Thou shalt love thy neighbor as thyself."

Commandments are not given for those who are in heaven, but for the people of this world. Many as may be the excuses offered by those who really know their sins forgiven, for delaying to enter the Beulah land of perfect love, they must all fall short of justifying them in the sight of God. Every hour of postponement must grieve the Holy Spirit, weaken the believer and hinder the coming of Christ's kingdom on earth. Oh, how many suffer themselves to block the way of the progress of Emmanuel.

II. *Indecision injurious to the believer.* Another and quite different class of believers might well bear in mind the great harm which must come to their own souls, and to Zion, by an equivocal attitude towards "holiness to the Lord." These dear ones think they will do best for the cause of God by saying but little definitely as to their personal experience of perfect love, but will live it out. They mean to let their lives speak about that of which their lips are silent. But the Scriptures say, "Ye are My witnesses," and a person on the witness stand who would withhold the testimony of his lips, would be instantly dismissed or receive the censure of the court. Another injurious method of showing indecision is to accept the teaching of the Scriptures on the subject of holiness, and even to claim its experience, but to hesitate on the employment of Scriptural terms to designate it. Can it be that man can give a better name to this grace than that by which it is known in the Scriptures? We are not undecided in naming conversion; and if we were to designate it by various dubious names, would there not come a serious loss to the important teaching of the new birth? There should be no more uncertainty in the mind of any candid observer, as to whether one possessed perfect love, than as to another enjoying the witness to pardon of sin. The indecision resultant from an indefinite knowledge of either pardon or heart purity, must be a stumbling block to other souls. On the other hand, let us bear constantly in mind, that the "day of the Lord is near in the valley of decision." But do you ask, are we to precipitately, and therefore without proper consideration to profess this blessing? We reply, do not profess what you do not posess: but seek for it at once, and with all your heart. Go down deep into the valley of humiliation, because of all the light you have possessed, the many chidings of conscience given you that you were not living up to the standard of the Scriptures, and because of the multiplied and neglected tender drawings of the Spirit, leading you to that standard. Is it so, that you are not now in the possession of this blessing? Call upon God most earnestly, to deeply humble you, to break your heart in pieces, in view of the loss of influence which has come through your failure to have this grace. Persist in asking believingly for a clear sense of wrong, which the cause of God may have suffered through you. Do not hesitate to go down to the deepest depths of self-abnegation, " for the day of the Lord is near, in the valley of decision." Cease making excuses for yourself, or finding fault with others, or dwelling in the shadows of indecision because of the failure of some who profess holiness, to properly exemplify it.

III. *Be definite about this grace.* The history of Christian experience demonstrates that to obtain this grace of heart purity, we must seek it definitely as a "second blessing," having such marked characteristics of its own, bestowed upon it of the Lord, as to forever make it distinct from general bestowments of grace. The holy of holies in the temple of Solomon, is recognized by all to have been intended by the Great Architect, to be forever distinct from other parts of the same sacred enclosure. To confound pardon and purity, proves ignorance of God's way of salvation quite as much, as to say that the holy place of the temple was one and the same as the holy of holies. To confuse these things, is to unite parts of the temple which God intended to be distinct, and to contradict the facts of Christian experience, and the clear teachings of God's Word. One of the historians of Columbus brings to light the fact, that the great navigator was only on the main land of the American continent but a few hours, and then he was not aware of this important fact. He spread a boat sail for his shelter, under which he slept one night, and the next day re-embarked. This biographer remarks that Columbus had evidence enough to have known he was on the main land. All his biographers agree that his principal discoveries were in connection with islands belonging to the continent. We wonder why he did not positively ascertain that the lands he knew most about, were only adjuncts of a far greater land. Why did not he command his comrades in the little fleet, to weigh anchor, hoist sail, and steer definitely for the great second blessing, of the continent itself? The climate, soil, and fruits of the islands, were all excellent, as are all the blessings coming from the justified state, and are in no wise to be disparaged.

Columbus had overcome the greatest part of his difficult mission when he located those islands; and the soul which has the testimony of the Holy Spirit to its pardon, has accepted a very important part of the mission of the Lord in saving man. But the continent of holiness is near, and its vast area, and promise of superlative good, should incite us all and at once to weigh anchor, hoist sail, and definitely steer for the great blessing of heart-purity. Some have entered upon this blessing without a clear knowledge of that fact, and instead of remaining to explore, and to make permanent settlements, they have too soon re-embarked for the borderland of justification. They never will get into Beulah land without definite prayer, consecration and faith. Oh, that the great continent of perfect love, may incite them to say, "I will start at once."

There are some of the disciples of our Lord, who insist upon growing into this experience of holiness. They rest their belief on the command to grow in grace. Have they ever known or read of a Christian who has succeeded in obtaining it thus? No matter how long they have been in the way, Christians do not testify that they have entered the experience through growth in grace. Preparations to enter are, and of necessity must be, merely preparatory. No person could enter the holy of holies, even after the veil had been rent from top to bottom, except he should of direct purpose pass into its sacred precincts from the holy place. There could be no bridging from the islands to the continent. By the very way these important but outlying places were reached, so must the continent of holiness be entered upon by consecration and faith. Justification was obtained by a definite consecration, and a definite faith, and thus only may we realize the blessing of heart purity. Both justification and sanctification are gifts from God, and when the soul is entirely ready to receive, God instantly bestows.

IV. *The benefit of enjoying perfect love.* "The day of the Lord" may be understood as a time of special advantage, and divine power, bestowed upon the soul ready to receive it. For its own sake, and because of what may be done for others, every Christian should be possessed of that power. The law of co-operation between the believer and the Holy Spirit, is abundantly enforced in the Scriptures, and demonstrated in all the history of the church. It has been well said that " God is as much in need of good men, as good men are in need of God." The Bible is full of illustrations of the divine power, choosing some human agent through whom the Almighty purpose could be carried out. Who may say the kingdom of Christ on earth would not have been much further advanced, if the Lord had found agents made ready by the Holy Spirit to carry on His designs? Dear reader, can you say that God could not more rapidly send forth His light and truth if your indecision had forever passed away, and instead, you were graciously enabled to be all the Lord's?

Let it not be thought that there is any special danger of falling, associated with this grace. So many cling to the idea that they must climb to a high elevation, in order to be in this grace, and that those who are elevated are more liable to fall. But notice, that the day of the Lord is near in the valley of decision. The more deeply one sinks in the valley of humility, the more readily will the Holy Spirit come to that heart. While those who are entirely sanctified may fall, experience demonstrates they are less likely to backslide. The apostle, in writing to the Ephesians said, " Take unto you the whole armor of God, that ye may be able to stand in the evil day, and having done all, to stand." When we abide in the valley of humility, we so answer the conditions on which many promises of the Bible rest, that God is well pleased to verify these promises to our souls. With a multitude of others who have gone before you in this way, dear reader, you will find that it is a way of safety, and not a path of increased exposure. With the Psalmist you can say, " I will walk at liberty, for I seek Thy precepts;" and with Paul you shall know, that you have "been delivered from the bondage of corruption, into the glorious liberty of the children of God." If in this experience you may at times realize you are walking in an elevation of joy, it will not be on the edge of a precipice, but on the King's highway, cast up for the ransomed of the Lord, who shall come to Zion with songs and everlasting joy upon their heads. " They shall obtain joy and gladness, and sorrow and sighing shall flee away." If some have explained holiness as a process of ascent, and others of equal reliability, as a path of descent, we should know that both are correct.

V. *This grace, is a valley in the mountains.* The

sincere seeker of heart purity should not be embarrassed if told by well meaning Christians, who do not possess this great grace, that there are many valleys of humiliation, which they have known by experience. Yes, there are many occasions of humbling ourselves before the Lord, and great profiting results therefrom. But, there is one valley of humility which brings us near to the day of the Lord.

No one who has entered that valley can forget the initatory impressions written on the soul by the finger of God; some of these were a conscious and a very vivid sense of entire dependence upon God; the gladness accompanying the gift of every power of our being to the Lord; the soul's unreserved reliance on the promises of God to save to the very uttermost; the depth of purpose of the soul to walk by faith, and not by sight, as long as God should be pleased to withhold special manifestations of his acceptance; nor finally, of the quiet peace, accompanying the full conviction that once for all, everything now known or which should hereafter be discovered, was unreservedly given to the Lord.

This valley, like the celebrated Yosemite, is the most wonderful ever known to the traveler. Passing from the plains, into the foothills, one realizes the bracing air, and observes his extended power of vision through the clear atmosphere. As he further ascends, he finds he must make many descents. Now he may be on a "divide;" the water falling on one side of which, flows in one direction, and that dropping but two feet away, in quite an opposite direction. But still he keeps on his course towards the far-famed valley. What magnificent trees grow on many of these hills! It is thus the justified soul, finds valuable developments in the conscious experience of pardon. The traveler may think a home would be desirable, on some of these uplands. But into what deep canyons, he must yet descend to enter the Yosemite. He may be greeted by some settler in the vales through which he journeys who in a congratulatory way, asks him if he is going to *the valley*. The writer went down a very long and steep mountain-side, and as the shades of evening gathered about him, it seemed to be far longer than any of the other descents into the frequent canyons which had been passed. It was here that his older brother, acting as his guide said, "We are now getting down to the level of the Yosemite."

Further on we drove, and he said, "Now we are in the valley." But the darkness had come, clouds obscured the stars, and I could see nothing. "If it were light," he said, "you would see the most remarkable surroundings your eye ever rested upon." All I could do was to answer, "I can see nothing." Still further on he said, "We should cross a bridge over the river, about at this point." I felt about on the ground, for the entrance to that bridge. The light of a match directed us across that peaceful stream. On we went in the gloom of night, my guide saying, "Now, were it light, you would see the beautiful falls; the majestic *Half Dome*," etc. But I said, "I can see nothing." At last we were greeted by a light in the window of the hotel where we were to put up.

Refreshed with a good meal, we soon sought, "*Tired nature's sweet restorer, balmy sleep.*" The sun had risen high when I awoke, and rapidly dressing, I went upon the porch, and lo! before me, loomed up El Capitan, 2500 feet, in air. Yonder were the Cathedral tops piercing the clouds; on my right, that marvelous Half Dome fixed my wondering gaze. At my feet flowed the quiet Merced river, having leaped over great cascades and waterfalls, now to reflect each flitting cloud, and the massive perpendicular rocks of this wonderful valley. The language of man fails to describe fully the beauty, grandeur and sublimity of this scene. So reader, you may have entered many valleys of humiliation, but stay not, until you have reached the valley near which is the day of the Lord. You may enter it without rapture, or remarkable developments of any kind. But abide there in faith, until the Lord shall reveal Himself to your soul in great power. Remember if you are determined not to dwell in any other valley, or to build a tabernacle for yourself, on any mountain height of experience, but to press on to all your privilege as a Christian, your *elder brother Jesus Christ* will go with you, and will assure you when you have crossed into Beulah, even though no special emotion may then be realized. Go right on your way in faith, and it will not be long before the day of glory shall break upon you and you will be constrained to sing with joy,—

"I have entered the valley of blessing so sweet
And Jesus abides with me there,
And His Spirit, and blood, make my cleansing complete
And His perfect love casteth out fear."

XVIII.

HELP THROUGH UNEXPECTED CHANNELS.

ISAIAH REID, DES MOINES, IOWA.

"Likewise the Spirit also helpeth our infirmities : for we know not what we should pray for as we ought : but the Spirit itself maketh intercession for us with groanings which cannot be uttered" (Rom. 8 : 26).

HERE are some important items for the daily needs of life's journey. All travelers in the King's Country are furnished with a most excellent tourist's guide. Attentions to the above mentioned things would save from much needless mistake, regret, blunder, and fall, it may be. God would have us all real students. He expects us to read and think for ourselves. He arranges place and time for us to sit in His library and feast on its treasures, and learn for ourselves the wonders of His kingdom that now is, and that which is to come. He wants us to look into His text books, walk with Him amid the beauties and glories of the natural world. The seas are His, the stars in heaven are His. The secrets of air and ether are His. The generative forces of nature all His. We are His children. He made this world for us. The world of mind and spirit are His. They are a step nearer Himself than the material universe. It is more to find, see

and understand God in the hidden spheres of spiritual life, than in the world of material things.

Our sonship involves and necessitates companionship and fellowship. These do not exist without community of understanding, aim and desire. To be "made in His image" means to be of similar organization as to kind; though it does not necessarily imply equality in degree.

Fatherhood in God implies likeness in the son. More, a father seeks to make the son know what he knows. He desires his son to see things as he sees them: to seek what he seeks, to like what he likes, to be as he is in quality and character. God desires our success. In His order, what we desire He wants to assist us to obtain. He wants us to have what we want, while we abide in the light.

Our want of success in spiritual attainment is a grief to Him. Our inability to compass what we want, and reach satisfaction, pains the very nature of all parentage, and so pains "Our Father," because He is a father.

To meet the difficulty into which the defection of sin brought us, He has furnished us a Helper.

This Helper, to be what we are not; this Teacher to teach us what we know not; this Reformer to bring us to that which we are not; this Transformer to make us like what we are not: this is the special office work of the personal Holy Ghost. He is a sympathizing Teacher. Please do not think of Him as a mere critic, convictor of wrong, and reporter of evil conduct or mere influence. While His office as responsible schoolteacher implies all this, think, on the other hand, of His office as Helper. He knows all things, for He is God. As the gift of Jesus, He has come in the spirit of love to fulfill all the good pleasure of His goodness in our behalf. Do you need love? His work it is to "shed it abroad in the heart." Have you "infirmities"? He it is who is commissioned from the Trinity to help you with them. Have you troubles about prayer? Carry them to Him, for He it is who sits as special Helper at your mercy seat. Did your preacher, like one I once heard, lump together infirmities, faults, mistakes and errors all in one vessel, and label them all "sins," and you have gone troubled, knowing that sin could be forgiven, and that one could be saved from it, but because you could not be saved from infirmity, you therefore reckoned yourself a continual sinner? It is false. If infirmities were sins, needing the remedy of forgiveness, the Holy Ghost would not " help " you in them, else He would help you in sinning.

Cruden defines infirmities thus: "Sickness, or feebleness of body; afflictions, reproaches and persecutions; spiritual weakness, and defects in grace; failings and mistakes, either through ignorance or weakness." This is Scriptural, and therefore practical. Who has not gone in some of these ways! How many go for years with a weak body, unable to carry the spirit on its errands of mercy and love! How many carry an enervated and over-sensitive nervous organization, with a brain consequently hindered in all work. There are those born with faults for which they can never be responsible. There are those injured for life through no fault of their own. But all this field is not so wide as littleness and lowness of a dethroned spirit. Now, we who have been teachers have been tried and perplexed and grieved with children who could study, but had no aptitude whatever to learn what we wanted them to know. Have you considered God's love in sending the Holy Spirit to help that infirmity which fell on us all on account of sin? This dullness of spiritual apprehension, how you have chided yourself for it! How you have lamented over it and blamed yourself for having it! Well, for this very thing the Holy Spirit came. Look up to Him this moment. Hunt up your infirmities and tell Him all about them. Pile them up at His feet, and rest from their burden.

Then there is your praying: how you have chided yourself, and perhaps let the devil worry you because you did not pray like some one else you could name. Perhaps the other one had been to the Teacher and found out what to pray for. You tried to pray in and of yourself. You did not count on the Helper, and because of this lack of trust, were left to yourself. Remember the text implies that not knowing what to pray for as we ought, is an infirmity for which there is help in the Holy Spirit.

The word "help" is suggestive. It is an inspired word. It does not convey the idea of pardon or deliverance. The thought implies a burden to be carried, for which there is somehow not strength sufficient. The Helper is the divine Spirit of God. He cannot help us in the carrying of a sinful thing. All the words he uses in connection with the adjusting of the sin question are different.

There is no thought here turning attention to pardon, or cleansing. The condition of being helped, so far as this connection shows, refers to a case in which all these things have been previously settled. The Father here speaks to His redeemed child, longing, ·n the deepest tenderness, to reach a feature of the hurt of sin, that can neither be pardoned nor cleansed.

Another thought I would not have you miss, is, that your infirmity is a possible extra chance for you to be associated with the Infinite. I have known those, who, after having met with some accident which maimed for life, found from that time their infirmity a peculiar channel of helpfulness and acquaintance with God. For some it seems needful, in order that they "may enter into life" over there, to be "maimed" and "halt" here; the better off by being bereft of some "offending member" or sense or outward opportunity in the time life, in order to gain the eternity life. Grieve not therefore, unduly, if the way of your going lies along some of these hard passes. Going down to Egypt was a hard pass for poor Joseph, but it resulted in a place hard by the throne of the greatest of kings. If the route be in the order of God hold still. The Helper is always there.

It is also in the thought underlying the words of the text, that we "ought" to do what we cannot of ourselves do. That is, God certainly requires of us that which cannot be done unless He helps us. In other words, the full measure of life's possibilities requires our association with the Infinite. Man's "ought" includes a definite participation in the Infinite Omnipotence. So, whatever man ought to do, man can do. There are, therefore, no impossible commands. This is evident from the nature of the case, and yet how strange to think we are required to do that which necessitates the positive putting forth of the divine energy. God so identifies himself with us and honors humanity with the gift of Himself. It seems bewildering, almost, to think that God would put the "ought" on us to do that which, of ourselves, we cannot, in order to get Him to help us! We should not shrink or complain of those passes in life, where, cut off from all other sources of help, we are forced to trust him and find out by actual contact what He is to the trusting soul. Run back along the trail of your experience, and find out how true this is.

If these positions be thus solidly true, it is evident in the next place that every man should keep his experience up to his knowledge and convictions of right. The oughtness in him should have right of way at all times, and he should be as good as he knows he ought to be. How far beneath this thousands live! So common is it for people to live beneath the oughtness hidden in their privileges, that the rightness of this law has been suspended in the high court of their conscience. This possibility to live beneath one's privilege is the bane of the race, and falls heavily on the people of God.

The oughtness in us is not simply the standard of rightness, but also the measure of the possible. We can be what we ought to be. We can be justly punished for failure to be what we can be. If we can be pardoned we ought to be. If God has provided to make us holy here, we ought to be. The can be, and the ought to be run in parallel lines with divinity between to make the connections.

To attempt what I know I cannot do of myself, appears useless and unjust to all who do not have faith. But, yet, when we consider that the doing of this very thing is the special thing that brings us into actual and personal contact with God, we ought, on the other hand, to rejoice that we are counted worthy to be called to such privilege. Here is the special field-work of the Spirit. He "maketh intercession for us with groanings." Some thoughts are too big to be contained in words. Some desires are wordless and unutterable in dictionary terms. Some features of love are inexpressible in word language. God really puts us in the line of real "mind reading"; that is, knowing others' thought without the use and locomotion of words. Possibly language may pass away, when the true spiritual life is reached — when the body is glorified. Other methods may supercede our present, so much superior that we will care no more for what is now of so much use.

At any rate, there is such a thing as wordless prayer. While the usual order is to "say" prayer, as Jesus said when instructing the disciples, it is possible to think prayer, and while about the usual activities of life to keep the prayer line in use; yet, after all, it is more to keep the soul in a prayerful attitude; a condition of mind, in which though you have not time to pray, you can easily, as if by habit, refer everything to

Jesus. True, wordless prayer is that which cannot be put into words. Its known expressions are groans and sighs. You have seen a sleeping child sob and sob again, even after all crying has passed. The vocal expression has passed away, but the sea of the spirit within has not reached quieted waves yet.

At such times the Holy Spirit "maketh intercession for us." Is not this then the best praying we do? Cannot heaven answer all such prayer? Possibly at such times you have been tempted to sink down into utter prostration, and perhaps thought yourself all but abandoned of the Lord. When we have prayed through, and can say no more, and the burden is still on, is it not time then to lie still and let the blessed Spirit make intercession for us? What we cannot say He can. What we fail to express to the listening court of heaven, He can. Our failure is his opportunity; but faith must hold steady. The searching is "according to the will of God."

Relationship is what is wanted in the prayer, and yet we are conscious of relationship without prayer. We love and are fully resting in our love when we have no petition. So, when the spirit gets back to God, like the forgiven child into its mother's arms, it is the office of the Spirit of God to make conscious this adjusted relation. It is more satisfying than all words. God rests in His love, and the child rests also. It is the rest of consciousness. It does not need words any more. It is better felt than told.

XIX.

THE HOLINESS OF GOD. OUR ASSIMILATION TO HIM.

L. R. DUNN, D. D., EAST ORANGE, N. J.

1 Peter 1: 15, 16.

It is one of the maxims of history and of philosophy that no person ever rises higher, in a moral and spiritual sense, than the god whom he worships. This is true of heathenism, with its multitude of divinities; and it is true of Christianity. But, it must be admitted by everyone, that the God whom the child of the Lord adores, is infinitely superior in His moral and spiritual perfections, to all the gods of the heathen. His infinite holiness is recognized and adored by the worshiping hosts of angels and archangels in the ever-repeated song, "Holy, holy, holy, is the Lord of Hosts!" Now this Being absolutely holy comes to us, His creatures, and says to everyone, "Be ye holy; for I the Lord your God, am holy." It is this possibility of the imitativeness of the Jehovah of the Bible, that ennobles and exalts man — while the revealed necessity of it often astonishes and even appalls him. Yet "it is written" so frequently, it is enforced so strongly, provision is made for its realization so abundantly and freely that we must consider and obey

THE HOLINESS OF GOD.

the divine command. The universality of the command is evidently shown; so that in heaven, in earth, and even in hell, this is the expression of the divine will.

It becomes us, therefore, to endeavor to understand, so far as we may be able, (1) *What is the holiness of God?* and (2) *What is the possibility of our assimilation to it.* The text teaches that God's holiness is Himself. "Be ye holy; for *I am holy.*" This involves all His other moral attributes and perfections. Justice, truth, goodness, etc., all are centered in this, and all radiate from this. If God is not holy, He is not God.

1. His holiness is absolute. It admits of no possibility of His erring, falling from this high estate, or, doing any thing that is wrong, unjust, impure, untruthful or unkind. As He has existed from the eternity of the past, so He has always been holy; and as He will exist through the eternity of all the future, so He always will be holy. Further, His holiness admits of no diminution, or decline, or decrease. And it admits of no enlargement, no increase. It is always and eternally the same.

2. His holiness is the most glorious thing in the universe. He is "glorious in holiness." "He sitteth upon the throne of His holiness." His "habitation is one of holiness and glory." He "swears by His holiness." These and many other forms of expression indicate the truthfulness of this. It is always called the beauty of holiness, the glory of holiness. The matchlessness of its splendor and glory is above the brightness of a million of mid-day suns. It is

delightful for us to know that Christ, the divine Messiah, is called by the Psalmist, " The Holy One." Gabriel in his annunciation calls Him, " The Holy One of God." Peter calls Him, " The Holy One." And we all rejoicingly know that the eternal Spirit is likewise called, " The Holy Ghost."

3. This holiness is uncreated, underived, it belongs to God, and to Him only. No one was before Him; no one will be after Him. " From everlasting to everlasting He is God, and we may add, He is holy. He is the fountain, all else are only streams flowing from Him. He is the reservoir; all the holiness of angels and archangels, seraphim and cherubim and redeemed men, is from this source. Well may we all sing,—

> " Holy as Thou, O Lord is none ;
> Thy holiness is all Thine own ;
> A drop of that unbounded sea
> Is our's — a drop derived from Thee.
>
> And when Thy purity we share,
> Thine only glory we declare ;
> And humbled into nothing own,
> Holy and pure is God alone."

What, then is the possibility of our assimilation to this holiness? We cannot, in very important particulars, be holy like God. We cannot be absolutely holy, nor infinitely holy, nor unchangeably holy. All the holiness we can ever have is derived from Him, and from Him alone. And yet the command is to " be holy: for He is holy." How far then, may we be like God?

We may be *like Him in our moral character*. By

sin we have lost His image from our soul. Our moral, our spiritual nature has been defiled. We cannot restore ourselves. We cannot bring ourselves back to our original likeness to God. But infinite wisdom has conceived the plan, and infinite love has accomplished it, whereby this divine likeness may be restored. Hear what Paul says, "And be renewed in the spirit of your mind; and . . . put on the new man, which after God is created in righteousness and true holiness" [of truth, margin] (Eph. 4 : 23, 24). Again, "Yield your members, servants to righteousness unto holiness;" "Have your fruit unto holiness" (Rom. 6 : 10-22). And in Heb. 12 : 10, it is declared that even our afflictions are for the purpose of making us "partakers of His holiness." These portions of Scripture teach us the possibility of being holy as God is holy.

What is the extent to which this likeness to God may be enjoyed? This is the summary which the Word of God presents before us. "Without blame," "unblamable," "holy in all conversation," or, more properly in all the course of our life. "Holy in all conversation." Here is a wide sweep. And remember all these things are "in the presence of God." This condition is not to be under the judgment of this world. God's command to Abraham was, "Walk before *Me* and be thou perfect." The standard of the judgment of these conditions is a moral one, and not according to the secular jurisprudence of this world. That only takes cognizance of outward actions and outbreaking sins. This looks at the heart, at the intention, at the will, and its volitions, at all the minute environments in which men are placed, and decides the character on these bases. Why, if men were to be judged by this standard of the world, then the holiest men would be denounced as the vilest sinners and punished as they only deserve. Did not the world, ay, and the so-called religious world say, that the holiest being it ever saw had a demon? Was not the great apostle Paul, perhaps the nearest like his Master of any one that ever lived, in holiness and righteousness, beaten, stoned, imprisoned and finally slain by the highest authority of this world? And have not countless thousands been thus treated by the men, the governments and authorities of the world? This poor, dark, blinded world scouts the very idea of holiness, hates to hear it mentioned, and scorns its possessors. And is it not a sad thought, that in proportion as worldliness exists and dominates in the soul of even the professed follower of Christ, it leads him to do similar things? Yet, after all, there have always been men and woman in this world whom God has regarded as holy — there are such men and women now; and there always will be.

Holiness is a spiritual condition. The very essence of holiness is love, pure, spotless love to God, and in a subordinate sense, love to the brother man. It is no wonder that Mr. Wesley thus defined it. It is no wonder that Paul declared love to be the "fulfilling of the law." This is not love for sin, or the love of sin, but God's love shed abroad in the heart, in its fullness, expelling everything contrary thereto, inspiring to all holy thought and desire, inflaming the whole being with its incandescent fire. But where this love exists it will be known, it will be felt, it will exert its power. It will be seen in a holy boldness against every form of sin, in ardent desire to be useful to others in a complete abandonment of every kind of iniquity, in a thorough consecration to the service of God, and a complete submission to the divine will. The holy man loves to tread in the footsteps of Jesus; for he knows that, "as He is, so are we in this world." He is an imitator of Christ, as Christ was a revelation of the Father; and holiness is the dominant principle of his whole heart, and his whole life.

But, if all this is true, what can you say about the *many weaknesses which these persons display?* I answer, weaknesses, errors, hasty words, shortcomings, and the like, are not sins charged against the soul, any more than blindness or deafness, is charged against the body. They are involuntary infirmities, and are unconditionally provided for in the great atonement of Christ. They often cause their possessor great agony of spirit, great regrets and great mortification; but they never produce condemnation. Many holy persons are troubled about temptations to evil. But temptation is not sin. The holiest being, the Son of God was tempted to do the worst thing that anyone was ever called by the tempter to do, viz.: to bow down and worship the devil. But it left no stain upon His soul, neither will the vilest temptation injure you unless you yield to it, and do what you are tempted to do. No cloud will come upon your soul. No darkness will shadow you.

How may this assimilation to the holiness of God be obtained? The answers to this question are clearly given. Of course every evangelical Christian will cheerfully admit that the atonement of Christ is the only meritorious cause of its existence in a human soul and life. Nothing else can produce, or effect it. The grandest evangel ever proclaimed in this world is, "The blood of Jesus Christ, His Son, cleanseth us from all sin." This is the hope of humanity, of the world. This is the fountain, the source of all heart purity. The primary work of every sinful soul, is to cordially and fully accept this provision, and rely upon it alone for pardon and salvation. And the primary work of the believer in seeking holiness is the fuller, higher and completer trust for purity or holiness in the same fountain of blood. This is not all of the divine provision. Just as when the sinner is pardoned and justified by the blood of Christ, he is also regenerated by the power and presence of the Holy Ghost; so the believer, seeking holiness, is not only cleansed from all sin in the blood, but is sanctified, transformed, metamorphosed by the power of the same blessed Spirit. He hallows, or makes holy, the soul. He separates from it everything vile, impure and unholy. He abides with it, not as a transitory, but as a permanent abode. Thus this great Executive and Representative of the Godhead is secured by the redemptive work of Christ, and makes complete the work of holiness. Nor is this all: The Truth — the Word of God, the holy Scriptures

— is a wonderful factor in this work. Does not Christ teach us this when He says, "Sanctify them through Thy truth, Thy word is truth"? Is it asked, "How is this?" I answer, "It is this truth which proclaims the divine command. It is God speaking to us, saying, 'Be ye holy, for I am holy,' and repeating it over and over again in many forms. It is this, and this alone, which tells of the infinite provisions made for the fulfillment of this work in us. It is this also which breathes out the exceeding great and precious promises that this work, upon the simplest conditions, may be performed. And it is this that contains the prayers of saints during the centuries for the full enjoyment of this promised gift.

But this assimilation is a constantly developing and growing condition in the faithful, persevering believer. Hence all saints are called upon to "*perfect* holiness in the fear of the Lord." Thus, while the blood is ever cleansing, and the Spirit ever hallowing, and the truth ever inspiring, God, in His providence, is constantly working for the same end. Do you doubt this? Hear then what He says. "He chastens us for our profit, *that we may be partakers of His holiness.*" So that sickness, pain, loss of property or friends, temporal disasters, are made to work for good to them that love the Lord, to mature them in holiness, and fully fit them for heaven. The saintly and sainted Rutherford writes, "O how much I need my Lord's hammer, and saw and file." The idea, no doubt suggested by Satan, that affliction and pain are the result of sins, and need not be suffered by saints, is contrary to, and contradictory of the Word of God, and has led many a one astray from the truth and from God. Some of the sweetest and loveliest saints whom we have ever known, have been the subjects of deepest affliction and of severest pain. Christ's people are a suffering people. They fill up the measure of His sufferings for them. "They suffer with Him, that they, also, may be glorified together." We return now to the question, *What must I do, that I may be holy?*

1. You must make a *complete, full, and everlasting consecration of yourself to God.* If you are given up to the world, to self, to sin, or to Satan, you can not be holy. That is an impossibility. All you have, or are, must be given into the hands of God now and forever. There must be no holding back, no mental reservation.

2. *Complete submission to God's will.* Your own will and your own way must be abandoned. God's will must be chosen as the dearest, sweetest thing in the universe. You must be willing to be regarded as only the bond-servant of your Lord, the steward of the Lord. You are to do His will, and His will alone; and to embrace it, and follow it whatever it brings, and wherever it goes. This, indeed, is the most important work we have to do, the complete surrender of our will to God. We are the only creatures in the universe, so far as we know, who are endowed with a will. Suns, stars, moons and constellations may shine and glow in the heavens; but they have no volitional powers. Men, only men, have these. And they are the grandest natural powers which we

possess. This is God's great condition of conformity to Himself. This relates to His wondrous plan. Will we voluntarily, cordially, embrace it? Will we trust in it alone for holiness and endless life? Then, the question is settled; then the work is done.

3. But we must dwell more largely on this *trust* in God for this work. What is this trust? It is not only complete submission, although that is its base, but it is also complete confidence in God, that He will do this work for us. Herein is the difference between consecration and holiness. Consecration is our work; making us holy is God's work. The instrument by which this work is wrought is faith. How many there are who have consecrated themselves to God thoroughly, and have wondered why it was that the answer to their prayer for holiness was not received. The simple reason is, that they have not believed that God will receive all we give to Him, and that He will *now do this work*. Faith not only regards the fact of the doing of this work; but also the *time* when it will be done. It says, He doeth it; and He doeth it *now*. Otherwise, the person might say, "Yes, He will do it at death, or in some more convenient opportunity, or amid some more favorable environments." God's time is now: and faith says, "Now He maketh me holy." Do not say it is presumption. No, it is not; it is God's truth. All His promises and assurances of this work are in the present time. Death has nothing to do with it; it is no factor, it has no power. This procrastination on the part of the believer, until death, is unwar-

ranted, and dishonors God. Look at it but for a moment. This is to say, that the blood of Jesus Christ *cannot* do it; that the eternal Spirit *cannot* do it; but that what they cannot do, death, itself, one of the fruits of sin, can do, and does for the Christian. Away with such unbelief. O Christian, O child of God, hesitate no longer, but now believe and be fully saved, and fully made holy. Let me say as I close this sermon :

1. This command obeyed, is the only thing that can save the church and the world. It is painful to look at the present condition of the church. How many of her ministers never preach on this subject; never refer to God's holy command. Almost everything else is uttered but this, God's first and greatest command. And what a multitude of her members utterly ignore this divine command. Worldliness, dress, fashion, show, the theatre, the dance and the card-table, are more fully patronized and attended to than the Word of God, or the holiness of God. Yet, all the while this command is ringing in their ears, if they would only stop to hear it. "Be ye holy, for I am holy." "Be ye holy in all manner of conversation." Can it be possible that God wills His church to be only a club, an association, or a monument of worldliness ? And is not this about all it is in certain places? And if it is so, can we expect judgment to "linger, or damnation to slumber?" (2 Pet. 2: 3). The most important work the church can do, or which can be done for it, is to be converted first of all; and then to be holy. How soon then would every

form of vice hide its head! How soon the saloon, the brothel, the gambling-hell, the race course, the theatre and the card table disappear: how soon would corrupt politics and legislation be banished from the land. And how soon the ends of the earth would see God's salvation! But all this will yet come. It will not, however, until the most fearful judgments have swept over our land and the world, and the glories of a millenial day shall burst over the world.

2. If, after you have carefully and prayerfully read this sermon, you can turn aside from it, you can ignore its truths, and go on still, in worldliness and in sin; it will show your blindness and your folly, your unbelief and disobedience, the possibility of your total apostacy, and your endless ruin. O, "awake thou that sleepest, and arise from the dead: and Christ will give thee light!" "Follow peace with all men, and holiness, without which no man can see God." Never forget. It is *God* who says, "Be ye holy, for I am holy."

XX.

PERFECT LOYALTY TO GOD.

WILLIAM TAYLOR, BISHOP OF AFRICA.

The first essential pre-requisite to Christian perfection, and a leading characteristic of it throughout, is a cheerful, perfect submission to the will of God.

"But," says one, "I had to submit myself unreservedly to God's will before He would even pardon my sins."

So had I, and so must every sinner. God will not receive any sinner into His kingdom unless he will, without the least mental reservation, confess and forsake his sins.

Well, then, what is the difference between the sincere, unreserved submission of the penitent, and this cheerful, perfect submission of the seeker of perfection? The submission of the penitent is very much like the submission of the manslayer fleeing from the avenger of blood. As he approaches the open gate of the city of refuge, in his fright he sees it not, but cries with a loud voice, "Open the gate! Open the gate, and let me in!"

The porter says to him, "Will you submit to the will of the governor of this city, and keep his laws?"

"O, yes, I will, I will; do open the gate, and let me in. Do save me from the avenger!"

That is a sincere, unreserved submission. Why? Because he was so much in love with the will and laws of the governor of the City of Refuge? Practically he knew nothing about them, for he had never been inside the walls of that city in his life. He submits because his life is in jeopardy — his all is at stake; the avenger is close after him, and he fears that every jump will be his last. Poor fellow, he will gladly do anything to save his life. A sincere, unreserved submission, but the leading motive prompting it is fear. There is intermingling with that motive, to be sure, a strong degree of desire, a degree of gratitude that a refuge has been provided, a degree of hope and faith which leads him to direct his feet with all possible dispatch to its open portal; but the leading motive is fear.

What is the penitent sinner doing? In the days of John the Baptist such were "fleeing from the wrath to come." In St. Paul's time he speaks of himself, and of all the believing Hebrews, as having "fled for refuge to lay hold on the hope set before us," employing this very figure of the manslayer to illustrate it. Human nature is the same now as then, and the demands of God's laws, and his gospel supply, the same now as then. His "sins that are past," and their dreadful consequences, present and prospective, constitute the great burden of the penitent sinner's heart, for the removal of which he weeps and prays, and flees away to the gospel refuge. While he is driven by the law, he is attracted by the great love of God in preparing a refuge for his poor soul, and for sending his Holy Spirit to show him the way to enter into it; but it is not until after he enters, that he feels the renewing love of God shed abroad in his heart.

Now, after he is admitted into the city of refuge — adopted into the family of God indeed — he is placed in the school of Christ, under the tuition of our divine teacher, "which is the Holy Ghost," to learn, and to prove that which he could not learn and prove in the darkness of carnal enmity, "what is that good and acceptable and perfect will of God." Some are very "dull of hearing," and learn very slowly. Some, who appear sharp enough to learn well, learned too many crooked dogmas before they entered, and it is very hard for them to unlearn all these, and hence they make very slow progress in learning " the way of the Lord more perfectly."

Some are naturally and habitually too lazy to apply themselves. Some are unduly curious and speculative. They want to learn all about the conditions of man's pristine state in Eden; whether or not there were carnivorous animals in Paradise before sin entered; whether the serpent that tempted Eve was a crawling reptile, or an animal of the monkey tribe; and a world of curious questions pertaining to this life. They want to know, too, all about heaven, the second advent of Christ, and the end of the world. Their attention is so occupied with speculative inquiries and theories, that they have but little time or heart left for the great practical duty of going on to perfection.

Some, through an unsettled, roving disposition, and through a want of discipline or mental training, readily play truant from the school of Christ; not by a wilful revolt, for that would cause their expulsion at once. No wilful sinner would be allowed to abide in this refuge a single day. But they "are children tossed to and fro," and may often be seen loitering about the gate, and occasionally saying one to another, "Oh! did we not have a good time down in Egypt? We remember 'the fleshpots, the onions, the cucumbers and the leeks,' how savoury they were. But for that horrible avenger of blood outside, we would go out and visit our old friends." We may readily measure the extent of their fidelity. But for their fears, the leading motive prompting them to flee to this refuge, they would be off on short notice. When you hear a Christian laughing and talking over his great exploits while a servant of sin, you may be sure he is loitering about the gate, and entering into sympathy with those things which should never be thought of but with humiliation and shame.

These various classes thus get out of harmony with God's arrangement for perfecting them in holiness, and hence become restless and unhappy, and seek for something else to supply the lack. As the gate stands open to let poor sinners in, they look out hoping to see some new attraction, and such now coming within range of their vision in a rapid succession of varieties, they are induced to venture out, just a little, so as to enjoy themselves, and though warned of their danger by frequent experiments of this sort, they become emboldened to venture further, and wander off quite beyond their own designs; and then, when again pursued by the avenger, they run to the gate and beg for their lives — "O do let us in this once. We will be obedient; we never will turn back again." They are truly penitent, and sincerely intend now to lead a holy life. God kindly takes them in and gives them another trial. Some learn by the bitter experience of their backsliding, and become true and steadfast. Others, alas! acquire such a habit of compromising with the world, that before you are aware of it they are loitering about the gate again, and wander off like lost sheep, and the avenger seizes and leads them into bondage. These are commonly called backsliders. The first fatal ground of their failure was their neglect to leave the principles and go on to perfection. That neglect disjointed their right relation to God, which gave place to the devil, who plied them with their old habits and associations until they "were entangled and overcome."

In this school of Christ the obedient disciple sits at the feet of Jesus and learns of Him; runs in the way of His commandments, and learns of Him; enters the arena of struggle and conflict, and learns of Him. He soon ascertains through the light of the Holy Spirit upon his heart, and his relations to God and society, that the will of God is much more comprehensive than he could have anticipated before he entered the school of Christ. But he, meantime, acquires such confidence in God — in His wisdom, His goodness, and His will, as the reasonable rule of his life — that he makes a consecration of himself to God, differing from that of the penitent sinner in several important facts; not different so much in kind, for it is all through the same Spirit, the same atonement, and in himself a development of the same work of salvation, commenced by the spirit of bondage to fear, carried on to saving effectiveness by the Spirit of adoption, but is now being perfected by the Holy Sanctifier, which is the same Holy Spirit that graciously commenced the work of his salvation when he was away in the wilderness of sin. But this development, nevertheless, brings out some distinct phases of the work, which I will state and explain.

1. This is an intelligent submission and consecration. As a penitent he could not practically know much about the details of Christian experience and duty, because it was a life he had never experienced. But having had a regular course in the school of Christ, he has reached a standpoint from which he can have an appreciative view of his relations to God, and the laws of the spiritual kingdom, and he now cheerfully adjusts his entire consecration of heart and life to his enlarged perceptions of these relationships.

2. It is based on different motives. The first, as I have shown, was based mainly on his fears. This is not. He has escaped the avenger, and abides in the city of refuge, where he knows he is safe, but has acquired such confidence in God, that he can appre-

ciate the grand fact that God's will is perfectly right in itself, and perfectly consistent with his own best interests in time and eternity, and hence gladly accepts God's will as the rule of his heart and life. It embraces the "field" containing "the hid treasure." He will cheerfully sacrifice everything necessary for its purchase. He knows that God does not require him to give up something for nothing, but to give up everything opposed to perfect heart purity, because it is but rubbish and death, to be taken out of the way to make room for "the gift of God, which is eternal life." He knows that if God should require a sacrifice of his rights for great spiritual ends, even to life itself, that it will not only be for God's glory, but for his own eternal well-being; and that, at any rate, his whole being belongs to God, and he now has too high an appreciation of God's lovely character to allow himself to parley with any motives that would tend to rob God of His rights, or mar His gracious purpose in saving him from all sin. He now fully acquiesces in the doctrine of St. Paul on this subject — "Ye are not your own, for ye are bought with a price; therefore glorify God with your body and with your spirit, which are God's." If you buy a lot of goods and pay for them, and the merchant puts them all up carefully and delivers them to your order, you don't think he did any great thing. It was just the right thing — common honesty — but if he keeps back a few articles embraced in your purchase, it is an outrage that you cannot readily pass over. To "glorify God, with our bodies and with our spirits, which are God's," is but common honesty in our relations to God. Again, St. Paul, pleading the reasonableness of God's requirements, says to his strange brethren in Rome, "For of Him," — God — "and through Him, and to Him, are all things; to whom be glory for ever. Amen. I beseech you, therefore, brethren, by the mercies of God," not "by the terrors of the Lord," "that ye present your bodies a living sacrifice, holy, acceptable unto God, which is your reasonable service." To lay the sacrifice of our entire being and all our interests on God's altar, as wholly devoted as a burnt offering, yet not a burnt offering, but a "living sacrifice," to be accepted and employed by the Holy Spirit according to His own good pleasure, is but "our reasonable service." The candidate for perfect holiness gladly establishes the fact of his entire sanctification to God, and steadily maintains that fact — and will allow nothing contradictory to it to remain in his heart — because it is right and reasonable, pleasing to God, and immeasurably profitable to himself. The righteousness and reasonableness of the thing constitute the basis of his action; but like good old Moses, he cannot lose sight of what God did not design to conceal from him — "the recompense of reward."

3. This perfect submission embodies such a development of the principle of obedience in his heart as will perfect his loyalty to God, and at once and forever preclude the question as to whether or not he will do his whole duty to God. The question, "What is my duty?" is always open, as manifested daily by all God's gracious modes of teaching me, but the question

whether or not in any and every case I will cheerfully accept my duty is not debatable. The perfectly loyal heart has but one question to settle in any matter of duty, and that is the simple fact of duty. This principle of cheerful obedience can only be developed in the school of Christ. Whether the period of its development embrace years, or simply minutes, that is the place of its development, and not prior to his admission into the kingdom of Jesus. Its development is promoted and demonstrated often by specific tests of obedience, rather than by a universal application to every imaginable possible duty that may arise in the future of our warfare. It was so in the case of Abraham. When he promptly offered up "his son, his dear son Isaac," as a burnt-offering, we have in that fact a demonstration of heart loyalty equal to any emergency involved by any command that God could issue — heart loyalty to the death.

This perfected principle of obedience in the heart will lead us to "abhor that which is evil," because it is abhorrent to God: and "cleave to that which is good," because it is pleasing to God. It will lead us to settle all questions of doubtful propriety pertaining to our relations to God and to society. These questions of doubt may pertain to things essentially right, and must be done; or things essentially wrong, and must be discarded; or to things comparatively indifferent in themselves, but in view of their relation to our hearts, or our influence upon others, they become questions of doubt.

Christian expediency is a very different thing from

worldly expediency. The one usually involves a sacrifice of principle for self. The other usually involves a voluntary sacrifice of self for the sake of high Christian principle. A man forfeits no rights in becoming a Christian; but if he sees in any given case that a strict maintenance of his rights will, through the perverted, disjointed conditions of society, work injuriously to the souls of others, he voluntarily foregoes his rights, and for the sake of Jesus, and his love of souls, cheerfully denies himself of property rights, by not "going to law with a brother before the unjust," or of personal gratification, declining "to drink wine," or do "anything whereby a brother stumbleth, or is offended, or is made weak." Why should I, for the sake of personal gratification, "cause a weak brother to perish, for whom Christ died"? He denied himself, even to death, to save that very man; and can I, possessing "the same mind" of self-sacrifice "that was in Christ," indulge in anything that would jeopardize the soul of another? Now, what I ask of any Christian man or woman in the name of the Lord is that they deal honestly with themselves and with God. Do not allow the accuser to take advantage of you, and break down the law of obedience by making the way so narrow as to render it impossible for you to walk in it, nor the assumed angel of light to make it so wide as to lead you to hell instead of to heaven, where you want to go. Avail yourself of all the sources and facilities of light which God hath furnished you. Give your own common sense and conscience fair play. Do nothing simply because the honorable Mr. Presumption does it. We are responsible for the exercise of our own powers, and "every one of us shall give account of himself to God." Settle all those questions of doubt affirmatively, if you can: "This is right," and "that is right." Maintain and vindicate the right; but if there are any of you who cannot settle in the affirmative, then give your poor soul the benefit of the doubt. "He that doubteth is condemned." Just in proportion to the doubt, whether the thing in itself be right or wrong, so is the guilt and condemnation.

The development and demonstration of the heart-principle of obedience, up to perfect loyalty to God, must embrace the settlement of all those questions, and at once and forever preclude the debate even in our hearts, whether or not we will decline any possible duty that our gracious God will enjoin. It is by no means a severe principle. In a subordinate sense, you expect that much of every servant you employ, in whatever department of business. If your servant is guilty of disregarding your orders, and of indulging in things forbidden and offensive, and you call him to answer, and he offer such apologies as we hear from the lips of professing Christians, would you keep such a servant in your employ?

"Did you not know that it was your duty to do thus, or so?"

"O yes."

"Well, why did you not do it?"

"O, I didn't feel like it."

Indeed!

You do not allow a sailor to debate the question of duty. When he goes in the shipping office and "signs the articles," and reports himself to his captain, he well understands that navigation demands authority and subordination; and while he is not responsible for the conduct of the ship, it is his duty to obey orders, no matter how hazardous. In the rising gale, when the master orders him aloft to "close reef," you will hear him respond, amid the thunder of the hurricane, "Ay, ay, sir;" and up the rigging he runs with his life in his hand.

You expect that much of every soldier. You expect him to be loyal to the death.

That seems hard, and yet you say, "The honor and stability of our great nation, and the prestige of our arms, demand just such unswerving, uncomplaining, heroic loyalty." Granted, but is it not a poor, pitiful thing if we can't have perfect loyalty to God — cool, unflinching fidelity to the death? A shipmaster may be tyrannical; a general may err; but the all-wise God cannot err. The immutably righteous God cannot be tyrannical. His service "is a reasonable service." "His commandments are not grievous." What a scandal to the religion of Jesus, that men and women professing to love God should, so far from conforming to this most reasonable principle of perfect loyalty to God, set themselves against the principle itself, and maintain that "it is even impossible for poor human nature to attain to such a standard." Cannot any man, even with the smallest development of common sense and piety see the reasonableness of this principle, and of its necessity in order to the attainment of that "holiness without which no man shall see the Lord." If the Holy Spirit hath graciously given you light on this vital subject, "walk in the light while ye have the light, lest darkness come upon you." If you say, "Well, I will think about it," but fail to act, you will "quench the Spirit," and injure your spiritual receptivity more than before you received this superior light of the Spirit. Bring your sacrifice, my dear Christian reader, "bind it with cords," lay it on God's altar, and steadily keep it there till the day of your death.

XXI.

THE SANCTIFIER AND THE SANCTIFIED.

ANDREW CATHER, WERNERSVILLE, PA.

"Both He that sanctifieth and they who are sanctified are all of one: for which cause He is not ashamed to call them brethren" (Heb. 2: 11).

"Jesus Christ the same yesterday, to-day, and forever" (Heb. 13: 8).

I. THE unity of the Sanctifier and the sanctified.

II. The divine proclamation of this fact to the universe.

III. The unchangeableness of the character and relations of Jesus Christ.

1. There is a Sanctifier, and there are the sanctified. Here are two facts. Here then, is God, and here is the work of God. Here is life, and the life traced to its origin. The sanctified ones go forth so simple and natural that they are scarcely conscious of the prominence of the place they occupy. They are the handiwork of the Sanctifier and His representatives. See the context, "We see Jesus, who was made a little lower than the angels for the suffering of death, crowned with glory and honor; that He by the grace of God should taste death for every man. For it became Him, for whom are all things, and by whom are all things, in bringing many sons unto glory, to make the

Captain of their salvation perfect through sufferings." Here is a vast programme. The beginnings of it, like the reservoir in the great mountains, overflowing into streams and rivers for the refreshment of vast stretches of the earth, and then rolling into the great ocean.

Back in the infinite depths of the divine bosom lay these fountains of life, waiting for the fullness of time, that they might bubble up in human bosoms and overflow in all the joys and victories of sanctified lives.

The teaching of the Word on the subject of sanctification is so full and clear, that the surprise one feels is that it can be misunderstood by anyone. It must be demonstrated through experience to be understood. The sanctified, like the Sanctifier, must demonstrate the divinity of the work and Worker, and if the world will not regard their testimony, one rising from the dead would not be heard. "We speak that we do know, and testify that we have seen; and ye receive not our witness." If Christ bore testimony to divine facts as well as principles, and dull ears did not hear and dull hearts did not appreciate, shall it be less so now?

Redemption in Christ from the guilt and power of sin to the believer is an ultimate measure for all men forevermore. Not one jot or tittle shall be changed to accommodate the exasperating demands of carnal reason or the deep cravings of hell-born lust. The doctrine of sanctification may be thus stated. "Our Lord's humanity is an all-perfect type of humanity in general; but its personal perfection is not transmissible, even by Him as a federal representative of humanity, save by His offering of Himself as an atoning sacrifice." In this character only is His perfection communicable to us; while, by virtue of His atonement, His entire humanity as a redeeming power is given to us; and all the redeemed and saved, through the washing of regeneration and renewing of the Holy Ghost, stand through the ages in His stead, and as His representatives. In this way, "He that sanctifieth and they who are sanctified, are all of one."

The sanctified and the Sanctifier are all of one origin and nature. "Of His fullness have we all received and grace for grace."

It is of but little moment whether "all of one" is used of a common fatherhood of Christ and His disciples or refers to their community of nature. Brotherhood may depend upon a common fatherhood, but it may be more properly referred for its origin to a common nature. We are able to cry in most rapturous strains, "Abba! Abba! — Father! Father!" because "we are made partakers of the divine nature," and "heirs according to the promise." The rapture is the result of the creative Word. "He spake and it was done, He commanded, and it stood fast."

This conscious unity is between the Sanctifier and the sanctified, first of all, which is the deepest and richest experience poor sinful man could have in the marvelous change "from darkness to light and from the power of Satan to God," and associated with it at once, the union with all the sanctified. This conscious and delightful union and fellowship of soul with all the sanctified, comes instantly with the conscious union with the Sanctifier, and the one lives with the other in every conscious moment of existence, even forever, if there be no lapse of devotion or faith. "He that dwelleth in love dwelleth in God and God in him." This is the perennial bloom of all the flowers of grace in the clean heart and pure life. They all drink from the same living fountain. "That rock was Christ." "Whosoever drinketh of the water that I shall give him shall never thirst; but the water that I shall give him shall be in him a well of water springing up into everlasting life."

This is the blessed experience of a multitude of the saved. This upspringing is shared by all in whom He lives. So, also, are burdens, sorrows, toils, fears, hopes, joys. "They shall be one, as Thou, Father, art in Me and I in Thee, that they may be one in Us."

The law of action and re-action that is working throughout all the domain of God, is at work here between the Head and members, and mutually between all the members of the body. This mighty acting and re-acting force going and returning in all the realm of spirit and matter causes the circulation and distribution of all the resources of the universe. This mighty force at work is but the pulsing of the heart of the God-man, already enthroned Lord of lords and King of kings. Thus is being accomplished that divine purpose that God may be all in all.

How inspiring; how enlarging is this experience. What a programme for the redeemed and saved! What resources! What upliftings! "What are hallelujahs for," cried Dr. Hodgson on one notable occasion, "if not for a time like this?" Thank God that time is always. Let us not be afraid of raptures. They are divinely given preparations for conflict and toil, victory and rest. They are the throbbing challenges to all the forces of evil. They are deeper in the soul than all the tests of toil and suffering. The adoring spirit, conscious of the continual possession of divine resources at command every moment, cries out "Thanks be unto God who giveth us the victory through our Lord Jesus Christ."

2. The proclamation of this fact to the universe. He is not ashamed to call them brethren. Our Joseph will when the time comes delight to acknowledge His brethren. He is not ashamed of His poor relations. He is not ashamed of the former slaves of Satan. He has redeemed them with His own blood out of every kindred, and tongue, and people, and nation, and made them kings and priests unto God. This language points to the final consummation. The struggle between sin and holiness, between Christ and Satan is ended. Satan is vanquished. Christ is acknowledged as the head of all principality and power. Even death, the last enemy, is put under His feet. But all the principles of that finality lie coiled up in the bosom of the sanctified.

"The testimony of Jesus is the spirit of prophecy." This includes the entire scope of prophecy before the mind of the Omniscient Spirit. Through all eternity the Holy Spirit is unfolding the great purpose of God in redemption, and the enthroned Elder Brother of the saints is waiting till all enemies, all the incorrigibles, are put under His feet. The executive power of the Holy Spirit will accomplish it. He will accomplish it through a consecrated, and sanctified, and holy people. It is a misrepresentation of His great purpose that Jesus must come in person and stay here a millenium of years to accomplish what the eternal Spirit working through the endowed and empowered church could not do.

The Holy Ghost is very God, and through Him all the attributes of the eternal Godhead are pledged to make His holy people a triumphant host conquering and to conquer. No doubt the devil will be chained and cast into the bottomless pit, to give the church time to recruit her energies and demonstrate to the witnessing universe that she does not go to war at her own charges, but that thus let alone awhile to gather breath, she will be prepared for the final struggle between sin and holiness, between Christ and Satan, and the universe will bear witness that a holy church endowed by the power of the Holy Ghost is more than a match for all her enemies, and that she represents the divine gift of a "broad religion, broad glory, and broad salvation."

"Whoso eateth My flesh and drinketh My blood dwelleth in Me and I in him." Every time this is done the proclamation goes forth that the Sanctifier and the sanctified are of one, and that the triumphant host of heaven and earth are being prepared for the great consummation. We are permitted to have a glimpse of the vast sweep of this eternal purpose of God respecting His bride, the church; "In whom we have redemption through His blood, the forgiveness of sins, according to the riches of His grace; wherein He hath abounded toward us in all wisdom and prudence; having made known unto us the mystery of His will, according to His good pleasure which He hath purposed in Himself: that in the dispensation of the fullness of times He might gather together in one all things in Christ, both which are in heaven, and which are on earth; even in Him, in whom also we have obtained an inheritance being predestinated according to the purpose of Him who worketh all things after the counsel of His own will: that we should be to the praise of His glory, who first trusted in Christ. In whom ye also trusted, after that ye heard the word of truth, the gospel of your salvation: in whom also after that ye believed, ye were sealed with that holy Spirit of promise, which is the earnest of our inheritance until the redemption of the purchased possession, unto the praise of His glory" (Eph. 1: 7-14).

Who can comprehend and appreciate all that is involved in this vast and massive statement of the thought, and purpose, and work of God in and through His church, the Bride, the Lamb's wife. When Adam awaked out of his sleep and was fully conscious of the origin of his bride that was presented to him, he said, "Thou art bone of my bone, and flesh of my flesh," so the saints are "members of His body, of His flesh, and of His bones," who hath redeemed us and saved us.

Thus, in the blazing light of this revelation of God's purpose in His church, "to make all men see what is the fellowship of the mystery, which from the beginning of the world hath been hid in God, who created all things by Jesus Christ: to the intent that now unto the principalities and powers in heavenly places, might be known by the church the manifold wisdom of God" (Eph. 3: 9, 10).

The eyes of several hundreds of millions of people if they were intelligent enough, have been turned to a young man twenty-six years of age. Why? Because the imperial head of a great nation was dying and the searching gaze of a multitude was fixed upon the Czarwitch of Russia. Deep questionings were in many anxious hearts, as to the spirit in which this young man should ascend the most important throne of Europe.

The innumerable myriads of the entire universe are gazing upon the enthroned Jesus, studying the problems of His relation to His redeemed and saved ones in heaven and earth, and their relation to all other beings of His vast and immeasurable realm. He is not ashamed to call them brethren. Lift up your heads, ye saints! The unsolved problems of your life and destiny are being unfolded as rapidly as the Meditorial Sovereign can do so to the adoring gaze of those who are watching the majestic sweep of His plans.

Ye saints! little and unknown, lift up your heads. Your divine Elder Brother is enthroned and is waiting to celebrate your coronation as joint heirs with Him to thrones and principalities and powers. One with Him you shall share His glory forever.

3. The unchangeableness of the character and relations of Jesus Christ. He is the same yesterday, to-day and forever. In the light of the Scriptures already quoted there is nothing more important than to fix our gaze upon Him as unchangeable. This involves His divinity. His existence is an "eternal now." "From everlasting to everlasting Thou art God." This is the wide-sweeping statement by inspiration of the Jehovah of the Old Testament. His character is described as "without variableness or shadow of turning." "Christ fills eternity." All is well. Hallelujah! He is "Emmanuel, God with us." We devote all to the Sanctifier, and by the power of the Holy Ghost, the thrill of the heavenly life takes possession of our whole being, and we enter into full sympathy with Him in all His plans and work. He is now to us the Christ of yesterday and all the infinite past. He is the Christ of to-day and of the changeless forever. Here is the guarantee of the saints. From eternity to eternity, He changes not. The kindled fire of love is an earnest of a boundless and never-ending bliss. Every promise of His Word is an anchor to the soul, both sure and steadfast.

I was told of the wonderful courage of a lady who suffered great agony from an injury through an accident. She felt every fibre of the injured part throbbing with almost unendurable pain. She bore all with Christian resignation that was considered remarkable by those about her. I was introduced to her afterward, when she was trying to secure a situation. I spoke of what I had been told of her endurance and cheerful courage. She replied, "How could it be otherwise, when I had thirty thousand promises of God's Word to draw upon? Oh, thank God for all these resources of our unchangeable Friend."

One has said that "everything earthly is spoiled by mutability." We must in due time pass out of the realm of exhausting change. Our hearts are sick of lapsed friendships. "Age changes us, affliction presses upon us; riches make a difference; poverty causes separation. The world is changing — we ourselves pass away — but there is One who is unchangeable. "I will never leave thee nor forsake thee."

Jacob saw the glory of his Joseph coming on beyond the power of change. Joseph is a "fruitful bough, even a fruitful bough by a well; whose branches run over the wall: the archers have sorely grieved him, and shot at him, and hated him: but his bow abode in strength and the arms of his hands were made strong by the hands of the mighty God of Jacob: (from thence is the shepherd, the stone of Israel), even by the God of thy father, who shall help thee; and by the Almighty, who shall bless thee with blessings of heaven above, blessings of the deep that lieth under, blessings of the breasts, and of the womb. The blessings of thy father have prevailed above the blessings of my progenitors unto the utmost bound of the everlasting hills: they shall be on the head of Joseph, and on the crown of the head of him that was separate from his brethren."

Our Joseph, who is the author and finisher of our faith, "for the joy that was set before Him, endured the cross, despising the shame, and is set down on the right hand of the throne of God." His relation to the believers who "have entered into His rest," is always the same. His is the unchecked and unchangeable sympathy. "He ever liveth to make intercession for us." Intercession! blessed word! He is our eternal go-between. "He can be touched with the *feeling* of our infirmities." In His enthronement He has lost none of that delicacy of feeling He had when He suddenly stopped and said, "Who touched me?" when the poor exhausted woman touched the hem of His garment and was made whole. The jostling crowd did not hinder the divine sympathy.

> "This, this is the God we adore,
>   Our faithful, unchangeable Friend,
> Whose love is as great as His power,
>   And neither knows measure nor end.
>
> "'Tis Jesus, the first and the last,
>   Whose Spirit shall guide us safe home.
> We'll praise Him for all that is past,
>   And trust Him for all that's to come."

And now the evening is coming on. The grand *finale* is looming up before the gaze of the saved in Christ. The unity between the Sanctifier and the sanctified is a fact of import wide as the universe. Shout! fight! triumph, ye saints! Ye saints of God, claim your birthright! Let the whole universe hear our hallelujahs! Join the unnumbered of the saved in heaven in adoring love and service. The saints should make more ado about the wonders that are theirs already, and of "the length and breadth and depth and height" of their portion, which passeth knowledge.

The Sabbath of eternity — that glorious rest — that indescribable calm — that immeasurable wideness of unchallenged possession is coming, is here now to the individual saints, who have the "earnest of the inheritance" in their experiences, and for the saved in heaven, who are looking, with intensity of gaze, for the great day of vindication and of final coronation. That Sabbath rest in the kingdom of the Father, is the "goal of all things." That *rest* "lasting as eternity, glorious as God." That is *love*. The great fountain principle of the universe is *love* the pure river of the water of life proceeding out of the throne of God and the Lamb. This is His rest, in Himself — in His universe. *Love.* Love the resurrection power, love the crown of immortality. Everything in man's history as a creature and as redeemed, points to the last and eternal Sabbath as the *rest of love*.

"It is finished." "The great redeeming work is done." The Sanctifier and the saints are of one and shall be *one forever*. This fact shall be proclaimed to the utmost boundaries of time and space. They must be vindicated in Him and He in them *forever*.

The Alpha and Omega, the First and the Last, the Beginning and the Ending, Jesus Christ the same yesterday, to-day and forever proclaims that "Man's Sabbath is *God*." Amen! Hallelujah!!

XXII.

JOHN THE BAPTIST; OR HOLINESS STAG-GERING UNDER TRIALS.

A. J. JARRELL, D.D., ST. LOUIS, MO.

"Art Thou He that should come, or look we for another?" (Luke 7 : 19).

THERE has been no lack of sermons on the life and character of John the Baptist. The world has needed them all. We have been thrilled again and again by the story of his heroic fidelity to God and man. The pulpit will never see the day when it will not need such thrills, from such a source. But who has heard a sermon on his religious experience? Who has read one? In all my life I have seen but one comment that gave me satisfaction, and that comment, I desire to unfold into the sermon for this hour. The explanation is from the pen of Canon Farrar, not a few of whose magnificent sentences appear herein.

John had his home among the lime-stone cliffs and caves of the wilderness of Jordan. He spent more than half-a-score of years in these deep solitudes. In the noon-tide heat of that tropical climate he would retreat into these caves and commune with God until they were lit up with a radiance that came from neither sun nor candle; by night he would walk out under the spangled heavens and lift up his soul until it lived and talked with the shining ones of another world. He had denied himself until there was no self left to deny. He had feared God until he had nothing else to fear. He had thought about the coming kingdom until Cæsar's great empire faded from his sight. For years he had known he was to be the forerunner of that kingdom, and his great heart had bounded with the glory of his message. At last, God said, "Go preach, the kingdom of heaven is at hand."

He came up "like a lion from the swelling of Jordan." His voice shook the nation. All Jerusalem and Judea, all Galilee and the regions round about, poured forth to hear him. Never had man borne so great a message. Never had divine message a nobler bearer. No "reed shaken with the wind" was he. He was man, and therefore must stagger under some trials, but he was too great to fall. All Jewry could not have moved him. No time-serving, ease-loving voluptuary, was this prophet of the wilderness. He was not sent to prophesy smooth things and to court the favor of the great. There was enough and to spare of such conventional teachers. "But what went" they "out for to see? A prophet? Yea, and I say unto you, more than a prophet." A Nazarite from his mother's womb, he stood in that valley with the world under his feet, and the light of heaven streaming on his head. "Whatever might be the class that flocked to his solitude, his preaching was intensely practical, painfully heart-searching, and fearlessly downright." His sword had lost its scabbard, his axe lay at the root of the tree. He respected no person, he spared no sin, he feared no man.

The sweetest tenderness goes hand in hand with the divinest terror. The hardest hearts trembled at John's preaching, but the bruised reed was never broken. His great Prototype, like an angel from heaven, could make Mt. Carmel quake and smoke under his denunciation of idolatry, and then, like a mother, could bend and weep over the dying child of the widow of Sarepta. It is of no little significance, that, under such preaching as this — midway a sermon of terror and tenderness — Jesus suddenly appeared in the throng, hardly a rod from His undaunted prophet. Kinsman though He was, John had never seen His face before. Twice he repeated it that he knew Him not, but the Spirit whispered, "It is He." Soft as the flush of morn on the brow of coming day, the Spirit rested on His head. It was the dove — the promised sign by which he was to know his Lord.

"When the Holy Ghost descended upon the apostles," says Archbishop Leighton, "He came as a flame of fire, there was something in them to be purged away; but when He descended upon Christ, in whom was no need of cleansing, He came as a dove, the symbol of the spotless purity of His nature." John was overawed in a moment. "To others he was the stern, uncompromising prophet; kings he could confront with rebuke, Pharisees he could unmask with indignation, but before this presence all his lofty bearing falls. As when some unknown dread checks the eagle in his flight and makes him settle with hushed scream and drooping plumage on the ground, so before the radiant purity of that sinless life, the wild prophet becomes as submissive and as timid as a child." The sermon was forgotten — unfinished forever — or, ended, as all sermons ought to end, by pointing to a Saviour in full view, and crying, "Behold the lamb of God."

It is a thrilling moment when the soul gets its first unclouded view of its Redeemer. It is unspeakable, when it gets such a view as John had, with such witness and such insight as was this day vouchsafed unto him. A thousand glimpses may afterward be enjoyed, and ten-thousand revelations of his love and pity, but, there is a sweet surprise — a divinely exhilarating novelty — in this first sight, never to be repeated afterwards. John is now in the meridian of his matchless experience. The midday will not decline, but clouds will gather, and storms will lower, until we shall hear a wail from his lips enough to melt a heart of stone.

He had already said of his Lord, "He must increase but I must decrease." Yet he rejoiced in that. No other proof is needed, that, "Among those that are born of woman, there hath not risen a greater than John the Baptist." Millions long to see Christ "increase," but they long to "increase" with him, and they pine and sulk if they drop out of sight and prominence. Two of the very chiefest apostles could not wait for him to be crowned. Their applications for office, and for the highest offices in his gift at that, must be on file in advance. The last carnal affection to die out of the heart is the love of prominence. When supposed to be dead, it is not dead. And when it is, it "being dead yet speaketh." Its death was only a "trance" from which it awakes in a more insidious form. A kingdom, a kingdom, for the man who can rejoice in his own "decrease," so his Lord may "increase."

John preached his congregations clean away from himself, and bound them over to Christ. There are two kinds of pulpit magnates: those who attract men to themselves, and those who attract them to the Lord. Neither is to be despised. Happy the pastor who can draw men to himself, but thrice happy, he, who can lead them beyond himself and wed them to his Lord. The former becomes a necessity to his church. It is held together by a rope of sand without him. The latter lifts his church to a plane where no living man is a necessity to it. "Not as in my presence only, but now much more in my absence," was the triumphant report of one of these. No man can doubt to which class John belonged. "Behold the Lamb of God" was his ceaseless cry.

He never saw his Master again. His fearless preaching had brought down on his head the unrelenting hate of at least one guilty wretch,— the adulterous wife of the adulterous Herod Antipas. The hate of such a woman is never quenched but in blood. She never rested until he was cast into prison. Josephus tells us it was in Machaerus, a gloomy fortress on the eastern shore of the Dead Sea. Into that rocky dungeon was this eagle of the skies thrust, and chained to the stone floor. He will never come out alive. His wings will beat against those rugged walls and iron bars until they droop in death.

"Not once or twice alone," says Canon Farrar, "has God seemed to make His very best and greatest servants drink to the dregs the cup of apparent failure, called them suddenly away by a sharp stroke of martyrdom, or down the long declivity of a lingering disease, before even a distant view of their work had been vouchsafed unto them; flung them, as it were, aside as broken instruments, unacknowledged and unhonored of men, ere he crowned their lives with an immortality of blessings and success."

Matchless Moses! while his eye was yet undimmed and his natural force unabated — just as he had suffered all the afflictions of the people of God, and had endured the brunt of their wanderings and privations,— when the promise of four hundred years was in his grasp — ere he could set one foot on the everlasting inheritance, God called him up into the mount to die. Spotless Savonarola! with hardly a peer, and never a superior, in the Roman Catholic Church — a very Elijah, in his day, for relentless war on the corruptions of the church — seized in the midday splendor of his transcendent career, hanged and burned at Florence at the age of forty-six.

Poor John the Baptist! He seemed forgotten of God in heaven and deserted of God on earth. The very day Jesus heard that he was cast into prison He turned His back on Judea and departed into Galilee. "John pining in prison and his Lord preaching in glad simplicity among the lillies of Galilee." John perishing for a crumb of comfort and Jesus feeding the thousands around Lake Genesaret. There was no sick man He did not bless, no poor man He did not pity, no aching heart He did not soothe, none, but one, and that one, the noblest of them all. Never one visit did He make to him nor send one message of loving sympathy. Had not his life been blameless? Had not his ministry been faithful? Were not these chains upon his ankles because he dared to rebuke a king and a queen for their sin and shame? " If his work was done, why not let him depart and rest with God? If his work was not done, why not free him from his prison and let him finish it? What wonder that the eye of the caged eagle began to film!"

"Art Thou He that should come? I thought so once. I knew it. I looked into that heavenly face. I saw the holy dove descend and rest upon His head. I heard the voice from heaven declare, Thou art My Son. I knew it all then — I seem to know it all now — but, oh, how different all things from what I expected!" Go ask, "Art Thou He that should come, or look we for another?"

The Master did not answer the question in words. He could not. To answer a question is to settle it. And this question was too great to be settled in words. But he had ready a reply that would settle it forever. On those boulders to the right recline two lame men, with their crutches at their side; they never have walked a step: by that tree in front stands a blind man leaning on his staff; no ray of light ever did enter his eyes: on His left is an eager mute trying to catch His sermon from the motion of His lips; no sound had ever entered those ears: in that winding sheet in the edge of the throng lies a lifeless body. The greatest question of the world is about to receive its greatest answer.

"Art Thou He that should come?" mournfully ask John's disciples. "Come and see," was the sweet response. They saw Him lift these lame men to their feet, and saw them throw their crutches away. Before their face He touched the eyes of the blind, and a new world flashed into view. He put His finger on the ears of that mute, and the music of earth broke in on his soul. Then, He spake the word, and the dead man threw back the winding sheet and sprang to his feet. "Go tell John what things ye saw." This was His answer to the great question. It was the only one possible. The veriest imposter could have answered "Yea" and the world had not been one whit wiser — and the staggering prophet not one whit steadier in his faith and hope.

Great moral questions can never be settled by words. Pity we are so slow to believe it. Is Jesus able to save to the uttermost? Take care what reply you make. Shall it be in words only? Then, the veriest hypocrite can make the same reply, and then, you need not make reply at all. To the minds of others the testimony of our lips is the least of all the evidences we can furnish of a pure heart. Great was "the word of testimony" of which John wrote in his apocalyptic vision, but it was testimony preceded by the entire eleventh chapter of Hebrews, and backed up by the whole book of the Acts of the Apostles. Such testimony overcame in that day and it will overcome in this. Nothing else ever can. Produce the man! Produce the heart saved "to the uttermost." Let the "salvation appear to all men." There is but one rule by which men are to be judged in this world or the next: "By their fruits ye shall know them." The world will not credit a testimony unsupported by life. It ought not. The argument is exhausted. We have reached the farthest limit possible by theological disputes and wrangling. If we go farther, we must do it by shining our way. Titus forced his way to the great silver Gate in the walls of Jerusalem, hard by the Temple. That Gate was more than a match for his legions. Two whole days thundering against it with his battering-rams failed to effect an entrance. He had absolutely to melt it away by fire. The gates in our front are closed, and ram-proof. They will never yield to anything but the loving fire of the Holy Ghost. Men will "be constrained" when our "light so shines;" never until then.

"Tell John what things ye saw." Then the Master's eyes grew misty, and His lips quivered a bit, as He added one personal message to His troubled servant. Tell him, "Blessed is he whosoever shall not be offended in Me." I know it all. My eye has not been off him since the day he was cast into prison. Tell him, if I never come to him — never send another message, all shall be well. I know him. I can trust him alone. Though he stagger, yet will he not fall. Tell him, no matter what I do, or suffer to be done unto him; no matter where I lead him, or allow him to be led; if every earthly expectation prove vain, and every providence of My hand disappoint, still, "Blessed is he whosoever shall not be offended in Me."

Small men have to be propped up on every side. They walk by feeling — not by faith. Unless God and men are forever honeying them up, they are doomed to go down. Not a few go down in spite of all the honey. But, there are men great enough to be trusted alone. God can turn His back on them with perfect safety. He may hide His face until the great day, and they will answer to the roll call. The fancy is allowable that He takes special joy in such heroes. He turns them over to men and devils, then hides His face from them, and watches what honor they bring to His name. Great glory have all they whom the Lord can thus trust.

At last the message reaches the prophet's dungeon. Every word is devoured through the iron bars. When the last words of personal assurance were repeated, a light broke into John's heart, and lit up that dungeon above the brightness of day. He clapped his hands and paced the floor to the full length of his clanking chains. "Blessed is he whosoever shall not be offended in me," rang to the echo, through those prison rooms. "It is enough! It is enough! It is He! It is He! I look for no other. I want no other. Thou shalt guide me with Thy counsel and afterward receive me to glory. Whom have I in heaven but Thee, and

there is none upon earth that I desire beside Thee."
Glorious servant of the most high God! Not another
shadow ever fell across his brow. Never again did he
reel under trial.

A few months later, a Roman soldier entered his
cell, broadsword in hand. John knew what it meant,
and smiled. He hung his head over the block and
whispered the golden message of his Lord. The sacred
head rolled off on the floor, and the spotless soul —
freed from its prison-house — mounted the skies, an
heir of glory. "Lift up your heads, O ye gates, and
be ye lifted up, ye everlasting doors, and let this
'heir' of glory come in!"

XXIII.

THE TRUE TABERNACLE; OR, THE THREE EPOCHS OF EXPERIENCE.

J. B. FOOTE, SYRACUSE, N.Y.

"The true tabernacle which the Lord pitched and not man" (Heb. 8: 2).

GOD must adapt His revelations to the growing capacity of His disciple. This is true of the race and of the individual. Our schools have a graded course. You cannot teach a child logarithms. God cannot teach a guilt-beclouded heart its own inbred corruption or the supernal purity of holiness. So God has taught the race by successive events or epochs; writers say three — the patriarchal, the Mosaic pointing to Christ, and that of the Holy Ghost. These are the three dispensations of time. In like manner comes individual progress. And there are three events here — conviction, conversion, and entire sanctification.

God also adapts His methods. In the early ages he used types and symbols. On the east of Eden were placed the typical flame of fire, the winged cherubim and an altar, a germ of Moses' tabernacle, as the word "placed" (Heb., *shaw-kan*) means "caused to tabernacle." These were symbols as were Abel's altar and Noah's and Abraham's.

Moses' tabernacle was a great symbol, and the inquiry is, *a symbol of what?* This book of Hebrews gives the answer. It is "*the true tabernacle.*" The symbol was constructed from a *pattern* shown to Moses, a pattern of "heavenly things." This term heavenly, used several times in this book, refers not to the abode and reward of the saints after death, but more broadly and more specifically to a spiritual condition of nearness to God unobstructed by sin. This heavenly pattern was not a material structure nor a form of ritualism. Rotherham translates it a model. Olshausen calls it a plan. It was the plan of salvation. The underlying idea of this book is that in the true tabernacle there are no limitations of place and time. Hence all that was material and ritual in the Levitical priesthood was adumbrative of realities in the spiritual realm. And those realities constitute the elements of God's plan of saving men, that is, of that system of divine doctrine, divine work and divine force, and also in the believer's life that divine fact which came to be called Christianity.

The tabernacle then, was a teaching of the fact and order of God's unfolding of Himself to sinful man, and hence of the appointed method and successive steps of his approach to God. After the decalogue in the same chapter appears a supplemental direction to build an altar and offer sacrifice. Foreseeing that they would break those laws God provided for their return as sinners, and the order is pointed out by the structure and rites of the tabernacle. *The true tabernacle* then is Christianity, considered as an unfolding of God especially in His character of love to sin-blinded and self-ruined man, and of the required steps of his return to God and the personal salvation secured thereby.

The most rudimental fact about this great type, albeit a point much overlooked, was *its three-foldness*. The three parts were the court, the holy place, and the most holy place. Correspondingly the true tabernacle is three-fold, having its basis in the doctrine of the Trinity, which is the starting point and foundation both of theology and the Christian life.

In following out this subject our aim is to be practical and get the spiritual significance and value of the teaching in the interpretation of Moses' tabernacle in this book.

This three-foldness with the special services appointed, was well fitted to teach the order of God's revealment, and the steps a man must take to come to know him, that is, to give him the knowledge first of God the Governor, then of God the Saviour bringing grace to sinners, and then of God the Holy Ghost bringing perfect holiness.

The fore court symbolizes God's moral government. It is the place which says you must reverence the law, and keep the commandments, and as you have broken them you must repent. It represents conviction. Now, looking at the brazen altar at the door of the holy place, the Jewish inquirer gains an intensified sense of the crime and shame of his sins, and learns of an atonement. Presenting his offering in faith he receives the Christ-grace in the remission of all his sins (Lev. 6: 7). The holy place presents the essential suggestions of holy living. From the candlestick comes instruction in the truth, from the shew-bread spiritual sustenance, from the altar of incense, worship and prayer through a Mediator. The most holy place with its ark of covenant, of typical manna and budding rod, the communion mercy seat, the cherubim, the Shekinah and its high-priestly services continually point the mind to those privileges of fellowship and purity, of spiritual light and fullness of holiness, of which the Pentecostal Holy Ghost is the agent and source. Here are the three steps of knowledge and epochs of experience, through which every one passes that makes the flight from sin to heaven.

Look again — look closely — into this book of Paul to the converted Hebrews. This trinality of experimental knowledge corresponding to the trinality of the tabernacle places, and to the triune personality of God, is an underlying line throughout the book. Distinctly apparent in its back-ground are the three dispensations, of God the Law-giver, of God the Son and Saviour, and of God the Holy Ghost. To the same end are its references to those certain conspicuous events, which distinctively mark out the respective dispensations — the event of the decalogue occurring on Sinai, the mountain of "fire, blackness, and tempest;" the event of redemption on Calvary where Jesus "suffered without the gate," "tasted death" and "offered one sacrifice to put away sin;" and the event of Pentecost on Mount Zion, "Ye are some to Mount

Zion" — an event of law, of grace to transgressors, and one of holy power. And these successive events are in the order of the three places of the tabernacle. Correspondingly, the true tabernacle in individual life has these three epochal events. God's revealment to each man is, first, one of law, ordering a government for the maintenance of righteousness; secondly, one of saving grace, a revelation of Jesus; and, thirdly, one of purity, perfection and power, by the indwelling of the Holy Ghost.

Now you will bear in mind that this book of Hebrews was written to persons already converted. They had passed through the fore court of conviction, come under the justifying grace of the brazen altar, and received the spiritual bread and light and answers of prayers figured by the priestly services in the holy place. The apostle writes them this epistle having in view their liability of apostacy and their need of a further work. To prevent the one by leading them to secure the other is his aim in writing — "On to perfection" is his key-note. This is the goal of the book. By compact arguments, earnest warnings, historical allusions, referring them to their Canaan possession, typical of the Christ-rest, exhorting them to hasten to enter it by faith, he urges them to pass from a child condition to an adult experience; to prove an uttermost salvation; to have the sanctifying process perfected, and the Holy Ghost's witness to it, and to lay aside — get rid of — the closely clinging sin, inbred sin, and improve the inward scourgings and chastenings of the Spirit with a view to partake of Christ's gift of holiness; and to follow after it, warning them against refusal, till every shakable thing is burned up by the consuming fire, and they receive the unshakable kingdom in which they can render service well-pleasing to God in devout reverence and godly fear.

A definite and very special part of his appeal and argument are his references to the two places of the tabernacle or tent of meeting (Rev. Ver.), the holy place and the most holy place and the priestly services in each respectively. He tells them (chapter 9; 6-14) that the priests accomplishing the service in the first compartment and the high priest entering the second, were figures by which the Holy Ghost signifies Christ's entering the holy places (plural in Greek) of his more perfect tabernacle, which *includes* both the provisions and the resulting work achieved in the believer, viz., his conversion and secondly his perfecting by the purifying of his nature. He indicates two things: first, that the priests' service in the first compartment could not make perfect. Yet it must be kept in force, "imposed till the time of reformation." Rotherham and Clark put this word "rectifying." It means perfecting. The tabernacle work could not do this while the worshiper kept the first, *i.e.*, the holy place service still "standing," or staying in his purpose and faith, not making the proper effort to advance to the exercises of the second or most holy place. Secondly, he tells them that as the high priest went into "the second" carrying the blood, so Christ entered in His greater tabernacle with His own blood, and that the high priest's offering was for "errors," typifying the full atonement as covering not only personal guilt, but the whole ground of the fall — all unholiness of nature and imperfections of character in the sight of God. This is "the time of reformation" or perfecting the holiness begun before. This is the eternal, hence a complete, redemption. He shows that the high-priestly service of the most holy place symbolizes that work of Christ which results to the child of God in a second salvational experience, which he expresses here in such terms as rectifying, perfecting of the conscience, a purifying from dead works — from the inbred sin, which is the corrupt root of dead works — and in the complete putting away or destruction of sin.

So he appeals to them again and again to draw close to God into the holiest place leaving behind them the second veil of sin, and in sacred spiritual exclusion enjoy with God a delightful unity of will and fellowship of love which make up the essence of what is meant by "the right hand of His throne" where Christ is seated.

For fifteen centuries these tabernacle services were kept up as continuous types and instructive object lessons. Their discontinuance was indicated by the complete destruction of the second veil of the temple — its rending from top to bottom, which occurred at the moment our Saviour's torn flesh rent the sin of the world — provisionally destroyed, and took away the innate sin of man. These typical services thus closed, the apostle shows the reality continuous on the line of faith without the symbol, as indeed so many full-faith men in the past had enjoyed the reality with the symbol.

The practical sum for us is this: Every man should enter the fore court of considerate thought, take cognizance of God as Governor, reverence the law and repent of his transgressions. Then, secondly, every awakened person should go on to a *holy place* experience. We have seen that the parts and services symbolize Christ's work in giving salvation to the penitent sinner: the brazen altar, giving pardon for his guilt and the new life to conquer his habit of sinning; the candlestick, Christ giving light; the shew-bread, Christ giving bread to the soul; the golden altar of incense, Christ our Mediator, through whom we offer worship of love and prayer and upon whom we are to lay our living sacrifice. Every one should go from conviction to conversion.

But the service in the holy place could not make perfect. So the teaching seems plain — the believer is to go with boldness by faith and obtain complete redemption and a purified conscience in the experience typified by the most holy place. This innermost compartment beyond the second veil, having no opening or window on the sides or above where were the ark, the wings, the light, and fire, (for the Shekinah was both) with its high-priestly services, symbolizes the soul's complete separation unto God, beyond the second veil of our "original or birth sin" for which Christ's rent flesh became as a sin-offering and bore away, and typifies also its conscious purification by the all-cleansing blood, and its divine fellowship and care under the wings of the cherubim, and in the shining light, and refining fire, of the Holy Ghost. Going into the holiest is the transition of the believer, not to his reward and abode after death, but to a state of full holiness — to what the apostle refers to in Eph. 2: 6, "And made us sit together in heavenly places in Christ Jesus" (Greek, *the heavenlies*). This is a Christ-fellowship unhindered by sin.

In other words every one should come to have three dispensational events. A period of reverence for law, a time of gracious justification and a period of perfect holiness; a *Sinaitic* event, revealing the majesty of government; a Calvary event, in which comes the regenerating and conquering grace; a Mount Zion event, when the Pentecostal Holy Ghost fills, baptizes, purifies and empowers.

Thus we see the book of Hebrews is a call to holiness, and the tabernacle under its interpreting light presents helpful suggestions to him who hungers and thirsts after the fullness. He can see that Christ is not only the brazen altar to whom he came when guilt-burdened, and through whom he has been quickened from his death in trespasses and sins, but also the golden altar upon whom he can now lay himself as a living sacrifice and by whose blood seven times sprinkling and cleansing him, (Lev. 16: 19), he may come to enjoy a fullness of love and joy in his divine Shekinah.

Behold the high priest entering. He carries the blood. He puts aside the veil. The smoke of the incense goes in with him. He is alone with God. Every converted person has full right of way, and trusting the blood, laying aside sin, should put on faith and courage to enter the holiest — move right forward to a complete separation unto God, where he will stand environed by the divine presence, with no window of external glory to attract or divert.

He may go gladly and hold communion with his great Lawgiver whose law is now to him a covenant, like a bridal covenant, for he will take the law into his affections. He may abandon all hesitation, for he will find himself welcomed in the secret place of the Most High and abiding under His wings, and in the beaming light and fire of the Holy Comforter of Pentecost. Many significant lessons follow.

Every Christian should have the whole tabernacle experience as an ever-present reality. This trinality of experience, coming according to the trinal order of the tabernacle places, must come to blend in a unity of knowledge of the triune God as present in each of His personalities — just what Jesus meant when He said, " We," My Father and I, and also the Comforter " will come and abide continually." The Bible puts God as the first person, the Son follows, and the Holy Ghost proceeds from both and the Three act in unison. So Calvary follows and endorses Sinai and the Zion Pentecost makes both effective. So the brazen altar confirms the decalogue, yet the most holy place alone ensures the value of both. So conversion fixes the purpose of obedience started in conviction, and entire sanctification makes the whole will of God our delight. Ever after the principles of all are co-existent. Full holiness is a climax without which conversion is not an entire success; as a clear conversion must follow conviction or the good desires of the penitent become a failure.

And there is a trinality of divine leadership— Providence, the Word, and the interior conviction wrought by the Spirit. These three must always agree. Some on the plea of following the Spirit have plunged into the floods of fanaticism. Such are said to go too far. Rather, they do not go far enough. They must go from the impressson to the Word, and on to Providence. Half-guided or third-guided is misguided. They should find and follow the threefold guidance and thus be safely guided.

Finally let us draw near *now*. Let us come close to God at once. Enter into the holiest right here. Having boldness let us enter into full assurance of faith. Carry the blood and all is sure.

> "You by faith may now prevail,
>   Enter by the blood of Jesus;
> Pass beyond the second veil,
>   Enter by the blood of Jesus.
>
> Beyond the second veil,
> Pure love and joy prevail,
> God's promise ne'er can fail
>   Enter by the blood of Jesus."

XXIV.

FULL SALVATION.

H. C. MORRISON, LOUISVILLE KY.

"Abstain from all appearance of evil.

And the very God of peace sanctify you wholly; and I pray God your whole spirit and soul and body be preserved blameless unto the coming of our Lord Jesus Christ.

Faithful is he that calleth you, who also will do it (1 Thess. 5 : 22-24).

In the text we have a commandment, a prayer, and a promise.

The commandment is contained in the twenty-second verse. "Abstain from all appearance of evil."

The prayer is contained in the twenty-third verse. "And the very God of peace sanctify you wholly. And I pray God your whole spirit, and soul and body be preserved blameless unto the coming of our Lord Jesus Christ."

The promise is contained in the twenty-fourth verse. "Faithful is he that calleth you, who also will do it."

In these three verses we have set forth the great doctrine of perfect obedience, and perfect purity,— "full salvation."

The text is addressed to Christians. We cannot conceive of the apostle Paul exhorting sinners to "abstain from all appearance of evil." Addressing the

Thessalonians he says, "But ye, brethren, are not in darkness, that that day should overtake you as a thief, ye are all the children of light." To them he also says, "Rejoice evermore. Pray without ceasing. In everything give thanks."

Every reasonable Bible reader will see at once that these Thessalonians were justified believers, but they were not *wholly sanctified;* hence the prayer that, "the very God of peace sanctify" them "wholly." I call your attention to the fact that this inspired commandment, or exhortation to outward holiness, and this inspired prayer for entire sanctification and perfect preservation until the coming of our Lord, immediately followed by the inspired promise that God will grant the petition, ought to settle all dispute as to the teaching of God's Word on the subject of the possibility and necessity of entire sanctification.

We cannot conceive of a just God who would be satisfied with less than perfect obedience from His servants, or of a holy God who would be content with less than perfect purity in His children. We nowhere find Christ or His apostles praying for the entire sanctification of the sinful and unbelieving. We nowhere find Christ or His apostles exhorting the unregenerated to seek holiness, entire sanctification, or perfection.

Notice Christ's prayer for the disciples. These disciples had been born again. Christ says they "are not of the world." To them He had said, "Rejoice because your names are written in heaven." For them He prayed, "Sanctify them through Thy truth."

He said, "I pray not for the world, but for them which Thou has given me, for they are Thine."

Turn to any of the letters of Paul; where does he exhort unregenerated sinners to seek sanctification? Where does he fail to exhort regenerated persons to go on to sanctification, or perfection? Take for example his earnest words to the elders of the church at Ephesus at his parting with them. "And now, brethren, I commend you to God, and to the Word of His grace, which is able to build you up, and to give you an inheritance among all them which are sanctified" (Acts 20: 32). To the Hebrews he says, "Therefore leaving the principles of the doctrine of Christ, let us go on unto perfection; not laying again the foundation of repentance from dead works, and of faith toward God" (Heb. 6: 1). He charges Titus to preach Christ as one, "who gave Himself for us, that He might redeem us from *all iniquity*, and purify unto Himself a peculiar people, zealous of good works" (Titus 2: 14). Paul could not leave entire sanctification out of his preaching and writing for he was commissioned in his call by Christ "to open their eyes, and to turn them from darkness to light, and from the power of Satan unto God, that they may receive forgiveness of sins, and inheritance among them which are sanctified by faith that is in Me" (Acts 26:18). To this call Paul himself testifies that he was ever faithful. "Whom [Christ] we preach, warning every man, and teaching every man in all wisdom; that we may present *every man perfect* in Christ Jesus whereunto I also labor, striving according to His working, which worketh in me mightily" (Col. 1: 28–29).

It is certainly clear to my readers that the apostle Paul taught all believers to go on to "perfection," to entire sanctification, even as he prayed God to "sanctify them wholly." Would Paul have been continually at this if these believers had been wholly sanctified at the time of their justification? Certainly not. But you say, "Is entire sanctification a necessity, or is it a luxury that may be sought or rejected as the believer may choose?" We will let Paul answer. "Follow after peace with all men, and the sanctification without which no man shall see the Lord" (Heb. 12: 14. Rev. Ver.).

But you say, "Can a justified person be lost?" We answer no, but a justified person can lose justification; all who refuse to follow the calls of God will do so.

Does any suppose that when the Israelites crossed the Red Sea from Egyptian bondage into the wilderness, that if they had refused to go forward, the pillar of fire would have remained with them? If they had rebelled against God, and His servant Moses, and refused to believe there was such a land as Canaan, or if there was, refused to seek it, would the manna have continued to fall? No one believes it would. The only way to keep in the light and secure the manna which sustained life was to follow the cloud. In the end those who refused to enter into Canaan perished in the wilderness.

Then beloved, we warn you that those who are justified by His grace, and suppose that they can remain in that justified state without going forward to that sanctification "wholly" for which the apostles prayed, deceive themselves. To have refused to "stand still and see the salvation of the Lord" at the Red Sea, would have been to be recaptured and carried by the Egyptians into a more grievous bondage. To refuse to cross into Canaan at Kadesh, was to go back and perish in the wilderness.

When the sinner convicted by the Word and Holy Spirit of his lost condition, refuses to repent and believe on Christ for justifying grace, the Spirit of God departs from him, his convictions wear away and he becomes more hardened and wicked than before.

When the justified believer is taught of the Word and the Holy Ghost to go on to "perfection" to that entire sanctification for which the apostle prays, and refuses, the Spirit is grieved, He will not always strive. There can be no standing still. Those who will not go forward go backward. The manna ceases to fall, the cloud vanishes from him, the Holy Spirit is quenched, rejected, disobeyed, and He takes His departure. "The last state of that man is worse than the first." Some of you who read this know what I say to be awfully true to your own deep sorrow. But you answer, "Where is the ground of the necessity for this second work of grace? Why should I pray or sing with Charles Wesley,

> 'Speak the second time "Be clean,"
> Take away my inbred sin'?"

We will call on that great commentator, Adam Clark, alike eminent for piety and scholarship, to help us here.

Commenting on 1 John 1: 9, Clark says, "Observe here,

1. Sin exists in the soul after two modes or forms (*a*), in *guilt* which requires forgiveness *or pardon* (*b*), in *pollution*, which requires *cleansing*.

2. *Guilt* to be forgiven must be *confessed*, and *pollution* to be *cleansed* must be also *confessed*. In order to get a *clean heart* a man must know and feel its deformity, acknowledge and deplore it before God, in order to be fully sanctified.

3. Few are pardoned because they do not feel and confess their sins; and few are sanctified or cleansed from all sin because they do not feel and confess their own sore and the plague of their hearts."

The forgiveness of your sins placed you in a state of justification; regeneration placed the new life, the divine life in your soul; entire sanctification will eradicate the natural depravity from your heart. It will cast out the "old man." It will destroy the "root of bitterness" within. It will be the answer in you of this gracious and comprehensive prayer of the apostle, "And the very God of peace sanctify you wholly."

Is it necessary that I should reason with the justified believer, who is singing,

> "Prone to wander, Lord I feel it,
> Prone to leave the God I love,"

to convince him that there is in his heart a proneness to leave God, "a bent to back-sliding" — a conflict in his soul. Beloved, you know full well that often doubts and fears arise, jest and pride and lust, and vain imaginations and unholy tempers. You often wonder and strive, and weep and pray for deliverance from them, that is if you retain your justification. Many surrender and sink down beneath the trampling hoofs of sin. Some of you sadly sing —

> "Return, O holy dove, return,
> Sweet messenger of rest,
> I hate the sins that made me mourn,
> And drove Thee from my breast."

While some of you say, "I am rich and increased w.th goods, and have need of nothing; and knowest not that thou art wretched, and miserable, and poor, and blind, and naked."

That entire sanctification is not wrought in conversion is not only recognized by Christ in His prayer for His disciples, and Paul in his prayer for the Thessalonians, but this Bible truth has been recognized by all churches and creeds of the world.

Churches have differed as to their views with reference to the time and manner of the removal of the "remains of sin" in the justified, but they have been a unit in their agreement that the "root of bitterness" remains.

The Methodist Church has given special prominence to this doctrine from the days of John Wesley to the present time. Listen to the bishops of the Southern Methodist Church in their address to the general conference of 1894:

"The privilege of believers to attain unto a state of entire sanctification, or perfect love, and to abide therein, is a well-known teaching of Methodism. Witnesses to this experience have never been wanting in the church, though few in comparison with the whole membership. Among them have been men and women of beautiful consistency and seraphic ardor, jewels of the church. Let the doctrine still be proclaimed, and the experience still be testified."

So my readers, you will see at once that these bishops agree, and unite their voice with all Christendom, that the regenerated are not wholly sanctified; also that they speak out in harmony with the history and doctrines of Methodism, that those who are justified, may be sanctified, that from the first such persons have been in the church as living witnesses to the fact that Christ can sanctify, "save to the uttermost, and keep unspotted from the world."

You will notice also that they say, "Let the doctrine still be proclaimed, and the experience still be testified." Time would fail me to point you to the sermons of John Wesley, the songs of Charles Wesley, and the writings of Fletcher, Watson, and a host of others who plainly taught that inbred sin remains in the justified believer, and that it must be cleansed away in order to entire sanctification, and that this cleansing is not of works, growth or physical death, but by the precious blood of Jesus. "Wherefore Jesus also, that He might *sanctify* the people with His own blood, suffered without the gate" (Heb. 13 : 12).

Can you conceive of a truly regenerated believer saying, "I am unwilling to be entirely sanctified from sin." Would not such a will be in rebellion against the divine will? "For" says Paul to the Thessalonians, "this is the will of God, even your sanctification" (1 Thess. 4: 3). Could one rebel thus against God, and remain in peace with God, and justified in His sight? Every intelligent, unprejudiced mind answers, no! So far as committing wilful sin is concerned, the penitent forsakes all sinning before he is pardoned. Pardon or justification is impossible so long as he continues in actual sin. Hear the Word of God:

"Let the wicked forsake his way, and the unrighteous man his thoughts, and let him return unto the Lord, and He will have mercy upon him, and to our God for He will abundantly pardon" (Isa. 55: 7).

Is any one of my hearers so stupid as to suppose that any one must forsake all sin in order to become justified, and then can return back to the wilful commission of sin, and remain justified? I trust not. The doctrine that we can remain justified before God, at the same time wilfully sinning and violating the law of God, is the doctrine of devils.

If you would remain at peace with God you must subdue the indwelling remains of sin, and keep the mastery over it, so that it shall not break out in actual transgression. It is for this very reason that the apostle says in the text, "Abstain from all appearance of evil." (Rev. Ver., "Every form of evil.") Those who would come into the blessed experience, for which Paul prays in the twenty-third verse, must see that they walk in perfect obedience to the exhortation contained in the twenty-second verse.

Those who would be entirely sanctified must abstain from outward sin, the meanwhile offering themselves to God a "living sacrifice," calling upon God in the prayer of faith to sanctify them wholly from inbred corruption.

John is quite in harmony with Paul in this matter. He says, " If we walk in the light, as He is in the light, we have fellowship one with another, and the blood of Jesus Christ His Son cleanseth us from all sin."

Those who desire inward holiness must practice outward holiness. Those who lift up holy hands, hands that commit no wilful sin, will doubtless receive from God a holy heart. Let no one deceive you. You cannot sanctify the depravity out of your hearts, you cannot grow it out, death will not destroy it. Christ alone is able. He is our Sanctifier. Depravity is the work of the devil. " For this purpose the Son of God was manifested, that He might destroy the works of the devil " (1 John 3 : 8).

The twenty-second verse of our text is to the *sanctification wholly* in the twenty-third verse what the Jordan was to Canaan. Those who would come into the twenty-third must come through the twenty-second. It is but a short step from the obedience of the twenty-second, to the entire sanctification of the twenty-third. That step is the step of faith. Join your prayer with that of Christ and the apostle, and take the step this moment. Cast yourself upon Christ, He is the altar. He will sanctify you. He died that He might do it. " Faithful is He that calleth you, who also will do it." Commit yourself without reserve, and have no fear; He will " sanctify you wholly," and preserve you " blameless," " spirit and soul and body unto the coming of our Lord Jesus Christ."

In the operating room of a great surgeon, a frail woman lay prone upon a table; her husband stood by her side, holding her delicate hands, which clung to him as never before. They had talked it all over. It was her only hope for life. She had put her home in order, and said farewell to friends and relatives. She said, " Husband, you will stay with me, and hold to my hand." " Yes, wife," said he, " I will not leave you a moment." The surgeon adjusted his apron, and arranged his instruments conveniently; the attendant stood by ready for service. " Now," said the surgeon, " we are ready, but madam, you must let your husband step in the other room, and close the door. He is liable to faint, he can do you no good, and will be in our way." She hesitated a moment, and with one long fond look, she sighed, and answered, " Just as you say doctor." The husband stooped silently and pressed a kiss upon her forehead, and with heavy heart stepped quietly away, and closed the door behind him. A trembling voice said, " Now doctor I trust all to you, save my life if possible."

The attendant applied the anæsthetic; the pallor of death spread over the patient's face, she breathed more quietly, she dropped into unconsciousness. The surgeon applied the knife. " It is just as I expected," said he, as he laid open the diseased part. The knife was sharp, the hand was strong and steady, the delicate task was soon performed, the wound was closed. The anæsthetic was removed, the patient opened her eyes, tears of gratitude rolled down her face, and she said, "Thank you doctor."

Health and vigor soon returned, she was hale and strong again. Will any one say that she should not testify to the skill of her physician?

Would you be circumcised in heart? Would you have the depravity entirely removed? Would you have the "old man" forever crucified? Then come to the Great Physician. Bid all the world farewell, and shut yourself up with Jesus only. Take the anæsthetic of a full surrender. Lose all consciousness of surroundings and die to self. Fear not, trust the mighty Christ. Now believe; believe with all thy consecrated heart, "I will not let Thee go, until Thou bless me." Oh, the day is dawning. The Sun of Righteousness is rising. There are floods of glory everywhere.

> "Jesus comes, He fills my soul,
> Perfected in Him I am,
> I am every whit made whole,
> Glory, Glory to the Lamb."

XXV.

COMPLETE CONSECRATION NECESSARY TO ENTIRE SANCTIFICATION.

D. COBB, LOS ANGELES, CAL.

"For Moses had said, Consecrate yourselves to-day to the Lord, even every man upon his son, and upon his brother; that he may bestow upon you a blessing this day" (Ex. 32 : 29).

THE marginal reading is, "And Moses said, Consecrate yourselves to the Lord, because every man has been against his son and against his brother," etc.

This is a most thrilling account of giving the law to Moses, and the general defection of Israel. Their excuses for their course are few and remarkable: a desire for a leader, and the long absence of Moses. Excuses for wrong-doing are never numerous, nor of any force. God has wisely removed all ground of complaint or excuse from every responsible soul. Aaron was their agent in carrying out their idolatrous request, but when he came face to face with Moses he shrank from the responsibility, and was ashamed of it. Our text, and especially the marginal reading, shows that man cannot sin but its results touch damagingly the interests of others. Every man, without exception, "*has been against his son and against his brother.*" Their going back to idolatry, by the creation of the "golden calf" for worship, took wives, children and all within the camp, in its destructive path. A large proportion of the wayward and wicked in every age are the product of bad example, and a vicious home administration. Consecration to God,— a setting apart ourselves, families and all we control to sacred uses, and to the service of Almighty God, would largely remedy this evil. God made man for Himself — in His own image, for the high and noble purpose of representing and honoring His creatures, in his Head-ship of the race. But what a wreck of Edenic plans in a little time was realized, in the use of delegated powers by which freedom of agency was conferred upon the now fallen pair. This being the beginning of the development of the race a remedy must be found. Adam and Eve alone were responsible, and the race was seen only in them. The satisfaction of a broken law, only, was necessary to place man where he could by his intuitive advantages, and grasping the *first* promise made to them with hope, lift himself out of his dark environments, and give him sufficient light to walk with his companion in perfect obedience to the commands of God, in their state of humiliation, and learn the lesson of faith by what they had suffered.

Christ Jesus, the Son of God, paid the price of these advantages, leaving man to improve them. This brings us to the question under consideration, namely: consecration.

I. *What is consecration?* In a religious sense, "*All for Christ.*"

1. All professions involve the principle — as law, medicine, etc. Consecration to these several callings is a stern necessity to success in their prosecution. This is secular, or a setting apart one's self wholly to a special work, with this motto: — " One business for one man."

The lawyer declares himself set apart for the adjustment of civil matters between man and man. The physician says, by his professional sign, "I have prepared myself to look after the ailments of our physical being." The terms of consecration are such that you can call me out at any hour of the night, to face any storm, to go any reasonable distance, to put myself into contact with any disease however contagious — and suffer no violation of terms of contract, or professional justice. I will give you one sample of a higher type of consecration than the professional, and a lower than that which prepares us for entire sanctification by the office of the Holy Ghost. I refer to the marriage contract. Parties agree to take each the other, to love, cherish, protect — and forsaking all others, keep themselves for each other so long as they both shall live. This consecration stands next to consecration to God in Christ, and is used by Christ and His apostles to illustrate, as far as it may, the relation existing between Christ and His church. Christ says of it, that, "He gave Himself for it; that He might sanctify and cleanse it . . . by the Word, that He might present it to Himself a glorious church, not having spot, or wrinkle or any such thing; but that it should be holy and without blemish" (Eph. 5 : 25–27).

2. The highest type of consecration must take the whole man: body, soul and spirit; and is a complete surrender of all to God in Christ (1 Cor. 6 : 19, 20). Paul cries out, as though much surprised at the ignorance of the church at Corinth: "What? know ye not that your body is the temple of the Holy Ghost which is in you, which ye have of God, and ye are not your own? For ye are bought with a price: therefore glorify God in your body, and in your spirit, which are God's."

What sublime sentiment! Peter corroborates this wonderful truth, in his *first* letter to the churches, general — (18th and 19th verses). "Forasmuch as ye know that ye were not redeemed with corruptible things, as silver and gold . . . but with the precious blood of Christ, as of a Lamb without blemish and without spot." These passages put the Holy Ghost within us, as its temple — and establishes ownership to the casket and all there is in it.

No person with a properly instructed conscience, can read these Scriptures for light, and not be impressed with the necessity of "cleansing ourselves from all filthiness of the flesh and spirit, perfecting holiness in the fear of God" (2 Cor. 7 : 1).

(1.) The apostle Paul, in his epistle to the church at Rome (12 : 1), "I beseech *you* therefore, brethren, by the mercies of God, that ye present your bodies a *living* sacrifice, holy acceptable unto God, which is your reasonable service."

In the opening of this letter to the Romans, he addresses them as the "beloved of God, called to be saints." You can see by this that the term "brethren" means something more than national ties, as in the ninth chapter and third verse, where he speaks of his "brethren and kinsmen according to the flesh." These were brethren in Christ, exhorted to complete consecration. Evidently the presentation of the body here is put for the whole man, and is to be a constant, rational sacrifice. The sacrificial victim is a *dead body* — the Christian's is a living, active body — the former a mere animal service, while that of the Christian is a rational one. The body is the "house we live in." We will repair and protect the *literal* dwelling, to preserve it from the decay and wastage of time; so we should care for the house of the soul — the temple of the Holy Ghost. We should observe strictly the laws governing its purity, its longevity, and thereby conserve its strength. "I beseech you *brethren;* called to be saints, beloved of God." In no case are sinners urged to seek holiness; reconciliation, the primary step, for sinners, but sanctification of believers.

(2.) *Our mental faculties are also to be set apart to God's service* — that we will have "the mind that was in Christ." So that we will agree with Him in thought — in our likes, and dislikes, and will take pleasure in what pleases Him. Will "search the Scriptures," to find out God's will concerning us. Will *study* the Scriptures, for the love we have for them, and the light that is in them. A consecrated mind will turn away instinctively from everything that dishonors God. Our tastes will be pure, under the sealings, and sanctions of the Holy Ghost.

(3.) *We are to consecrate our property to God.* He provides the capital on which He permits us to do business, and provides the necessities of physical life, and justice requires an adequate return for its use. This is clearly taught in Jacob's contract with God at the city of Luz (Gen. 28: 20, 21, 22). God's revealings to him on this *first* night out from his home convinced him that something must be done, more than to flee from his wronged brother. Not having a religious basis for action, his mind turned on the commercial side of his enterprise, and there he "vowed a vow," that if God would be with him in his journey, and give him bread to eat, and raiment to put on, and bring him to his Father's house ultimately in peace, then, shall the Lord be my God, and these stones shall be God's house, and of all given to me, I will surely give in return, a "tenth."

This was a commercial transaction, and embraced a principle in Jewish finances during the long history of that race. When in their backslidden state, they had failed to bring a tenth of their income to the storehouse, for sacred uses, he charges them with robbery, (Mal. 3:8) and declares a curse is upon them, on that account. He proclaims a remedy in the tenth verse, "Bring ye all the tithes into the storehouse, that there may be meat in Mine house, and prove Me now herewith, saith the Lord of Hosts, if I will not open you the windows of heaven, and pour you out a blessing, that there shall not be room enough to receive it." Sometimes we sing: "Fill me with Thy hallowed presence, Come, oh come, and fill me now," etc. Have you emptied yourself? Have you brought all the tithes into the storehouse? If not, stop your song-pleading until you have attended to this matter. A bridge over the chasm is a necessity, but entirely useless without an approach to it. Sanctification, the bridge; consecration, the approach to it.

When stationed in Minneapolis in '75 a member of my church, a lumberman, had made a very successful sale of logs to a firm in St. Louis, and came to tell me about it that I might rejoice with him, as he knew of my strong personal friendship. He said, "I have made a clean twelve thousand dollars in the sale." I was heartily glad of his success, and asked him what about the Lord's part of the profits of the sale? He did not seem quite to understand the full import of my remark. I explained the Jewish plan of giving a tenth of their income, in silver and gold, in flocks and herds, and grains and fruits, etc., and so far as I knew the obligation had never been repealed. He studied the question a few minutes, and then taking his note-book and putting down the amount of profit, and cutting off the right hand cipher, and then looking at me seeming much surprised, and said, "That would be twelve hundred dollars. Do you think it would be my duty to put that much into the Lord's treasury at one time. Now, my dear brother, I will tell you what I think about the tenth business. It may do for small incomes but not for large ones."

What overwhelming benevolence on the part of our heavenly Father to furnish all the capital and ask only one dollar out of ten of the income in return for its use. This is a matter of income and not of capital. I am convinced that there are thousands of professed Christians who are withholding the Lord's part of their income and using it to further their own selfish ends. Many of these are not realizing this fact, nevertheless they are robbing God. It is plainly embezzlement.

Here lies the difficulty in reaching a satisfactory experience. To bless you as you desire, would be a sad endorsement of your course, an injury to you and all others under your influence. When we are right in our position it is God's pleasure to bless us until we cry, "Stay Thy hand." " Bring all the tithes into the storehouse." Some are doubtless antagonizing their convictions, and these retained funds burn in their pockets.

(4.) *We should consecrate to God our influence — social and official.* Every person has an influence for good or for evil. Its operations are subtle and silent, but none the less effective, like animal magnetism — operative, yet unseen.

Like the " leaven "— doing its work without observation — we are not aware, not alarmed, until results no longer can be concealed, and it is too late to correct.

A son, a daughter, a whole family injured, possibly ruined religiously, by an influence, undermining foundations, and pillars of truth, so that confidence and faith are lost. The agencies in this work are parents, or guardians, who could not be induced to do such work for any consideration; and yet in the above supposition, *do that very thing* without fear or solicitation. "Awake thou that sleepest, and arise from the dead, and Christ shall give thee light." "How shall we escape if we *neglect* so great salvation?" A salvation touching our soul's interests, and of those around us. In a consecrated life the influence can but be right.

Official influence is the product of conferred gifts. Delegated powers are representative, and are to be used for the benefit of society. It is base for an officer in the civil or political realm to use these powers for personal ends, and much more so to injure and oppress the represented. Officially their motto should be, "Do right though the heavens fall." God will care for results.

And finally: *We are to consecrate our soul, life and heart love to God.*

This is the main-spring of all religious action, "Thou shalt love the Lord thy God with all thy heart and with all thy soul, and with all thy mind. This is the *first* and great commandment." The strongest evidence of supreme love to God is obedience. "If ye love me keep my commandments" (John 14: 15).

This consecration should be so complete and so sustained by our convictions that it should never be *modified* nor *withdrawn* (See Gen. 15: 13).

II. *Reasons for consecration.*— Having shown what we should consecrate in the foregoing, we come now to consider the reasons. Jehovah says, by Isaiah, "Come now let us reason together." It would seem sufficient to an honest inquirer, that God should authorize it — and yet by many reasons are required.

The first we bring is the Fatherhood of God. That He has a *right* in us as His children.

"He made us, and not we ourselves" (Psalm 100: 3). A paternal administration, human or divine, is founded on this right. God says of Abraham, "I know him that he will command his children and his household after him, and they shall keep the way of the Lord to do justice and judgment," etc. (Gen. 18: 19). God has a *right* to require that all we have and hope to be, shall be devoted to His service. You have the *right* to command your children, because they are yours, and God your Heavenly Father has the right to your consecration, because you are His by creation. You have no right to question the justice of this claim.

Again: He is our *Redeemer*, so we are His by purchase. Paul tells us; "we are bought with a price: Therefore glorify God in your body, and in your spirit, which are God's." Peter declares, (1 Peter 1: 18, 19), "That we know that we were not redeemed with corruptible things, as silver and gold . . . but with the precious blood of Christ." The apostle Paul, in his letter to the church at Rome, gives an exhaustive argument, on the redemptive office of Christ's death for us, as found in the fifth chapter of that letter, which we commend to your careful study; and let the Word do its work.

Again: we are his by adoption. This is clearly taught

in Romans eighth chapter. He says, "For as many as are led by the Spirit of God, they are the sons of God. For ye have not received the spirit of bondage again to fear; but ye have received the Spirit of adoption, whereby we cry, Abba, Father." In these and the following verses he clinches this whole question to an honest conscience.

The fourth reason is given by Christ in His sermon on the Mount, "No man can serve two masters." All perons capable of choosing, are serving one master; to which are you rendering service? Since you cannot, in the nature of things, divide your service, *dual* worship cannot be satisfactory to either God or Mammon. No man can be neutral, "He that is not with me is against me; and he that gathereth not with me scattereth abroad" (Matt. 12: 30). Again, in the spiritual kingdom there can be but *one will* (John 6: 38). Christ says, "For I came down from heaven, not to do mine own will, but the will of him that sent me." In the garden he says, "O my Father, if it be possible, let this cup pass from me; nevertheless, not as I will, but as thou wilt." In his inimitable prayer, Christ teaches us to pray, "Thy kingdom come. Thy will be done in earth, as it is in heaven." This teaching shows us that not even the will of the Son could oppose the will of the Father. One will only can be recognized in His administration. In this consecration we must surrender our wills to His. *Thy will, and not mine, be done.* Unity of will — a necessity to a successful administration.

Finally: a *complete* consecration will give us *power*

with God and men. A successful religious life hinges on this, — power with God and man. What are we here for — to enjoy ourselves? We are here to *win the world to Christ.* Now what will prepare us for successful work? *Entire* devotion — sanctification.

Here is the battle-field — here is use for the "enduement of power." The harvest is ripe; the fields are white; are the reapers ready? God has promised His agents the aid of all His attributes in the work assigned them. We must be right to claim this help. "If we depend on Him we cannot fail." If we ask, and work in faith, it shall be done. "He that goeth forth and weepeth, bearing precious seed, shall doubtless come again with rejoicing, bringing his sheaves with him" (Psalm 126: 6).

III. *Time of it,* "to-day." The text declares our consecration due to-day. To-morrow is *one day too late.* "To-day, if ye will hear his voice, harden not your hearts." "Procrastination is the thief of time," and opportunities as well. "Put not off until to-morrow, what ought to be done to-day," is a safe adage. Convictions, should heed no delay. It is an antagonism that we cannot afford to maintain. The hazard is too great.

An *opportunity* is priceless. No mathematical value can be put upon it. Once gone it can never be recovered. To-day you can, to-morrow you cannot — can you calculate the difference? The loss to your own soul, and to others you might be instrumental in saving, is beyond computation. Let us analyze a little.

1. God claims all our time and resources in His

service. He reckons this from the time of our knowledge of good and evil. Grown to manhood, without a proper rendering or accounting, see what a fearful indebtedness has accrued. It cannot be paid, it must be forgiven. And if unforgiven, eternity itself cannot lessen the obligation, nay, but increase it. Like an unpaid mortgage it will eat, until all is consumed. Sin in its results, never decreases by time. Again, the promises of God are good to you to-day but not to-morrow.

2. To delay is a *risk* without the *least* compensation. The commercial motto is, "Will it pay!" No person yet gained any advantage by hesitation or tardiness in the discharge of a religious duty.

We stand or fall alone. If we do not succeed, the blame will rest wholly upon ourselves. However involved in the wreck and its issues, environments and outside agencies may be, their responsibilities will stand apart from our own, and we be judged by our deeds alone. Who will comply with the exhortation of the text, and put all into God's "*to-day*," and say in the language of Charles Wesley — Hymnal, Hymn 470, verse 3.

> "Take my soul and body's powers;
>   Take my memory, mind and will;
> All my goods, and all my hours;
>   All I know, and all I feel;
> All I think or speak or do;
>   Take my heart, but make it new."

XXVI.

BAPTISM WITH THE HOLY GHOST.

P. F. BRESEE, D. D., LOS ANGELES, CAL.

I indeed baptize you with water unto repentance: but he that cometh after me is mightier than I, whose shoes I am not worthy to bear: he shall baptize you with the Holy Ghost, and with fire (Matt. 3 : 11).

For John truly baptized with water; but ye shall be baptized with the Holy Ghost not many days hence (Acts 1: 5).

THE dispensation of the Holy Ghost was ushered in soon after the ascension of Jesus, by His coming upon the apostles and disciples in sanctifying and filling power. This was in accord with this prophecy of John the Baptist, in reference to Jesus and His baptism, and Jesus' own statement just preceding His ascension, after referring to John's prophecy, and emphasizing his work, that it should be fulfilled not many days hence. This He also declared was in accord with the promise of the Father, which they had heard of Him, evidently referring to His statement to them in view of His expected departure, that He would send the Comforter — the Holy Ghost — who was to abide with them forever. All of this was fulfilled as they were gathered together in one place, of one mind, waiting with prayer and supplication, believing the words of Jesus.

No doubt that up to that time, that was the greatest day the church ever saw. It was the ripe fruitage of all the dispensations which had preceded it. It was the beginning of the time of the fullness of the gospel of Jesus Christ. It was, in a more general sense, the establishment of the kingdom of heaven in human hearts. John the Baptist had said, "The kingdom of heaven is at hand." Jesus, Himself, when He began to preach also said, "The kingdom of heaven is at hand," He commissioned His disciples, when He sent them out, to say the same thing; but now the kingdom is set up and established within. Believers on Jesus Christ are brought into closest unity and fellowship with Him, their King, being made partakers of the same baptism, and thus of the same nature.

There are two questions connected with this subject which I desire to ask:

1. *Does Jesus still baptize with the Holy Ghost?*

2. *What did the Holy Ghost baptism do for the early church?*

First: *Does Jesus still baptize with the Holy Ghost?* I ask this first, as it makes but little difference to us what this baptism did for believers eighteen hundred years ago, unless Jesus is still in the midst carrying on His ministry of baptism with the Holy Ghost. But if this is the day of this ministry, it is of the utmost importance what was done in and for them, as the same will be done in and for us.

It would not seem necessary to urge at length that these are the days of the Holy Ghost baptism. It would not seem as if any student of the Word could doubt it. It is certainly the teaching of all prophecy bearing upon this sending of the Comforter, which was the Holy Ghost, by the ministry of Jesus: that it was not to be a momentary flash, not an aurora which was to fade away into darkness, but a glorious day — a consummation — a blessed fruitage of all that had preceded it. Joel had said that in the last days the Spirit was to be poured out upon all the flesh; sons and daughters were to prophesy, servants and handmaidens were to receive this divine blessing, and their mouths were to be filled with this new prophecy. This certainly takes in a wider scope than a few disciples and a few days.

Jesus said that the Comforter would abide forever. Certainly, not simply through the lives of the first disciples, for in the same connection Jesus prays for all that should believe on Him through their word, and the promise seems as broad as the prayer. Jesus said it was better that He go away and the Comforter come. Evidently not a temporary gift, but to abide in the church and in the hearts of believers, while He was absent, or until His coming again.

The great gift of God to man is the Holy Spirit. It was His coming that was to pierce the hearts of men, convince of sin, of righteousness, and of judgment. It is He always who regenerates. His coming is incomprehensible, but brings birth into a new life. "The wind bloweth where it listeth, and ye hear the sound thereof, but cannot tell whence it cometh and whether it goeth, so is every one born of the Spirit." It is also He who sanctifies and endures unto the end. As Paul says,

"Being sanctified by the Holy Ghost." Jesus' great promise of the Spirit, the first time, so far as we know that he alluded to the Holy Spirit in his teaching, is, "Ask and ye shall receive," etc. And then after referring to the earthly father's faithfulness to give what his child asks, adds as an explanation of our heavenly Father's faithfulness and what the great gift is, "If ye then being evil know how to give good gifts unto your children, how much more shall your heavenly Father give the Holy Spirit to them that ask Him." This certainly was not a temporary promise, but as Peter said, amid the glory of the Pentecost, "The promise is unto you and to your children and to all that are afar off, even as many as the Lord our God shall call." It was regarded by the early church as the inheritance of all believers. They were everywhere prayed for and urged, and led on that they might receive it. Paul did receive it, three days after his conversion, through the ministry of Ananias. The converts at the city of Samaria, who were so clearly and wonderfully converted through the ministry of the evangelist Philip, received the baptism with the Holy Ghost, through the ministry of Peter and John, who were sent down from Jerusalem, evidently for the purpose of leading them in. At Corinth and Philippi and Ephesus, those who had not received this baptism were prayed for and urged to enter in.

It was in reference to this that Peter said, the Lord had put no difference between Jew and Gentile — not only no difference because of race, but there was no difference because of the time which had elapsed between the baptism at Jerusalem and that at Cornelius' house — and there was as much difference in those few years, as unto this day, for with the Lord one day is as a thousand years and a thousand years as one day.

The church in theory believes that this is the dispensation of the Holy Ghost, and that the last of the last days has not yet passed. We say in our creed, "I believe in the Holy Ghost." It is in our songs. We still sing —

> "Holy Ghost no more delay, —
> Come and in Thy temple stay;
> Now Thine inward witness bear,
> Strong and permanent and clear;
> Spring of Life, Thyself impart :
> Rise eternal in my heart."

How often we lift up our voices and sing —

> "Oh, that it now from heaven might fall,
> And all my sins consume;
> Come, Holy Ghost, for Thee I call, —
> Spirit of burning come."

Better than all, it is in the experience of the church. Many of God's dear children have taken His yoke upon them, and learned of Him, who is meek and lowly of heart, and have found that rest to the soul, — that second rest — of which Charles Wesley speaks when he says —

> "A rest where all the soul's desire
> Is fixed on things above;
> Where fear, and sin, and grief expire,
> Cast out by perfect love."

This is the day of the Spirit's power. Jesus still baptizes with the Holy Ghost and fire.

Perhaps I ought to say that no one can be a candidate for the baptism with the Holy Ghost but one who is a child of God — one who is living in conscious favor with the Lord. If you are not converted, there is but one thing that you can do, and that is to repent, to surrender to God, and get saved. The one great thing for you is to receive pardon, and be adopted into the family of God. Then being a child, you are an heir, and may press your claims to the inheritance among them that are sanctified. It seems that the question was pressed in the early church, "Have ye received the Holy Ghost since ye believed?" I am aware that some who have confounded the witness of the Spirit, with the baptism with the Holy Ghost, have thought that the translation in the revised version indicates that, whatever was meant by that question, it was received at conversion. The revised version reads, "Did ye receive the Holy Ghost when ye believed?" But the literal rendering of the text is, "Having believed, did ye receive the Holy Ghost?" and the circumstances preclude its meaning anything but a further blessing after conversion.

When Paul asked the brethren at Ephesus this question, John the Baptist, whose disciples they were, had probably been dead for twenty years. John the Baptist preached a gospel of salvation. The Holy Ghost said of him that he was "to give knowledge of salvation unto his people by the remission of their sins." These men were his disciples, and had been evidently walking in the light for all these years. They were doubtless faithful men of God, for they were ready to receive the truth which Paul preached to them. Now, it is evident that they did not receive the Holy Ghost when they believed. They did not yet know of the baptism with the Holy Ghost. But as soon as they did know, they pressed in — a good example to all converted people. And this is the way that those who are converted and are walking up to the light they have, will do. The question really was, " Did you, in your early Christian life, receive this baptism? Did you early come to your Pentecost?" The apostles were converted before they received the baptism with the Holy Ghost. Probably no one would question this. But Jesus sets the matter at rest in His prayer the night before He suffered, in which He says of them to the Father, " They are Thine, they are not of the world, even as I am not of the world," etc., certain evidence that they were converted men. Peter, who had fallen by the way, had been restored and re-commissioned by Jesus, who after thrice probing him as to his love for Him had told him to feed His sheep, and after holding before him the martyr's death, by which he should glorify God, had bidden him to follow Him, which he had gladly done. They were converted, and not backslidden, when the blessed baptism came.

Now, as such, what did it do for them? We know they needed something more, for Jesus told them to tarry at Jerusalem — not to attempt to carry out the commission He had given them, until they received the fulfillment of the promise of the Father — the baptism of the Holy Ghost. No student of their lives can fail to see how great their need was and how completely the Pentecost baptism supplied their needs. So, we ask again, "What did the baptism with the Holy Ghost do for them?" And we ask it with the assurance that it will do the same for the children of the Lord to-day.

It purified their hearts. This, Peter clearly declares in the council at Jerusalem, telling them how God led him, and justified his going to Cornelius, a Gentile, by the fact that the Holy Ghost fell upon him and those gathered, as it did, upon them in the beginning, and put no difference between them — "purifying their hearts by faith" — evidently declaring that the baptism of the Holy Ghost purifies the heart. This was the case with the apostles. Before, they had worldly ambitions, fear and selfish purposes. Afterwards, these had disappeared, and in their place, ardent zeal, holy loves, and lives swallowed up in God. We have but to appeal to the deepest experiences of Christians all about us, who are converted and earnestly walking in the light, to have witnesses on every side, of the need of a further cleansing. Christians who confess that their love to God is not complete; that they do not always seek His glory; that there are in them many selfish and worldly aims; that they do not always burn with desire for the salvation of men; that they do not have love towards all; that there is not always an amen in their hearts to the will of God; that close, earnest preaching is not always acceptable to them — such can scarce doubt their need to have their hearts purified through the same baptism that purified the hearts of the apostles and disciples on the day of Pentecost, and Cornelius and his house, when Peter preached to them. The Holy Ghost baptism will meet this need.

This baptism also reveals Jesus, the King of Glory, in the soul. There is a very precious meaning in the words of Paul, when giving his experience; he says, " When it pleased God, who called me by His grace, to reveal His Son in me." The promise of Jesus in reference to the ministry of the Comforter, " He shall glorify Me, for He shall take of Mine, and shall show it unto you." It is the office of the Holy Spirit to reveal Jesus in the soul. Those baptized with the Holy Spirit are to see visions — evidently revelations to the soul — of the Lord Jesus Christ. This is true in experience. Never was Jesus so near and precious. He who was with us, is revealed in us, never before so completely — " the chiefest among ten thousand, and altogether lovely." It is in the coming of the Comforter, in the baptism of the Holy Ghost, that this is promised and received. In the abiding presence of the Holy Ghost there is the continued revelation of Jesus Christ. This is the marvelous and blessed life to which we are called.

In this baptism the Holy Spirit becomes also a revealer of the Word of God. The Holy Ghost is the Great Teacher. Under the light of His fire the Word yields up its mysteries. By His presence, the veil is taken away, and we are initiated into the blessed mysteries of redemption. To eyes not anointed, the Bible is largely a sealed book. Flashes break out here and there — enough to guide the wanderer's feet to Calvary — and on to gaze up to the ascended Lord, and receive this great gift that makes the sacred page flame with light, and gives to these sacred messages of God a sweetness and glory that is altogether inexpressible. The Book, that before had but little real interest to us, and was read as a duty and studied professionally, now becomes our joy by day and our solace by night. This baptism with the Holy Ghost imparts power to the soul. We see that when this baptism came upon the early church, it at once became a conquering army. It brings not the power of great deeds. Great men and great deeds have little place in the thought of men illuminated by the Holy Ghost. But the power of humility, of gentleness, tenderness, power to be broken-hearted and contrite; power of unworldiness, whose gaze is on the unseen glories — the power of being so lost to self, that God can shine. Not the power of genius, or human learning, or eloquence, but the power to be an empty vessel, that God can use to pour the water of life through. Power, not to do great things, but to testify to the abounding grace of our Lord Jesus Christ. " Ye shall receive power after that the Holy Ghost is come upon you, and ye shall be witnesses unto Me."

Such may lose many things. The apostles suffered the loss of all things. Saul of Tarsus counted the things that were gain unto him as loss for the excellency of the knowledge of Christ Jesus. So, to-day, a man may lose position, and friendship, and worldly gain; but he will not be left alone. The inheritance among them that are sanctified far outweighs all else. Nothing is sacrificed, but highest, sweetest privilege to give all to Jesus our Lord, and to have Him and be with Him forever.

XXVII.

BE YE HOLY

W. L. GRAY, PHILADELPHIA, PA.

"Be ye holy, for I the Lord your God am holy."

What an impressive argument! There is no reference to angels, however flaming with holiness. There is no reference to men, however they may be like God; but God Himself is made the example of our holiness. We admit the standard is so high that it seems dreadful; its brightness so dazzling that we are ready to cry out in deep humility "Hide me beneath the shadow of Thy wings."

But this is the voice of the Father speaking from heaven to His unholy children on earth. What silence should reign everywhere? What obedience should begin everywhere? What earnest inquiry should be made by all respecting the exalted nature of holiness? O turn not away from the flaming words of the Lord. Has the church an aversion to the spirit of holiness? Shall we blot out this precious doctrine from our theology? Shall it no longer be preached by our ministers? Shall it be a divine doctrine buried in the Bible and not reach the hearts of believers? O ye voluptuaries enchanted with the beauties of nature, of art, of science; turn away from the adoration of your idols and "worship the Lord in the beauty of holiness."

I. WHAT IS THIS HOLINESS?
II. HOW IS IT ATTAINED?

Let us treat this subject a moment with respect to common sense.

What is this holiness? The regular combination of all the parts is called the whole — the parts are wholly made up. There is also a similarity of meaning between the word wholeness and holiness; wholeness is all the parts of anything; the state of being whole, entire, sound; holiness therefore in God comprehends all His moral perfections. Holiness in man comprehends all the graces and virtues with which he was originally endowed by his Creator, or those which are proper to his renewed nature.

Having thus in a particular manner defined the term in question, we remark that in approaching the awful subject of God's holiness, we shall better understand it as meaning the wholeness of the perfection of the divine nature; His moral character and conduct being whole, entire, sound; love, mercy, justice, faithfulness and all other moral perfections constitute His holiness.

Now it may be remarked with reverence, that if any one of these were absent or wanting, there would be no longer a wholeness; and it is true, as we do know that while some make out there is no God, others make out that He is an imperfect God, that He is not holy. They admire the divine love, but they controvert the divine holiness. They adore the mercy that pardons sin, but they deny the justice that punishes sin. But all the moral perfections of God abide in Him in harmonious agreement and action. "Thou hast loved righteousness and hated iniquity."

We remark further that this wholeness, this entireness, this soundness in the infinite and divine Being, forever precludes the very idea of wrong motive and wrong conduct. It is therefore said of God with great caution and distinctness, "In Him is no sin." "Thy ways are equal and not unequal." Moreover this holiness in God will not allow sin to exist in man without notice. His love therefore leads Him to give His son to the world, who has made an atonement for sin, and sin must be pardoned or it must be punished. With overwhelming majesty in this great plan of human redemption, drawn up by prophets, apostles, and our Lord Himself, published from the mount, published from the cross, published from the sepulchre, published from the throne of intercession, published from the Holy Scriptures, published by the ministry of reconciliation.

Let it be again repeated — sin must be pardoned or sin must be punished, sin must be destroyed or the sinner must be destroyed. There is nothing harsh, nothing cruel in this, since the doctrine of the divine holiness embraces mercy and justice — indeed the doctrine of the divine holiness is most amiable. While Jehovah is proclaiming from heaven in a voice so positive, so urgent, so commanding, "I, the Lord your God, am holy" the world should be awakened not to despair but to repentance, hope, salvation, while the church is admonished to sing, "Sing unto the Lord, O ye saints of His, and give thanks at the remembrance of His holiness." But why this rapture of praise at a holiness so consuming to sinners?

> "He wills that I should holy be
> What can withstand His will?
> The counsel of His grace in me,
> He surely shall fulfil."

What is this holiness? It is a wholeness of renewed nature and conduct, it is the heart wholly cleansed from sin, and the life wholly regulated by God's will. It is the affections so sanctified, that while it is possible to sin, there is no disposition to sin. It is the life so regulated that while we may step out of the narrow way there is no disposition to do so. But no more can you understand what this blessedness is, by a mere description of it in words, than you can understand what heaven is, for indeed it is heaven in the soul. Be ye holy, and then shall ye know.

But having defined it briefly, let us *explain* it. It is plain that holiness has but one fixed and unalterable nature, that there cannot be two different kinds, that it is therefore in its nature the same in man that it is in God. But further, that although it is ever of the same nature, holiness in His creatures has many degrees. In God it is infinite. In angels it is according to angelic law and obedience. In Adam it was a perfect being keeping a perfect law. In fallen man it is according to the law of grace. And a definite standard respecting this holiness is plainly laid down in God's Word,

Serious and intelligent minds will reason after this manner. Every work of the Holy Spirit in the soul is a holy work, conversion is the work of the Holy Spirit, therefore conversion is the work of holiness in the soul. This is true, and it must be true of every work of the Holy Spirit. Why, then, is so marked a distinction made between conversion and holiness? To understand this whole question Scripturally let us now inquire: What is *justification?* The plain, Scriptural notion of justification is pardon, the forgiveness of sins. It is that act of God the Father, whereby for the sake of the propitiation made by the blood of His Son, "He showeth forth His righteousness [or mercy] by the remission of sins that are past." Thus St. Paul, in the epistle to the Romans, declares, "Blessed are they whose iniquities are forgiven and whose sins are covered. Blessed is the man to whom the Lord will not impute sin."

What then is *regeneration,* or the new birth? Is it the same as the former? Not precisely. Justification relates to that great work which God *does for us* in forgiving our sins; regeneration, or the new birth, relates to the great work which God *does in us* in renewing our fallen nature. In order of time neither of these is before the other; in the moment we are justified by the grace of God through the redemption that is in Christ Jesus, we are also born of the Spirit; but in order of thinking, as it is termed, justification precedes regeneration. "Being justified by faith, [when that great act is performed, then] we have peace with God," — our nature is renewed.

What then is *sanctification?* Regeneration is a part of sanctification, not the whole; it is the gate to it, the entrance into it. When we are born again, then our sanctification — our inward and outward holiness — begins. Adoption also is ours; "For we have not received the spirit of bondage again to fear but the spirit of adoption whereby we cry, Abba, Father." The witness of the Spirit is also ours; "The Spirit itself beareth witness with ours that we are the children of God." This is true religion. The kingdom of God, of righteousness and peace and joy in the Holy Ghost. O brethren, this is a great work. We must be careful not to underrate it.

Now this — that is to say, regeneration — is the beginning of inward and outward holiness, but not the whole. There is a higher state most distinctly declared in the Word: "Having therefore these promises dearly beloved, let us cleanse ourselves from all filthiness of the flesh and spirit, perfecting holiness in the fear of God." The doctrine then in question, is not the beginning of holiness, but the perfection of holiness according to the promises. But does not this imply that the great work of regeneration is imperfect? By no means. It is profane to assert that God does an imperfect work. All the graces that constitute regeneration being present, it is one whole, complete, entire work; in a word, a perfect regeneration. But would not that make the perfect Christian? No more than a perfect babe would make a perfect man. Do not be offended at the distinction which the Scriptures themselves make. Do not deny these truths, for upon the same principle you may deny the power of the atonement or even the existence of God. Do not plead for sin rather than holiness.

> "Why should I, the world to win,
> Hug the filthy idol, sin."

But you say great obscurity still covers the subject. Then whatever may be the difficulty, for the love of the truth, inquire still further. Let us offer this prayer together: —

> "Open my faith's interior eye,
> Display Thy glory from above;
> And all I am shall sink and die,
> Lost in astonishment and love."

The Holy Scriptures present this doctrine under a great variety of terms, and it should be observed that the terms perfection, holiness, love and sanctification, have a most remarkable similarity of meaning. They make up part of the great spiritual rock and that rock is Christ. And, no matter on which side it is smitten by the rod of faith, it sends forth the same spiritual drink: For that rock is Christ. "Therefore leaving the principles of the doctrine of Christ, let us go on unto perfection; not laying again the foundation of repentance from dead works, and of faith toward God, of the doctrine of baptisms, and of laying on of hands, and of resurrection of the dead, and of eternal judgment. And this will we do, if God permit." How undeniable is it from these passages, that the whole of the experimental doctrine of Christ had not yet been accomplished in them. There was one doctrine less;

one work less; one blessing less than the whole; and so far they were imperfect or un-whole, and not until there is a regular combination of all the parts — that is the doctrines, graces, and blessings belonging to this state — will this wholeness be made up; and this will be holiness or perfection.

And how exactly does this accord with passages found in Thessalonians; "I charge you by the Lord, that this epistle be read to all the *holy brethren*." And yet respecting these holy brethren it had just been said, "And the very God of peace sanctify you wholly and I pray God your whole spirit and soul and body, be preserved blameless unto the coming of our Lord Jesus Christ." Does not this imply that some part of the soul, some of the intellectual powers, some of the affections, remain unregenerate? By no means,— the former is *entire regeneration;* the latter is *entire sanctification*. But why continue this argument? You cannot be saved by that. Will you then cry out,—

> "Jesus, for this we calmly wait,
> O let our eyes behold Thee near;
> Hasten to make our heaven complete,
> Appear, our glorious God, appear."

And now let us turn to the sublime reasoning of the Holy Spirit under the idea of love. "And we have known and believed the love that God hath to us. God is love; and he that dwelleth in love dwelleth in God, and God in him." "Herein is our love made perfect, that we may have boldness in the day of judgment, because as He is, so are we in this world." "There is no fear in love; but perfect love casteth out fear; because fear hath torment. He that feareth is not made perfect in love." What a gush of holy inspiration is this! How it inflames the coldest passions! How it awakens the slumbering powers! How it starts out Hope upon her strongest wings.

In connection with this argument of love, we remark upon the passage, " He that feareth is not made perfect in love." He loves, but is not wholly given up to love, hence the great command of our Lord, " Thou shalt love the Lord thy God." And many do this. This you do, but this is not the whole command. " Thou shalt love the Lord thy God with all thy heart, and with all thy soul, and with all thy mind, and with all thy strength, and thy neighbor as thyself." And this is perfect love.

Is this, therefore, a state of sinless perfection? Not as we suppose you understand it, as our opponents have seemed to understand it. The law of God is perfect, and perfect love is competent to keep it; for the heart, being filled with love, there is no disposition to sin, no will to sin, and hence we may be kept from sin, but the moment this perfect love ceases to fill the heart, which it may do, that moment we may sin, for "love is the fulfilling of the law."

The philosophy of it is plain; no two dispositions can reign triumphantly at precisely the same time. Consider the nature of these passions : hatred, anger, and fear. Now, when our sins are forgiven, they are all done away, and guilt and condemnation are all done away. The heart is entirely clear of these, but are these passions done away ? No one will assert this, but all will admit that these passions may be controlled by grace. And as they give rise to nearly every sin after justification, we desire to show in what relation they stand to entire sanctification. We do not believe, as we understand mental science, that these passions will be annihilated — indeed, those passions are only so-called because we know the heart to be capable of such and such dispositions, and do not exist as an entity. In what sense, then, are they extirpated? We answer: Let us go on unto perfection, not absolute, but of the Christian graces. Then, virtually, perfect love will destroy hatred; perfect meekness will destroy anger; perfect courage will destroy fear. And if these graces be in you and abound, these evil passions need no longer be the inlets of sin. Inbred sin ceases its unholy incubation. This is confirmed by St. John's unanswerable argument, "And every man that hath this hope in him purifieth himself even as He is pure." "Whoso committeth sin transgresseth also the law; for sin is the transgression of the law. And ye know that He was manifested to take away our sins; and in Him is no sin. Whosoever abideth in Him sinneth not; whosoever sinneth hath not seen Him, neither known Him. Little children, let no man deceive you: he that doeth righteousness is righteous, even as He is righteous. He that committeth sin is of the devil; for the devil sinneth from the beginning. For this purpose was the Son of God manifested, that He might destroy the works of the devil. Whosoever is born of God doth not commit sin; for his seed remaineth in him: and he cannot sin, because he is born of God." And if all this is said of one who is born of God, how much more, then, may it be said of one who is *filled* with God.

The expression, "He cannot sin," proves that there is power in the atonement both to pardon and to prevent sin, so long as the seed, or word, or grace of Christ remains in the heart. The Christian, however, is not a machine, constructed so that he cannot sin in an absolute sense, but he may be saved from the supposed necessity of committing sin; understanding by sin the voluntary transgression of a known law. This is the spirit of St. John's teaching. Do you differ from St. John? Then what have we to hope of you? Then you must be left to the issues of your own wisdom.

Second. *How is this great salvation to be attained?* Oh that I could answer this question as it should be answered. Many words need not be used. Who hath said, " Thou wilt show me the path of life"? " Blessed are they that do His commandments that they may have right to the tree of life and enter in through the gates into the city." But " Lord what wilt Thou have me to do?"

1. *Search the Scriptures*, and mark the numerous commands, promises, prayers and examples of holiness.

2. *Believe this doctrine;* believe that the blessing may be yours and yours now. " For God hath called us from the beginning unto salvation through sanctification of the Spirit and belief of the truth." This is most important. Believers, whatever they believe, can

never attain what they deny. They will not come until they believe they can come. Faith and volition and action unite. And is not ours a present salvation? May I not receive the blessing now? "No!" you say; "the doctrine I believe, but not the time of its experience — that must be in the future, especially in death." But this is human opinion, it is nowhere taught in the Scriptures; two plain passages are positively against it. Speaking of Christ, our example in holiness, it is said, "As He is, so are we in the world." "That He would grant us, that we, being delivered out of the hands of our enemies, might serve Him without fear, in holiness and righteousness before Him, all the days of our life."

3. *Perform the act of personal consecration to God*, deliberately and unreservedly in the strength of grace. All that you sought and found in the first instance was regeneration, and your first consecration extended no no farther. This work of consecration must now be completed. It embraces a stern determination under grace to commit no sin and avoid even the appearance of evil. Body, soul, life, property, means — and if there should be houses and lands and millions in prospect, all, all, is to be laid upon the altar of consecration. This will rouse your fallen nature — you cannot become a pauper. But grace will touch, will quicken your will, and you will be strengthened to act — strengthened to obey that strong, that encouraging command, "Come out from among them, and be ye separate . . . and touch not the unclean thing; and I will receive you, and will be a Father unto you, and ye shall

be my sons and daughters, saith the Lord Almighty."

4. Then in order to attain this glorious state, it is of the utmost importance to *believe in the faithfulness of God to fulfill His promise* in accepting our consecration. As it is written, "If ye believe not, yet He abideth faithful, He cannot deny Himself." Nay, more than this, it should be that faith that realizes the offering as already accepted, unchangeably, now and forever. "Therefore, I say unto you, What things soever ye desire when ye pray, believe that ye receive them, and ye shall have them." And may we not put this to the test of actual experiment? That is the very ground upon which God has placed it. He challenges you to the proof in language the most convincing. "I beseech you therefore, brethren, by the mercies of God, that ye present your bodies a living sacrifice, holy, acceptable unto God, which is your reasonable service. And be not conformed to this world: but be ye transformed by the renewing of your mind, that ye *may prove* what is that good, and acceptable, and perfect, will of God."

It remains for us to *urge* the language of the text, "Be ye holy;" not as man hath said, in the sense that we are to attain a state of sinless, absolute perfection above ignorance, error, infirmity, bodily imperfection, temptation, involuntary transgression; no! delivered from these we cannot be in the present life. We neither know nor preach such a perfection, nor is it demanded. "Be ye holy," not in a fixed degree and beyond which there can be no progress. Neither time nor eternity will prevent this progress.

"Be ye holy." The fullness of joy may decline but

that is not all the fullness, nor the fullness of all. Indeed, the deeper depths of love will only be attained by way of the cross. You will come to learn something of that mysterious state. "I am crucified with Christ: nevertheless I live; yet not I, but Christ liveth in me: and the life which I now live in the flesh I live by the faith of the Son of God, who loved me, and gave Himself for me."

Ah, Christian, when thou comest to learn what that means, the crucified Christian as well as the crucified Saviour, thou art within three days of a resurrection, a higher degree of spiritual life; and dying daily we thou shalt also be risen with Christ. May the Spirit teach thee this holy mysticism.

"Be ye holy." The present condition of the church demands it. The temple of Christendom is defiled, her priests are corrupt, her people are idolators; the leprosy of sin cleaves to her courts; the dove-sellers and the money-changers are too near the mercy-seat; the blood that sprinkles is not the blood of redemption; the brightness of the Shekinah is withdrawn; the voice of God is hushed in the noise of this world. "Holiness becometh the house of the Lord forever," but they have made it a den of thieves; the God of holiness is forgotten, the blessing of holiness is unknown.

But surely, surely, you exclaim, these are exceptions. Do you know them, brethren, then allow them; but "Be ye holy." The condition of the world demands it. The world is already redeemed. Christ has done His work, but the plan is to save it through human instrumentality, and if that be the plan, then if the instruments fail, souls are lost. In one day, how few, think you, rise to heaven; how many sink to hell! Who is responsible? God is clear. We are guilty. If the world really knew its claims, it might demand of the church, "Why do you not do you duty? Why do you let us perish?" Oh how shall we preach? how shall we live to do good? Well this idea of holiness is a power, a power to shake the throne of the devil, demolish the enterprises of wickedness, limit the reign of sin, curtail the empire of hell. Ministers, preach holiness! believers, seek holiness! and may the silver trumpet of the gospel, sound the sweet note of holiness to the end of time.

XXVIII.

HISTORY OF HOLINESS MOVEMENTS IN THE CHURCH.

C. MUNGER, OLD ORCHARD, ME.

"Blessed be the Lord God of Israel; for He hath visited and redeemed His people, and hath raised up an horn of salvation for us . . . to perform the mercy promised " (Luke 1: 68, 69 and 72).

In this text and context, the Holy Spirit by an inspired man, announces the one eternal purpose of God in redemption, viz.: a people so saved as "to serve Him in holiness and righteousness all the days of their life;" that is, of their earthly life, not after they were dead, nor while they were dying, but in all the legitimate relations of earthly society.

That was His "grant" given and attested by their king's seal, which had on it the words "Holiness unto the Lord," which words their high priest must always bear upon his forehead when he entered the holy of holies, as a condition of their acceptance and of his own life.

This grant was unfolded in a covenant, confirmed by an oath to our fathers, and to us, and the special joy expressed in the text is that God had raised up One to perform it — make it actual in experience.

Notice how this mercy was set before the Old Testament church.

They were bond-slaves in Egypt. God visited them — redeemed — delivered them by the hand of Moses, brought them to Sinai, adopted them in a covenant in which they promised to obey all God's words, and He promised on that condition that they should be to Him (1) a peculiar treasure; (2) above all people; (3) a kingdom of priests, *i. e.*, consecrated, purified worshipers and mediators; (4) a holy nation — a nation whose King was the Lord, and whose politics should be not only religious but holy. This was a covenant of holiness. The nature and mode of this holiness were set before them by an object lesson which they could hardly forget.

"Let them make Me a sanctuary," said God, "that I may dwell among them." It must be a freewill offering, in every item, after the pattern given by God. It was made, and then dedicated as God's dwelling-place; first by Moses and Aaron, then by God Himself. Moses sanctified Aaron by rites ordered of God; then Aaron sanctified the tabernacle by prescribed rites, and then God, according to His promise, sanctified both the tabernacle and the priests, by filling it and them with His glory — the symbol of Himself. God had said to man, "Thou shalt hallow [sanctify], the tabernacle," and "the tabernacle shall be sanctified by *My glory*."

Man's sanctification was gradual, by rites performed in faith during seven days. God's sanctification was instantaneous. When the last act of man's obedient faith was finished, *then* "the glory"—the symbol of God—filled the tabernacle, and the attesting fire fell upon the great altar, and the people shouted and fell on their faces. Possibly, some imagined that their experience at Sinai was the perfection—the fullness of the blessings promised. But God said, "Ye are not yet come to the rest and to the inheritance which the Lord giveth you." Mark the words, "the rest and the inheritance." Two things: the inheritance was the land-grant, even to the uttermost bounds named in the promise; the rest was the condition of the people in that land, viz.: deliverance from all enemies, and experience of all promises to them then applicable, so that they should serve God without fear in holiness and righteousness all the days of their life.

Again and again Moses points to the experience of loving and serving the Lord with all the heart and soul, as the chief glory of that rest and the pledge of continued victory. So, when God said to Moses at Sinai, "Arise, take thy journey before the people, that they may go in and possess the land," Moses said to them at the start, "And now, Israel, what doth the Lord require of thee but to fear the Lord thy God and to walk in all His ways and to love Him and to serve the Lord thy God with all thy heart and with all thy soul?"

This was a holiness movement—a movement, not a growth—a divinely inspired movement of God's covenant people, His forgiven people. It was a definite movement for a definite object to be obtained in this life, viz.: the rest of holiness, of whole-hearted trust, love and service in the land of promise all the days of their life. It was a movement for the fullness of the blessings of that covenant, which they had not attained by any or all antecedent experiences.

They came to it, but did not enter it. Why? The majority said they couldn't. Moses said they wouldn't. And Paul says it was because of "an evil heart of unbelief." What was the unbelief? Moses answers, "In *this thing* ye did not believe the Lord your God." What thing? Moses had said, "The Lord your God which goeth before you He shall fight for you." Joshua and Caleb had said, "The land is an exceeding good land. Let us go up at once and possess it for we are well able to overcome it." "If the Lord delight in us He will bring us into it and give it us." This was just what they did not believe. Their leaders— almost all, had talked their unbelief in two forms. "We be not able," and then by implication "It not desirable," for, said they, "It is a land that eateth up the inhabitants thereof." Then, the unbelieving man turned with evil intent against the faithful few, who had stood with God and for immediate entrance and possession. God called that report, "We be not able," "a slander," and its originators died by the plague, and the multitudes who believed it, died under the sentence of disinheritance. Is there anything like that example of unbelief in the church to-day: — any leaders saying, "*We be not able;*" any members covering a will not, by " We cannot;" any who are evidently hostile to those who are in the rest or earnestly seeking it; any who pity them as victims of delusion or persecute them by odious terms, misrepresentation and reproach? And is that unbelief less odious to God and destructive of the church now than it was then? Will the unbelief and slander which brought disinheritance and death to them, bring inheritance and life to us? Will our leaders open their eyes to the mischief this unbelief is working and the inevitable wreck to which it tends?

But another generation came, having another spirit, and in its history we see the church entering her promised rest by wholly following the Lord.

THE HOLINESS MOVEMENT UNDER JOSHUA.

Joshua was the visible leader, Jesus the invisible "Captain of the Lord's host." Forty years before at Kadesh, Joshua and Caleb stood up against the whole congregation and braved death for their testimony. "Let us go up at once and possess it, for we are well able." Now the people say, "All that thou commandest us we will do." Then the leaders ignored God and His Word and works, and looked only at themselves and the obstacles. Now they depend wholly upon the presence, power, and faithfulness of God, and say not a word about the difficulties or their impotency. The record of the first generation is one of alternate obedience and disobedience, of murmurings and revolts; in short, of all the good and evil of unsanctified hearts issuing in failure through unbelief. The record of this generation is one of an all-conquering faith, grappling with impossibilities and triumphing in spite of them; of faith without sight, steadily marching on, patiently submitting to the most crucifying disappointments, in exact obedience to orders which were plainly violative of all precedent, history, philosophy, science and common sense, save that which resolutely obeyed God; a faith which accomplished nothing in six days of going and blowing the trumpets of jubilee,— nothing but self discipline and crucifixion; a faith which nevertheless kept on going and blowing in six more abortive circuits on the seventh day till evening; and then the triumph came: the massive walls of Jericho dissolved into atoms at the touch of the Almighty Christ.

At the beginning of that movement Joshua told the people to "go after the Ark," and that, as soon as the priests bearing it touched the Jordan, its waters should stand upon an heap, and "Hereby ye shall know" said he, "that the living God is among you and that He will without fail, drive out all " the enemies who came out against them. That miracle accomplished, all the rest was assured. And it was accomplished right over against Jericho. And Jericho fell; and in seven years, " Joshua took the whole land acording to all that the Lord said unto Moses." Mark these words — "according to all that the Lord said unto Moses;" *i.e.*, respecting that generation, not everything said of every succeeding generation, but of them. Mark Joshua's testimony respecting the two tribes, Rueben and Gad. " Ye have kept all that Moses the servant of the Lord hath commanded you, and have obeyed my voice in all that I commanded you." Then he blessed and dismissed them with this charge: "But take diligent heed to do the commandment and the law, which Moses the servant of the Lord charged you, to love the Lord your

God, . . . and to cleave unto Him, and to serve Him with all your heart, and with all your soul" (Joshua 22: 2, 5). To all Israel just before his death he said, "But cleave unto the Lord your God, as ye have done unto this day, . . . and one man of you shall chase a thousand: for the Lord your God, He it is that fighteth for you, as He hath promised you" (Joshua 23: 8, 10).

Here was a people who had kept their covenant with God, and therefore God was with them, not in a human body, a man, but by an Almighty invisible presence. And so complete was their union with Him that future victories were assured if they did but cleave unto Him as they had done unto that day, *i. e.*, a period of twenty-five years. Now see God's faithfulness to them. "Ye know," said Joshua, "that not one thing hath failed of all the good things which the Lord your God spake concerning you; all are come to pass unto you, and not one thing hath *failed* thereof" (Joshua 23: 14).

Now of all the good things which the Lord spake to them — the command to love Him with all their heart and soul, and the promise that He would circumcise their heart to do it, were the first and sum of all. If they or He failed in that, all failed. But "Not one thing hath failed," said Joshua, and I am not disposed to contradict him. Thus the church of that period inherited the fullness of the promises, and became a type and prophecy of that era, possibly at hand, when Christ shall conquer every foe, by His almighty though invisible Presence, and give the kingdom and the dominion under the whole heaven to His saints, who follow Him wholly.

"And Israel served the Lord all the days of Joshua, and all the days of the elders that overlived Joshua." No charge of moral delinquency is found in their history. On the contrary, Joshua testifies that all the promises to them were fulfilled.

It required another generation to complete the example — a generation having possession, but keeping it only by following the Lord fully in the matter of enlargement by the extermination of outlying heathenism. Joshua and Israel, in obedience to God, exterminated every foe that came out against them. Except in the case of the Gibeonites, who deceived them, "they left none remaining." That was the condition upon which their children were to continue in their possession. They did not do it. There is no evidence that more than two tribes made any attempt to do it. "They did not," is the emphatic record respecting the other tribes. They suppressed their enemies somewhat and made them "tributaries," then made alliances with them, and in turn were suppressed by them. This went on till Israel became so corrupt that God gave them to the sword and the Ark to the Philistines. For this "all Israel lamented twenty years." Then came the national holiness movement promoted by Samuel and David. This movement continued about a century. In it, the church and nation attained an enlargement never known before. After it had been in progress over seventy years, David could write, "This is the generation that seek after Him — that seek Thy face, O God of Jacob." And a hundred years after it began, Solomon, at a national convocation said, "Let your hearts be perfect with the Lord our God . . . to keep His commandments *as at this day*." Oh, that our King could say that of His church to-day!

Now look at the life and methods of that movement. It began by Samuel — an itinerant preacher, whose parish was "all Israel," and his "circuit" was Ramah, Bethel, Gilead and Mizpeh. Wherever he went, this was his message — his hobby, "If ye do return unto the Lord, with all your hearts, put away the strange gods . . . and prepare your hearts unto the Lord and serve Him only, and He will deliver you." The Hebrew for "prepare" in this passage means, "to be erect," to stand up straight; also "to fix," "fasten." Samuel's meaning was: fasten yourself to God by an inflexible purpose to turn to Him with all your heart, and stand up straight and steady in your determination to "serve Him only." "All" and "only" were the Shibboleths of that movement. If Samuel were here, would he hold revival services on any other principles? And what would be his estimate of a pastor, deacon, elder or layman who should affirm or intimate that this Samuel was a crank, a fanatic, for nobody ever did or would "turn to the Lord with all the heart and serve Him only." But Israel believed Samuel and trusted God. Then Samuel called a national convention at which they confessed, fasted, prayed, put away their idols, offered sacrifice, and the Lord answered and smote the Philistines so they came no more in "all the days of Samuel."

David gives a glimpse of the inner spiritual life of that period. His terrible fall taught him his need of a

L. F. GAY.   J. R. JONES.   R GRANT.

pure heart. After bitter repentance and prayer for pardon, he cried, "Create in me a clean heart, O God, and renew a right spirit within me. Uphold me by Thy free Spirit. Then will I teach transgressors Thy ways, and sinners shall be converted unto Thee." And God answered his prayer, for the record says that, save in that matter of Uriah, "David did that which was right in the eyes of the Lord and turned not aside from anything that He commanded him all the days of his life."

The apostasy of Solomon and his successors necessitated another holiness movement. When Solomon was old his heart "was not perfect with the Lord," and "he went not fully after the Lord as did David." His successors followed his evil example, and "forsook the law of the Lord, and all Israel with them." Then they were vexed with all adversity. The kingdom was divided, the temple plundered, and there was no peace. Then God visited His people by raising the reformers, Asa and his son, Jehosaphat, Jehoiada, the priest, and Elijah. Asa's "heart was perfect with the Lord," and like Samuel, he put away all the idols and "commanded Judah to seek the Lord God of their fathers, and do the commandment and the law." This singular form — "the commandment " — points emphatically to the law of whole heartedness, or holiness, and so the people understood it, for, in a great national assembly, they bound themselves in an oath "to seek God with all their hearts"; and they did it. "And all Judah rejoiced at the oath, for they had sworn with all their heart, and sought Him with their whole desire, and He was found of them and gave them rest." They performed the condition of the promise, "The Lord thy God will circumcise thine heart to love the Lord with all thine heart and soul," and as God was true, He performed his part, and of course they found what they sought — clean hearts and perfect love.

Asa's son took up the work on the same lines. By a system of Biblical teaching throughout all the realm, the people were brought back to God and His covenant of holiness. In history we find a trial and triumph very much like those of Joshua. A great multitude invaded his realm, and threatened his capital. He had no forces to cope with them. But he and the people fasted, and prayed, and trusted God. As his army moved out, the king stood at the gate of the city, saying, "Believe in the Lord your God, so shall ye be established; believe His prophets, so shall ye prosper." Then the army moved upon the enemy, led by a band of singers, "praising the beauty of holiness." This was their ark and testimony, and their enemies were scattered as chaff by the wind.

A succession of kings who, with few exceptions did evil, brought Israel low and in sore distress. Then came Hezekiah, who sought the Lord with all his heart in every work, and prospered. Then, by a covenant, he sought to bring all Israel back to God, and the people, in great numbers, set their heart to seek God, and their "prayer came up to His holy habitation, even unto heaven." "So there was great joy in Jerusalem." But some scoffed. Among these were the Assyrians, who defied Israel and her God. But, in answer to prayer, the angel of the Lord smote them and delivered His people from a great peril.

But the successors of Hezekiah departed from God, and began the apostasy which sent the people to Babylon. But God inspired another holiness movement *the last before Babylon.*

Notice the testimony: Josiah "turned to the Lord with all his heart, and with all his soul, and with all his might, according to all the law of Moses" (2 Kings 23: 25). Then, as God was faithful to his promise, here is another man who sought and found a clean heart and perfect love. Not only that, but he "*did* right in the sight of the Lord . . . and turned not aside to the right hand or to the left." Notice his methods: He put away the idols, restored the temple worship, gathered the people great and small, to hear "the book of the law." Then, in the temple, and before all the people, he "made a covenant to walk after the Lord and to keep His commandments with all his heart and soul. And he caused all that were present in Jerusalem and Benjamin to stand to it. And the inhabitants of Jerusalem *did according to the covenant of God.*" Well, if they did, God did, and of course here was a goodly company who knew the bliss of perfect love in a pure heart, for that was just what God promised on that condition.

But this goodly company was a small fraction of the church. The great bulk ignored the movement — probably took little pains to know about it. At any rate there is no indication that they bound themselves by that covenant, for they rushed on in sin. They were the very class of people described by Moses, who would "ignore God's covenant, and walk after the imagination of their hearts, and yet promise themselves peace" (Deut, 29: 19). But they landed in Babylon, to be consumed, and with these terrible words put in their mouth by Jeremiah, "The harvest is past, the summer is ended, and we are not saved." And Jeremiah records God's estimate of all such in the startling words, "The Lord hath rejected and forsaken the generation of His wrath."

In that weary-footed procession of captives on the journey of six hundred or one thousand miles to Babylon, were two classes — good and bad — symbolized by the good and bad figs of Jeremiah's vision. The good were those who had made and kept the covenant of holiness in Josiah's reform. They could only "sigh and cry because of the abominations" that prevailed, and they were carried to Babylon for the sins which they could not help. But God assured them that it was "for their good." They and their children were to be the germs of the new nation which would serve God in the beauty of holiness. They had this promise, "Thus saith the Lord God of Israel: I will set Mine eyes upon them for good, and will bring them again to this land . . . and build them and plant them. . . . I will give them an heart to know Me . . . for they shall return unto Me with their whole heart" (Jer. 24: 1–7). A year later this promise was unfolded more fully in these words, "Thus saith the Lord: After seventy years be accomplished at Babylon, I will visit you and perform My good word to you, in causing you to return to this place. . . . Then shall ye call upon Me, and ye shall go and pray unto Me, and I will hearken unto you. And ye shall seek Me and find Me when ye shall search for Me with all your heart " (Jer. 29 : 10–13).

Here, in promise, was a visit of God, to perform His good word, to give His people a heart to know Him, and to turn and seek Him with their whole heart, and then they should find Him and be built and blessed according to His word. Prayer, individual and social, is specially designated as a method of that search. They shall not only pray, but they " shall go and pray and search for Me," plainly indicating a union of social effort.

The history of their restoration shows the exact fulfillment of these promises. His visit was announced in these words, " Sing and rejoice, O daughter of Zion, for lo ! I come, and I will dwell in the midst of thee, saith the Lord." The same year, and by the same prophet, God said, " I am returned to Jerusalem with mercies, and My house shall be built."

Later, this return of God was unfolded still more — thus, " I am returned unto Zion, and will dwell in the midst of Jerusalem, and Jerusalem shall be called a city of truth . . . the holy mountain . . . and I will save my people . . . and they shall be My people in truth and in righteousness " (Zech. 1 : 14 ; 2 : 6–10 ; 8 : 3–8).

How did God come and dwell with them ? Not in body — a man — but just as He does now, by His Holy Spirit. Hence, He said to the people and their leaders, then building at Jerusalem, " Be strong, all ye people, for I am with you . . . My Spirit remaineth among you, fear not " (Hag. 2 : 2-5).

In vision, the prophet saw their high priest cleansed and clothed with his holy garments and a fair mitre upon his head — that mitre which bore God's signet, the words, " Holiness unto the Lord," and he heard a voice saying to that priest, " I have caused thine iniquity to pass from thee," and also the promise, " I will remove the iniquity of the land *in one day* " (Zech. 3 : 1-9).

In a manual of devotion, supposed to have been written by Ezra, we get a glimpse of the spirit of the people nearly a hundred years after that movement began, " Blessed are the undefiled in the way, who walk in the law of the Lord. Blessed are they that keep His testimonies and that seek Him with the whole heart. They also do no iniquity" (Ps. 119 : 1-10). This was the seventh and last holiness movement of Old Testament history.

We can only glance at the unfolding of this " grant " in the New Testament. God set this same mercy before the Christian church as her rest — to be entered by faith.

In three epistles, the history of the generations which failed of entering their rest is referred to as a warning, "lest we come short " of the rest set before us. Blameless purity and love, producing whole-hearted service, with all accompanying blessings, is the mercy set before us, in command and promise, prayer and precept, example and warning. The history of Israel, from Egypt to their rest in the land of promise, is repeated in outline in the Christian church. Among the Jews in Christ's time were godly and ungodly men. From these Christ selected the founders of His kingdom. That He chose ungodly men, and ordained them as His ministers, is unthinkable. That those chosen were devout men, accepted of God, is proven by all His testimony and treatment of them. Like Israel at Sinai, they were His children in covenant, forgiven and " holy " in the sense of " set apart for God." But the mixed and variant life of the generation under Moses appears in all their history before Pentecost. Christ definitely pointed them to a sanctification which they had not attained, in which they were to " be made perfect in one," and thus be fully equipped as His witnesses. In His last address, before His death, He set this before them, in the promise of the fullness of the Holy Spirit. And His last promise was of the power of that Spirit coming upon them. And His last charge was, " Tarry ye until ye be endued with power from on high." They obeyed, and the Spirit came and purified their hearts, sanctifying them wholly — " suddenly "— just as " the glory," filled the tabernacle and sanctified it and the priests at Sinai. After this they knew no cowardice, no unbelief, no apostasy, no betrayal.

Outside the circle of Christ's personal disciples, we find the same phases of experience. The apostles exhort believers already justified, to " go on to perfection " — to " cleanse themselves from all filthiness of flesh and spirit," and pray " the God of peace to sanctify them wholly and preserve them blameless." Some obeyed so faithfully, that an inspired apostle could say of them, as of himself, "Herein is our love made perfect, that we may have boldness in the day of judgment; because as He is so are we in this world." Some sought and found "the end — the aim of the commandment — perfect love out of a pure heart," and kept it. Others swerved from it, and turned aside unto vain "jangling." Some recovered from the snare of the devil, others fell away beyond repentance and "drew back unto perdition."

Review the facts set in the inspired record, "for our admonition." Every reformation in Old Testament history, was a "visit" of God: was a holiness movement, in which the Spirit of holiness — the Holy Spirit — inspired men and women to "follow Him wholly," in the faith "We can" and in the inflexible purpose covenant and pledge, "We will." Then their faithful God cleansed their hearts to love Him perfectly and serve Him fully.

Those holiness movements were rare. In the record of a thousand years only seven. Between them, were eras of apostasy, which brought the church and nation again and again to the brink of ruin, from which they were saved by a revival and reformation on the basis of personal holiness of heart and life. What a startling fact this, and what responsibility it suggests. God's call to holiness ignored, and in some cases, a hundred years of apostasy with all its miseries followed.

Glance at the modern church history. The Lutheran Reformation, based on the doctrine of justification by faith, accomplished wonders, but was in full retreat before its enemies by reason of its internal decay. Then Pietism appeared as a protest against formalism and a dead orthodoxy, and a divinely inspired movement for spiritual life by the Spirit and Word of God. It was persecuted by infidels and formalists, but triumphed and blessed all Europe, till rationalism crept into its theological schools and then it died. But Methodism then appeared. Planted definitely upon the basal doctrine and experience and methods of primitive Christianity and of every reform in the Old Testament church — "Holiness unto the Lord" Methodism started on its mission "to raise up a holy people." And it triumphed gloriously.

The present holiness movement is simply a renewal of the spirit and power of Wesleyan Methodism by the explicit enforcement of the doctrine and experience by which, more than any other, its victories have been won, viz.: blameless purity and love by faith alone instantaneously wrought and divinely attested by the Spirit of God. The Salvation Army is moving on the same lines, and is winning the distinction once given to the Methodists: "God's flying artillery." That we are living in an era of reform and apostasy is most certain. The Spirit of holiness — the Holy Spirit — is poured upon the devout in all churches working in them self-abnegation, love, zeal, power, working out by them in the various societies, leagues, crusades, unions, and by the missionary, evangelistic, and philanthropic agencies, marvelous achievements. Satan also is gathering his forces for the furious — perhaps the last battle for the world's sovereignty. By the Spirit of holiness and the Word, Christ is leading His host into this battle. His triumph and reign are foreordained, foretold and seen. "The day of His power" approaches, perhaps is now, in which His "people offer themselves willingly in the beauties of holiness." Do we belong to that people? Do we accept their reproaches? Are we fastened to Christ by an unflinching purpose to follow Him fully? Do we stand up straight in the inflexible determination to "serve Him only?" If so, we already share their soul triumphs and are moving straight to the coming glory.

XXIX.

BIBLE MEASURE OF LOVE TO GOD AND MAN.

M. L. HANEY, NORMAL, ILL.

THE gospel was not designed to abrogate the moral law of God, nor lower its standard, but to furnish the divine outfit by which we could measure up to its demands. Without the sacrifice of Christ, this would have forever been impossible, but through His mediation, each child of Adam may keep the divine commandments.

We may not know, nor be concerned about God's law as given to angels, but His law to Adam's race, is found in the ten commandments. There is nothing in either the spirit or letter of these, which may not be obeyed by every completely ransomed soul. Hence it was not the design of the gospel to bring the standard down to the sinner, but to bring the sinner up to the standard. The sum of all obedience is reached in meeting the demand of the text, "Thou shalt love the Lord thy God with all thy heart, and with all thy soul, and with all thy mind. This is the first and great commandment. And the second is like unto it, Thou shalt love thy neighbor as thyself. On these two commandments hang all the law and the prophets" (Matt. 22: 37–40).

I. We inquire as to the nature and source of this love.

1. It must be pure in its essence and divine in its origin. It is not a superabundance of natural love. It is not now, never has been, and never can be, the natural outflow of any fallen soul. It cannot be attained by culture, or growth, or development. Millions hope to reach it through church membership, church activities, Christian ordinances, money sacrifices, brain culture, helping the poor and other Satanic subterfuges, who die without its possession! Here lies a great danger from false and unspiritual teaching in the Sunday School. Attractive statements are made relative to Christ, which suggest Him as a desirable person, as was Washington, and children prompted to love Him, without being born again. They easily admire Him as they do any other beautiful character, are asked to hold up their hands, or sign a card, to indicate their love; are pronounced converted, join the church, are urged to grow in grace which they never possessed: and sent on to perdition! As they mature, the church is now their party and its services their only hope. So they defend it against attacking foes, and by being active on its behalf, and complying with its ceremonies, they vainly expect eternal life! Millions there are of such, who have never known Christ as a Saviour, nor have their hearts been once thrilled with His love! Protestant Christians consider this truth as applied to the Church of Rome, and easily confess the hellish

delusion of its devoted adherents; but we, like them, will wake in the judgment to find that church relationships and ceremonies and cultured natural love, will fail utterly and forever as a substitute for the "love of God shed abroad by the Holy Ghost given unto us."

The Scriptures have not left us in doubt as to the origin and nature of this love. Rom. 5: 5, "And hope maketh not ashamed; because the love of God is shed abroad in our hearts by the Holy Ghost which is given unto us." Not natural love, increased by culture, and the round of church duties in an unrenewed heart; but the love which comes from God, and is shed abroad in our hearts by the Holy Ghost given unto us. This truth is verified by other statements of Scripture. Gal. 5: 22, "The fruit of the Spirit is love." Not the fruit of your fallen spirit, but the Holy Spirit; not the effect of culture, nor a result of human effort; but the imparted love of God by the Holy Ghost sent down from heaven. 1 John 4: 7, "Beloved, let us love one another: for love is of God; and every one that loveth is born of God, and knoweth God." This love being the outflow of the new birth, is forever impossible, till we are thus born of God; and it is newborn love made perfect, which alone enables us to love our neighbor as ourselves.

2. It is first imparted, and afterwards perfected, as seen by the following Scriptures: 1 John 4: 12, "If we love one another, God dwelleth in us, and His love is perfected in us." First it is in us, and then perfected. Any thing has first to exist before it can be

perfected. Verses 17 and 18, "Herein is our love made perfect, that we may have boldness in the day of judgment: because as He is, so are we in this world. There is no fear in love; but perfect love casteth out fear: because fear hath torment. He that feareth is not made perfect in love." The fear to be removed by perfect love is not the natural instinct of fear given of God for the safety of His creatures, but the fear which is born of sin, and gives torment, as to death and the judgment; and with many is the greatest barrier to obedience and the activities of Christian life. Millions are held by it in a life of sin, and multitudes who are true Christians are crippled by its agency, and kept in bondage all their days. Hence the Wesleyan statement of three classes of persons attempting to tender service to God: the first, a service of fear, without love; the second, a service of love, mingled with fear; the third, a service of love, without fear. These three represent the service of true penitence, of justification, and of sanctification. It is *perfect* love that casteth out fear.

3. This love in its impartation, is always supreme, and when perfected, it is the love of all the heart. We mean to say that, in every case, a newborn soul is at once enabled to, and does love God supremely, or above all other objects combined. When made perfect, it is the love of all the heart, and soul, and mind; and is called perfect, because that is the measure of love required. No man nor angel can love God with more than all the heart, but it is foolish to say we cannot thus love Him.

4. Supreme love may be possessed and exercised, with remaining moral evils in the breast; but perfect love involves the extirpation of those evils. All truly regenerate men love God supremely; but only completely sanctified men, love Him, or can love Him, with all the heart. A vessel with a pint capacity if completely clean, would certainly hold a pint of pure water; but if a stone were at the bottom, it would be eternally impossible for it to contain a pint of water till the stone should be removed. With the stone remaining, it could be supremely occupied with water, but never perfectly. If the Pacific Ocean were emptied into and out of it, it would still be as before — supremely, but never perfectly — filled. While it remains true that two substances cannot occupy the same space at the same time, it must forever be impossible to love God with all the heart and soul and mind, while antagonistic elements remain in the heart, or soul, or mind. But in the merely regenerate, such elements are not only found, but they rise and struggle for the mastery, as is proven by universal experience. Who in all the church of God has ever walked with Him a single year, in the regenerate state, without complaining of inward evils, and praying for their removal? Who, that has not testified of battles with inward foes, of besetting sins, and confessed the uprisings of unholy anger, the presence of depraved desires, conflicts with unbelief, enslaving fear, jealousy, enmity, or something sordid, or sinful within? Hence the universal prayer for deliverance from some, or all of these, by truly regenerated souls, in order to a satis-

factory experience and the exercise of unmixed love to God and man! This is the "flesh lusting against the spirit," the "roots of bitterness springing up to trouble" God's faithful child; the "carnal mind" held in check; the "old man" which has to be crucified; the "besetting sin," which has to be laid aside and left behind; the "body of sin," which has to be "destroyed;" the heart uncleanness which must be washed away by blood divine; the dross that has to be consumed by Pentecostal fire!

5. The extirpation of these evils is the work of God, and not the product of human development. The fact of their existence after conversion has been so universally felt and acknowledged, that through the ages, men have ever been in search of remedies. Wonderful as it may seem, the remedies thus suggested have always indicated an aversion to the immediate destruction of the evil complained of! This statement may be startling, but all history proves it to be true. It can only be accounted for on the ground of the two existing natures in converted men:— the one spiritual, and the other carnal. The new spiritual nature implanted in regeneration, if untrammeled by its opposite, would demand the immediate destruction of the old man, but the carnal nature has always insisted on longer life. The carnal mind being of Satanic origin, has always been his stronghold in believers, and for its life he marshals all the powers of hell. Hence the otherwise unaccountable array of subtle agencies, confederated against completed holiness, and the effort of centuries, to retain some sin!

Out of this mixed moral condition, correspondingly mixed propositions for deliverance have come.

1. It is proposed to attain complete purity by works of righteousness. Souls longing for deliverance from the inbeing of sin, are accordingly urged to greater Christian activities and sacrifices for the church. The hope is thereby enkindled, that by long and persistent effort, freedom may be attained; but those who have thus sought, never testify to having attained it.

2. Others propose the Hindoo, Pharisaic, Roman idea of attaining it by suffering. Hence the introduction of mental agonies, struggles, self-torment, torturing the body, painful fastings, crucifixions and seclusion from society. Such have suffered long and painfully, but thus never reach the end of sin. It would bring glory to Christ if there were less of this among Protestant Christians.

3. A large class are unceasingly seeking it by efforts at growth. Efforts! Nay, for such usually make a painful stagger at growing! Saying nothing of the eternal failure to reach a divine work of cleansing by growing, such persons will usually find themselves at the end of the years less spiritual, less like Christ and more like the world, than at the beginning! Failure must inevitably follow all these efforts and plans, as each of them substitutes human for divine agency — the efforts of man for the work of God — and persistently ignores Christ as the sanctifier of the soul. If complete sanctification is the inwrought work of God, by which we are cleansed from

all indwelling sin, the substitution of any number of human efforts is a mockery.

4. Both ministers and people would be saved from the gravest errors by studying the Methodist catechism, whose teachings are unmistakable on this subject. After having defined justification and regeneration, whereby we become the children of God, it asks, "What is sanctification?" Answer, "Sanctification is that act of divine grace whereby we are made holy" (No. 3, page 13). On page 39, "What is entire sanctification?" Answer, "The state of being entirely cleansed from sin so as to love God with all our heart and mind and soul and strength, and our neighbor as ourselves." It cannot escape the attention of the earnest reader that this is the exact teaching of this discourse, and hence the true teaching of Methodism; but the teaching of Methodism must be supported by the Word of God.

5. What saith the Scripture? Deut. 30:6, "The Lord thy God will circumcise thine heart, and the heart of thy seed, to love the Lord thy God with all thine heart, and with all thy soul, that thou mayest live." It might be expected that, when Infinite Goodness demanded perfect love from fallen men, He, Himself, would furnish the qualification to execute such demand. Hence this promise which followed the command from Sinai. This, observe, is not a human work, but a divine act; not an endless series of divine acts, but one act, by which those who are His recognized children are enabled to obey the first great commandment. Whatever this circumcision might be, it

cannot be a growth, or development, or the effect of culture, or the death of the body, or a series of self-imposed crucifixions, but simply one act of God which extirpates the barriers to loving Him with all the heart. The circumcision which symbolized this was an act of violence which took away the flesh and itself became a mark of utter separation from the world and a token of God's covenant between Him and His child. It might be well to notice that the covenant of circumcision was given to Abraham fifteen years after he was justified and at the time when God commanded him to be perfect (Gen. 17:1-14). It is quite common with those who discard the emptying, cleansing work of God in entire sanctification, to claim that they love God with all their heart, and soul, and mind. Such often, in the very advocacy of this claim, reveal a soul filled with the antagonisms of love. Let it ever be kept in mind that to thus love God is eternally impossible till all those antagonisms are destroyed. Hence the utter failure of those not fully sanctified, who ignore the cleansing, ever to reach this climax of love.

II. Loving God with all the heart is a necessity in order to love our neighbor as ourselves. Hence the second commandment is the outflow of the first.

1. Loving thy neighbor as thyself indicates that self-love is not to be destroyed. There is a measure of self-love divinely ordained and begotten of God, which is to be exercised in earth and heaven. This is a necessity to the highest happiness of God's children and in perfect harmony with His glory. (*a*) It secures

us against self-injury and compels the avoidance of all evil to ourselves. In like manner, we will forever scrupulously avoid injury to our fellow man — in his property, reputation or pursuit of happiness. This love will make every interest of our neighbor sacred to us, so that we can no more injure him than ourselves. (*b*) Self-love, in God's order, will lead to seeking the highest good to ourselves consistent with the divine plans. To love our neighbor thus, we will persistently seek his highest good; in his property, family, reputation, spiritual interests, and in everything involving his highest happiness. In the judgment of some, this would involve a community of goods and the dissolution of individual rights and possessions; but the plans of God recognize such rights and possessions. He has ordained the family and your love to your wife as Christ loved the church. This He makes a necessity to your highest happiness; and if so, in like manner to your neighbor's happiness. This being true, neither your own nor your neighbor's happiness could be secured by the dissolution of your family; but in the maintenance of those rights the highest good may accrue to both in time and eternity. In order to sustain the family, God has ordained the rights of property and made the happiness of each to depend on those rights being kept inviolate. If your neighbor could dispossess you of your home at will, it would result in desolation and horror. If, to-day, each Christian were to renounce the rights of property and disburse what he had to feed the poor, he would thereby be disqualified to farther materially benefit mankind. If you now had an income of one thousand dollars, and could use three hundred annually to help your neighbor, the transfer of your capital would destroy your capacity to further help him and make you dependent on the help of others. Pure love has always sacredly regarded the rights of property in man and moved its possessor in its use to seek the highest good of man.

2. This measure of love to our neighbor cannot be exercised till all carnal self-love is destroyed. The one is the opposite of the other. The one is of God; the other of Satan. The one is pure; the other impure. The one naturally seeks the happiness of others; the other begins with, and ends in itself. Hence the sin-extirpating work wrought by the Holy Ghost in entire sanctification, forever must precede the possibility of love to our neighbor, as ourselves. This measure of love to man, can only proceed from one who loves God with all the heart and soul and mind, which makes the second commandment the outflow of the first; and hence, love to our neighbor is the fulfilling of the law (James 2: 8).

3. It is discriminating as to character, and recognizes the divine distinctions between right and wrong. God loves a thief as a thief, and an honest man as an honest man. He loves a sinner as a sinner, and a Christian as a Christian. The one is loved with a love of pity, compassion and disapproval; the other with the love of complacency, approval and delight. In like manner, we will love our fellow men, always exercising a love toward saints that we cannot toward sinners.

III. This measure of unmixed love to God and man is the divine qualification for the service to be rendered to both.

1. It will forever be impossible in any true sense, to render to either a perfect service with a divided heart. But the heart must be divided, if incapable of loving with all its powers, and cannot be perfectly loyal to God while retaining His enemies within. Hence the difficulty with which many duties are performed by all ordinary Christians. Hence the painful fact that all such have to be incessantly urged to Christian activities. All who undertake the required service without complete sanctification ignore God's preparation for all good works (1 Tim. 2: 21; 3: 16, 17. Heb. 13: 20, 21).

2. The moral condition resulting from entire sanctification alone is sufficient with fallen men to produce an unmixed love service. Without it, service rendered to either God, or man, will often have to result from restraint, or constraint, and ever contain a perverted mixture of self interest, or selfishness. Let him who doubts the truth of this statement, fully analyze his own soul.

3. The life that springs from love made perfect, if maintained, cannot but produce the highest order of service to God and man. The soul possessing it has all the natural powers he had before receiving it. He has all the gracious ability he possessed in the regenerated state. He now has gotten rid of all the inborn moral evils which before hindered him. Then, added to this, his whole being is now filled and actuated by

unmixed love to God and man in a measure never before realized. It is inseparable from love to lavish itself on its object. Hence from such love to God there must proceed adoring worship and a glad obedience, to the outlimit of its powers, to give vent to itself. This is worship, as the spontaneity of love, and obedience, from heaven enthroned within. Divine love, completely ruling human powers, must result in the highest activities and lead to the best service rendered to man. It changes that which was imperative duty into love offerings, and the sternest commands into a service of delight. Real love with all the heart, demands the sacrifice of time, and ease and money and life itself, if need be, to bring glory to God and salvation to man! Yet this truth, glorious in its origin, divine in its authority, and so majestic in its results; is neglected by millions, and meets with greater opposition than all other truths in the gospel of Christ!

Hear it, from Sinai and the mouth of God; from Calvary and the lips of Jesus Christ, "Thou shalt love the Lord thy God, with all thy heart, and with all thy soul and with all thy mind; and thy neighbor as thyself! On these two commandments, hang all the law and the prophets!"

XXX.

THE FULLNESS OF CHRIST.

JOSEPH H. SMITH, NEW CASTLE, IND.

"Unto a perfect man, unto the measure of the stature of the fullness of Christ" (Eph. 4: 13).

SOME idea of the magnitude and of the importance of our subject may be gained by considering the relative position of the text. It is the practical center of the longest and most comprehensive sentence in the Bible. A focal point into which converges the great apostle's thoughts of an ideal ministry, and from which radiate his views of a model church.

Let us devote a share of time and attention to this gigantic context. It will prove our best commentary upon the text itself, and furnish the best groundwork for appreciation of the subject of the fullness of Christ.

Look at the lists of subjects — cardinal subjects which are dealt with here. (1) A diversified ministry with a unified aim. "He gave some apostles, and some prophets, and some evangelists, and some pastors and teachers . . . for the perfecting of the saints. (2) Christian perfection — the goal of all believers. "Till we all come in the unity of the faith and of the knowledge of the Son of God unto a perfect man, unto the

measure of the stature of the fullness of Christ." (3) Growth in grace both sure and symmetrical. "That we henceforth be no more children . . . but speaking the truth in love may grow up into Him in all things." (4) True church unity. "The whole body fitly framed together and compacted by that which every joint supplieth." (5) Normal and certain church extension and development. "Maketh increase of the body unto the edifying of itself in love."

This is a general analysis of this most remarkable sentence. And I call attention again to the fact that the logical center, the pivotal point of the whole is this expression, the fullness of Christ. This is the sun of this system of light and truth. This, the hub of each and every one of the wheels of Christian progress, both in the soul and in the world. For this the entire ministry is given to the church. In this is the believer's security against false doctrine, and his surety of development in that which is true. And upon this is hinged those two greatest of all desideratum to the church — her own unification and her extension.

We are interested then to ascertain: (1) What is the fullness of Christ? (2) Who may attain unto it? (3) How?

And, in the first place, inquiring, What is the fullness of Christ? we find that other Scriptures in representing this fullness, taken in connection with our texts, introduce the whole Trinity into the matter. We need not leave this very epistle for illustrations. In the apostle's prayer in the third chapter, he requests that we might be "filled with all the fullness of God." His exhortation in the fifth chapter enjoins us to be filled with the Spirit. And his declaration in the text before us is that all believers are expected and entitled to come unto the measure of the stature of the fullness of Christ. These we believe, are interchangeable expressions, and the fullness spoken of in the one instance is identical with that referred to in each of the others. Together, they represent what Paul elsewhere calls the "fullness of the blessing of the gospel." It is the fullness of the Father's provision, of the Son's propitiation, and of the Spirit's presence and power.

Another point of much interest is found in the grammatical construction of the text. Here we find the "fullness of Christ" is put in apposition with the term, "a perfect man." This is exceedingly significant and important, since it follows that the definition of the one must be the explanation of the other. Should we ascertain what Paul means by the "fullness of Christ," we will know whereof he speaks when he urges the church on unto "perfection;" when he commands us to be "perfect"; when he says, "We speak wisdom amongst them which are perfect;" and where he classes himself with others as being in the number of the "many that be perfect," etc.

Attention to this point of exposition — comparing Scripture with Scripture — will protect us against some of the current errors and misconceptions of this great subject of Christian perfection — full salvation. For instance, none who read the great apostle's language, as he makes out that the fullness of Christ is the necessary equipment and qualification for our growing up into Him, our living Head; and then observe that he is speaking of exactly the same subject or experience as when he uses the different term, perfection: can readily fall into the mistake of confounding this perfection with growth or the result of development as some do. It is, indeed, rather the divine preparation for a symmetrical growth, rather than the product or result of that growth; so, at least, reasons Paul.

Again, whoever studies carefully the apostle's language and how he conditions this attainment upon faith, and suspends it upon a gospel ministry in the power of the Holy Ghost, can hardly fall into that other error, so common amongst Christians and preachers, that New Testament perfection is to be reached by processes of natural growth, or by efforts of legalistic service. No! every one of us must hear, through these words, reiterated, the apostle's inquiry of rebuke, found in the epistle to the Galatians, "Are ye so foolish; having begun in the Spirit, are ye made perfect by the flesh?" For it is, he declares, by "the unity of the faith and the knowledge of the Son of God, that we are to come to a perfect man, to the measure of the stature of the fullness of Christ." Bless God!

Defining expressions, such as we find in our text, the theologians will tell us that what is meant is the "communicable" fullness of Christ. But what does that mean? This is exactly what we want to know. And in answer, we submit two negative and three affirmative declarations: First, then, negatively, it cannot mean, "The fullness of the Godhead." It is never intended that man, even under grace, nor yet in glory, should be possessed of God's infinite attributes, as his omniscience, or omnipresence, or omnipotence. Throughout eternity, even a saved man will be a creature, not a creator; and he will never be other than a human creature at that. The fullness of Christ must, therefore, be explained in a manner that will consist both with the finite limitations and the ever expanding capacities and capabilities of human nature.

Nor, secondly, can this reference to the believer's heritage as the fullness of Christ mean that man can attain that full degree or measure of the graciousness of the man Jesus. To state it more plainly: as we can never be as great as Christ, who was divine, so neither can we ever be as good as He with respect to the degrees or measure of goodness. The reasons for this will force themselves at once upon the mind. His growth in wisdom and in stature and in favor with God and man had never been delayed or interrupted by transgression or defilement. It proceeded steadily from His cradle to His cross. But with many of us, it was never even begun until adult age had been reached. In many cases it has been subsequently retarded by lapse and sin, as well as by ignorance of the simple way of faith. The man Jesus will ever be head and shoulders taller than the best and biggest of His followers. So that He is ever before us as our model and example for our growth up into Him in all things. No witness to full salvation may claim to have graduated from the school of Christ, nor to have equaled Him in the measure of virtue or power.

Nor do any intelligent advocates of this blessed state make any such claim.

Upon the other hand, then, we remark more positively that the fullness of Christ does mean, (1) The fullness of Christ's salvation. (2) The fullness of Christ's love. (3) The fullness of Christ's Spirit.

These three comprise that for which Christ lived, died and was glorified in behalf of men. First: salvation — that is, deliverance — deliverance from sin. Sometimes we analyze this, and say, "Deliverance from the guilt, power and pollution of sin." All we need to note here, in justice to our theme, is the extent of this salvation from sin, according to the Scriptures. Hear only a few of these: " He is able to save to the uttermost;" "The blood of Jesus Christ cleanseth from all sin;" "The oath which He sware to our father Abraham, that He would grant unto us, that we being delivered out of the hand of our enemies might serve Him without fear, in holiness and righteousness before Him, all the days of our life." Here, then, is an uttermost salvation — both as to extent and duration — from sin; from all sin; from all sin now; and from all sin now, henceforth and forever. Glory! How rejoiced our interested hearts are to find that Paul not only advocates but attests this great salvation! After having described in graphic figures the loathsomeness and human hopelessness of the bondage of sin's pollution, he leaps to the witness-stand in honor of his Master, and declares, "The law of the Spirit of life in Christ Jesus hath made me free from the law of sin and death." Oh! that someone may now, at this very moment, leap by faith into like liberty!

Secondly: Christ purposes not only to fulfill the law for us, but also to fulfill the law in us. That is, the law of love; and the fullness of Christ is likewise the fullness of love in the believer's heart. It was predicted of Him, and promised, that He would write His law in our hearts. Not only so, but that He would "cause us to keep His commandments and His statutes." Christ has emphasized and enforced these two great commands: (a) "Thou shalt love the Lord thy God with all thine heart." (b) "Thou shalt love thy neighbor as thyself." But He also doeth more. He makes obedience possible and delightful, by not only imparting, but also perfecting the love of God in our hearts. "The love of Christ constraineth us;" "The love of God is shed abroad in our hearts by the Holy Ghost which is given unto us." This is that "charity which is the bond of perfectness." A grace it is, which fully adjusts to God, who is all love, and to humanity, which is all in need of love. Thus does Paul's "fullness of Christ" and "perfection" agree with John's "love made perfect." They are all one. A distinct state, or stage of grace, wherein everything contrary to love is expelled from the heart and where all pertaining to love is enthroned and equipped for its reign over thought and feeling and volition.

Thirdly: The fullness of Christ means the fullness of the Holy Spirit. This, of course, is implied in the other, for it is by the Pentecostal baptism with the Spirit that our "hearts are purified by faith." And by this, too, that "the love of God is shed abroad in our hearts." Nevertheless, it requires here, as it obtains in Scripture, distinct and emphatic notice of itself. The gift of the Spirit is, without doubt, the crowning gift of a crowned Redeemer to the believer on probation. Everything prior to His ascension was made to point to Pentecost. Everything afterward dated from it. Nothing short of this in the church and in the individual believer sufficiently attests the glory of a risen and ascended Christ. All previously bestowed graces, or measures of the Spirit, are but preparations for and promises of this fullness of the Holy Ghost. They are as the "well of water" rather than as "the rivers of living water." And all subsequent gifts and growth, too, proceed from this indwelling Comforter, which the Saviour said should be given to them who, unlike the world, already knew and had fellowship with the Holy Spirit of Truth.

Would it not be well for every one interested in this theme to answer to himself, before we go farther, Paul's question addressed to this same Ephesian church some years before, "Have ye received the Holy Ghost since ye believed?"

It is left for us only to inquire, "Who may partake of the fullness of Christ? and how?" The answer has, to some measure, been anticipated. We have seen that all need a full deliverance, that all are required to love God and man perfectly, and that all are called to the fullness of the Spirit which meets this necessity and enables to the fulfillment of this obligation. So that we are prepared to accept the aim and purpose indicated by this text as the supreme calling of all the ministry and of all the church. "Till we all come . . . unto the measure of the stature of the fullness of Christ." There is no exception; there are no favorites under the divine administration; no pets in God's family. What Christ has bought and wrought for one of His followers in any age, He proffers to every one and incites us all to pursue it.

And how may we attain it? First: it is by a manifold and unified ministry — preaching and laboring to this very end. And we venture that there are to-day thousands living beneath this privilege for no other cause than that the ministry is not, with becoming unity and intensity, devoting itself to "the perfecting of the saints."

Second: it is by faith. As Paul expresses it, "By the unity of the faith." Experiences of those who have "entered in" bear uniform testimony that full salvation is received by a definite, distinct and specific act of faith for this very thing. At this point the case is parallel with conversion. No ministry of others; no works of our own; no feelings nor frames, can avail as a substitute for faith. We must believe, for the completeness of cleansing. Yea, we must believe first that we need complete cleansing, dismissing that fallacious reasoning that "if God has done any work at all in us, He has done this, since He does not do things by halves." For plausible as this may seem, it seems right in the face of multiplied Scriptures which present the fullness of Christ as something additional to, distinct from, and conditioned upon the beginnings of a spiritual life, previously introduced by the "new birth."

Believing we need it, and believing He wills it, we need further to trust that He doeth it. This is the point of crisis. It is here that an epoch is occasioned in one's spiritual history. It is for this that the throes of importunity and the sacrifices of consecration are designed. It is not a new intellectual assent to doctrine, though it must include that, but it is an affectionate confidence of the heart, by which the seeker, conscious that he has relinquished his hold upon himself, is now conscious too that he embraces Christ with the full strength of his soul, and that for a full deliverance from sin and a full possession in God. O beloved, have you entered in? Will you not now?

XXXI.

AFTER REGENERATION — WHAT?

C. A. VAN ANDA, EVANSTON, ILL.

"Having therefore these promises, beloved, let us cleanse ourselves from all defilement of flesh and spirit, perfecting holiness in the fear of God" (2 Cor. 7 : 1).

EXCLUSIVE attention to the experience of religion leads to neglect of religious work, and results finally in fanaticism. Such a type of religion will develop selfishness, and lead to a following of Jesus for the loaves and fishes.

On the other hand, an exclusive attention to religious activities, such as the means of grace, or benevolent enterprises, leads to formality and Phariseeism. Manifestly the true course is to secure a clear Scriptural experience, and then live according to the New Testament standard. Thus says Jesus, "If ye love Me keep My commandments;" "He that keepeth My commandments, he it is that loveth Me." That is, the heart filled with love for Jesus prompts to a life of loyalty to Him. How to secure this love and to express it is found by searching the Scriptures. And the precious promises preceding the text should stir us up to study the Word of God that we may know what our priv-

ileges are, and how they are secured. God says He will receive us, and be a Father unto us, provided we separate ourselves from sin.

Every child of God desires to know and do the Father's will. He is, in this respect like his Saviour, who said, "Lo, I come; . . . I delight to do Thy will, O My God; yea Thy law is within My heart."

Regeneration by the Holy Ghost is necessary to entrance into the kingdom of God. This is preceded by convictions of sin and a godly sorrow for it, leading to hearty repentance and to the act of trust in the personal Saviour, followed by the experiences of pardon and a new life. But what is there for the children of God in advance of the new birth? Can grace accomplish anything more? If so, how much more, and what more? If so, is it a definite grace, to be definitely expected, sought and secured? If it is, and we do not seek and obtain it, are we not disobedient? and if disobedient, can we retain the nature and relation of children of God?

The address is to the children of God — those "dearly beloved;" those to whom the promises in the closing words of the last chapter were given — "Having, therefore, these promises, let us cleanse ourselves from all defilement of flesh and spirit, perfecting holiness in the fear of God."

1. After regeneration then, is, beyond question, the privilege of growth in grace. Whatever be the kind or degree of grace received, it is accompanied with the command, "Occupy till I come;" and our retention of that grace depends upon our growth in it. "Unto

him that hath shall be given, and he shall have abundance; but from him that hath not shall be taken even that which he hath."

The conviction of sin, for example, is often slight to begin with, but if we are faithful to it, not only willing but anxious to know the truth, the light will shine more and more, unto the perfect day. So, when sins are forgiven and the moral nature so changed that sinful inclinations and habits no longer reign (Rom. 6: 12–14), being in subjection to the power of grace, then there will be the increase that follows a faithful use of the powers given, and the additions made from time to time by waiting upon the Lord (Isa. 40: 31; Eph. 3: 16).

Food and exercise make the healthy child stronger day by day; study, observation, discipline, application, secure increase of knowledge and of mental power. So in our spiritual nature, feeding on the sincere milk of the Word, we grow thereby.

The apostle condemns those who were so dull of hearing as not to be able to hear what he had to say. " For when . . . ye ought to be teachers, ye have need that one teach you again, which be the first principles of the oracles of God, and are become such as have need of milk and not of strong meat. For every one that useth milk is unskillful in the Word of righteousness, for he is a babe. But strong meat belongeth to them that are of full age, even those who by reason of use, or habit, have their senses exercised to discern both good and evil."

2. It is the duty and privilege of Christians to be

made perfect in love in this life; to "cleanse themselves from all defilement of flesh and spirit, perfecting holiness in the fear of God." But is not this the condition of every one born of God? Is not every child of God cleansed from all defilement, and perfect in love? In reply we must say, the Scriptures teach that the children of God do love Him, but not with a perfect love until, by a work of the Holy Spirit, subsequent to that of the new birth, all that opposes love is taken out of their hearts. Thus the disciples of Jesus were converted men before they received "the promise of the Father." They had received Jesus; did believe on His name, and to them had been given the right to become children of God (John 1 : 11-13). And, besides, He sent them out to preach, saying, "As ye go, preach . . . freely ye have received, freely give" (Matt. 10 : 8).

When Peter confessed, "Thou art the Christ, the Son of the living God," Jesus said, "Blessed art thou, Simon Bar-jona, for flesh and blood hath not revealed it unto thee, but My Father which is in heaven." In His prayer for the disciples, at the close of His ministry, Jesus said, "For I have given unto them the words which Thou gavest Me; and they have received them, and have known surely that I came out from Thee, and they have believed that Thou didst send Me" (John 17 : 8). And in verse 14, "And the world hath hated them, because they are not of the world, even as I am not of the world." And yet at the last supper — even after the announcement of the betrayal — there was a strife among them "which of them should be accounted greatest" (Luke 22 : 24).

Now He prays for their complete consecration. They do receive Him up to the light they have — as far as their Jewish prejudices will admit. Hence Jesus prays for their advanced experience. For (1) unity — like that between the Father and Himself — "that they may be one, even as we are" (John 17:11). (2) That their consecration to Him might be as complete as was His for them. "Sanctify them through Thy truth . . . and for their sakes I sanctify Myself that they, also, might be sanctified through the truth." These intercessions were fulfilled when the Holy Ghost was given. They received such clearness of vision as never again to doubt as to the nature of Christ's kingdom. They knew the kingdom was within them. They never again sought for ease or honor; never wavered in their devotion to their blessed Master. Toil, persecution, imprisonment, death, all that bigotry and malice could invent, failed to shake their faith or courage. The letters written to the early Christians reveal the same truth. They describe in clear and glowing terms their conversion from Judaism, or idolatry, and yet teach that they were not *wholly free from sin*. They do exhort them to grow in grace, and as definitely do they urge the churches to secure holiness. See, for example, the Corinthians. In his first letter, Paul says, "Unto the church of God which is at Corinth, even them that are sanctified in Christ Jesus, called to be saints . . . I thank my God always concerning you, for the grace of God which was given you . . . that in everything ye were enriched in Him in all utterance and all knowledge" (1 Cor. 1:2–9).

And yet notice the third chapter — the first and third verses inclusive. The apostle declares he could not speak unto them as *spiritual*, but as *carnal* — "as unto babes in Christ." Surely, they had been, and then were, converted, else they could not have been babes in Christ; and yet they were not entirely sanctified, else he would not have addressed them as carnal. Their inability to partake of meat was not because they were so young in the Christian life, but because of their envying, their strife and divisions. And again, in the second letter, written the next year, in the passage embracing our text and its context (6: 14–18), he exhorts them to completely break off sinful associations, to secure a thorough cleansing and to complete holiness in the fear of God.

The same truth appears in the first letter to the Thessalonians. Some time during the year 53 A. D., Paul was at Thessalonica, and planted the church there (Acts 17: 1–4). This letter was written in 54 A. D. Now, as moved by the Holy Ghost, he calls attention to their conversion and addresses them thus, "Unto the church of the Thessalonians, which is in God the Father, and in the Lord Jesus Christ." And then reminds them of the work God had wrought for them, "For our gospel came not unto you in word only, but also in power and in the Holy Ghost, and in much assurance" (1 Thess. 1: 1–4). Compare the fifth chapter, the twenty-third and twenty-fourth verses, "And the very God of peace sanctify you wholly: and I pray God your whole spirit and soul and body be preserved blameless unto the coming of our Lord Jesus

Christ." "Faithful is He that calleth you, who also will do it."

The work of salvation was begun in them when he was with them eighteen months or so before. Now he prays that it may be completed, and that they may be preserved in that wholly sanctified state unto the coming of — or in the presence of — our Lord Jesus Christ. Just as in the third chapter, twelfth and thirteenth verses, "And the Lord make you to increase and abound in love one toward another, and toward all men, even as we do toward you: to the end he may establish your hearts unblameable in holiness before God, even our Father, at the coming of our Lord Jesus Christ, with all his saints."

That the new birth does not completely destroy inbred, or original sin, is the view of the evangelical churches, and has been, from the beginning.

Upon the question, "Is there any sin in them that are born of God, or are they wholly delivered from it?" Mr. Wesley says, "I do not know that it was ever a subject of controversy in the primitive church." He says further that, in their writings, "they declare with one voice that even believers in Christ, until they are strong in the Lord, and in the power of His might, have need to wrestle with flesh and blood, with an evil nature, as well as with principalities and powers."

The ninth article of religion of the Church of England reads, "And this infection of nature [*i. e.*, inherited sin], doth remain — yea, in them that are regenerated — whereby the lust of the flesh is not subject to the law of God; and although there is no condemnation for them that believe, yet this lust hath in itself the the nature of sin." And is not this view confirmed by the general experience of Christian people? Mr. Wesley thought so. He says, "The generality of those who are justified feel in themselves more or less pride, anger, self-will, and a heart bent to backsliding."

We know that there are moments when our faith is strong, our experience definite, our desires for holiness intense, our zeal like a flame; then again faith is weak, doubts are troublesome, zeal dies away, service is irksome. Sometimes we can see the emptiness of the world; its ambitions, vanities and follies have no attractions for us —

> "Its pleasures can no longer please,
> Nor happiness afford."

Then, again, these things thrust themselves upon us, and, alas! often find that within which responds with some degree of favor to their demands.

This condition is explained by the fact that the new birth begins but does not complete sanctification. Alas! that through defective teaching, a large number of communicants in the evangelical churches, do not expect to be made perfect in love in this life; and it must be feared that many do not even wish to be. They desire to retain enough of the "old man" to receive the pleasures of sin, whereas the Scriptures demand that he be crucified; that we may be dead indeed unto sin, but alive unto God.

If asked why this work is not completed at the moment of justification, we can only answer, "Such is not the divine order, as appears from the Scriptures we have cited, and from many others equally plain." And as we have shown, experience confirms this interpretation of these inspired words. Further still, those who have carefully studied this question and had exceptionally good opportunities for such investigation, declare this is the result of their inquiries. Thus Mr. Wesley " We do not know a single instance in any place, of a person receiving at one and the same moment, remission of sins, the abiding witness of the Spirit, and a new and clean heart."

And Dr. A. Clark says, "I have been twenty-three years a traveling preacher, and have been acquainted with some thousands of Christians during that time who were in different states of grace, and I never, to my knowledge, met with a single instance where God both justified and sanctified at the same time." If there is no definite obtainment after justification set before the disciples of Jesus, there is great danger that the assurance of pardon will be lost and the spiritual power of the church will decline.

The extent and scope of the gospel is far greater than simply to secure the conversion of men. The soul needs to be saved from itsel. — from self-life.

Phillips Brooks says, " We are apt to let anxiety for the salvation of souls degenerate into a mere pity fo the misery into which they may be brought by sin. And the result of such a low thought is that when we have been brought to believe that a soul is, as we say, 'safe,' that it has been forgiven and will not be punished, we are satisfied. The thought of rescue has monopolized our religion."

Prof. Drummond said a few years since at Northfield, "Justification has been pushed to an extreme, out of its proper and due proportions, while the higher doctrines have been neglected."

In his sermon on "Wrestling Jacob," F. W. Robertson says, "A man whose religion is chiefly a sense of pardon, does not rise into integrity or firmness of character. A certain tenderness of character may very easily go along with a great deal of subtility."

Dr. John Hall says, "No church can be found in a high spiritual condition if the only definite standard is placed at justification . . . usually the experiences beyond justification are made so vague that little progress is made." Is it not, therefore, the duty of Christian teachers to present the Scriptural doctrine of holiness with the same definiteness that they present the doctrine of justification?

3. What then must the child of God do to comply with the text? What shall be done with a child growing and yet having the remnants of a deep seated disease? The appetite not always normal, digestion and assimilation imperfect; activities somewhat languid. In such a case, we would, if possible, secure treatment and continue it, until the desease is eliminated from the system. What the captive needs is not simply some degree of liberty, but entire freedom.

Jesus did not provide simply for a partial or occasional deliverance from sin, but for complete and continued emancipation (Isa. 61: 1-3). He says, "Whom the Son shall make free, shall be free indeed."

We must appeal, as the leper did — "Lord if Thou wilt, Thou canst make me clean." If we do, He will answer, "I will, be thou clean," and immediately we shall be made whole.

Then the child of God restored to perfect spiritual health, loses no time nor strength in contending against disease, but possesses the vigor and joy of health. Being made free from sin he has his fruit unto holiness and the end is everlasting life.

To be cleansed from all filthiness of the flesh and spirit is a better qualification for Christian work than to rest content with some seeds of sin which may germinate and trouble us. To change the metaphor, the branch purged by the husbandman, bears more fruit than if it were cleansed in part only. Is Jesus satisfied with the travail of his soul, in which He made a complete redemption for us, that we should continue to bear a part of our sins under the delusion that only death can relieve us of the entire burden? Having qualified Himself by humiliation and suffering to save to the uttermost those who came unto God by him, shall we deny that he possesses that ability or refuse to trust him for an immediate and complete salvation? No, let us secure to Him the honor He deserves, by an entire consecration to Him, and a complete sanctification through Him, and a life which shall be a continuous act of devotion to Him.

> "He breaks the power of canceled sin,
> He sets the prisoner free,
> His blood can make the foulest clean,
> His blood avails for me."

XXXII.

FREEDOM FROM SIN AND THE LAW.

J. H. SENSENEY, EVANSTON, ILL.

"For the law of the Spirit of life in Christ Jesus hath made me free from the law of sin and death. For what the law could not do, in that it was weak through the flesh, God sending His own Son in the likeness of sinful flesh, and for sin, condemned sin in the flesh: That the righteousness of the law might be fulfilled in us, who walk not after the flesh, but after the Spirit" (Rom. 8:2-4).

THERE is a wide difference between God and man as to man's salvation from sin. As soon as man is convicted of sin and wants to be saved, he invariably seeks salvation by doing something. That is, consciously or otherwise, he seeks to be saved by the doing. Hence one will reform his life, and rest in that reformation for salvation.

Another will depend on an outwardly moral life. He pays his debts, speaks the truth, and lives a manly life generally, and expects to attain eternal life as a result. Another adds the elements of charity and benevolence and in this way expects to be saved. Others set about the cultivation and development of the better elements found in man naturally, hoping thereby to develop a character commendable to God and fit for heaven. These are some of the devices which men resort to in order to save themselves.

Whereas the divine method of salvation is, that we should trust Jesus alone. It is salvation by faith only, in Christ as our all-sufficient sin offering, without regard to anything we do or can do as a means of salvation.

That which saves is faith in Christ. Faith joins us to Christ, and life is in Christ. Faith is the only golden link that joins us to Him as life's source. This conflict of means and ways of salvation is the conflict of the church's history. The church started on the line of salvation by faith but soon deflected to salvation by works. Several times, as in the ministries of Luther and Wesley, it has been called back to the way of faith to soon turn from it to the line of works. But what is true of salvation in its inception, is also true in its advanced stages; that is, as justification and regeneration are by faith only, so entire sanctification is also by faith only. That is, salvation in the sense of being saved from sin is always by faith, and by faith only; and never by works or by growth or anything else. If this is not so then salvation by faith is not a fact. The modern doctrine, that while we are justified by faith, we are sanctified by some other means, is a falling away just so far from the doctrine of salvation by faith only, as taught by the fathers.

The apostle, in the text, refers to several laws.

I. "The law of the Spirit of life."

1. By "Spirit of life" is meant the Holy Spirit, who

is the begetter of all life, whether it be vegetable, animal or spiritual life. He is the divine personal agent who generates life.

It was He who moved, or brooded, over the waters of the primitive world, and the result was that the waters and the land brought forth living beings, apparently without a distinct fiat of God. When man's body had been formed, God breathed into his nostrils the breath of life, and he became a living soul; yet the word "breath" is the same as "spirit," and probably the writer means that, under the touch of God's breath (Holy Spirit) man became alive physically, and also as a living soul in the full meaning of that term. The angel said to Mary, the mother of Christ, "The Holy Ghost shall come upon thee, and the power of the Highest shall overshadow thee; therefore also that holy thing which shall be born of thee shall be called the Son of God." Here by the power of the Spirit the nature of the virgin is not only elevated, purified and strengthened to become the mother of our Lord, but the human nature of Christ is a result of His creative touch. That is, He gave life.

2. He is also the generator of spiritual or Christian life. We are said to be born from above. Born of God. Born of the Spirit. It is the Spirit that awakens from death in sin. It is the Spirit who gives life. It is He also that enlarges and perfects the life of the soul. Paul says, "We all, with open face beholding as in a glass the glory of the Lord, are changed into the same image from glory to glory,

even as by the Spirit of the Lord." Jesus said, "If any man thirst let him come unto Me, and drink. He that believeth on Me, as the Scripture hath said, out of his belly shall flow rivers of living water. But this spake He of the Spirit which they that believe on Him should receive." These and other Scriptures go to show that the Holy Ghost not only generates life in the soul, but that he also carries it on to completion, until all death is swept from the realm of the soul, and the life of God reigns supreme. The power and authority by which He does this is revealed truth, and especially truth as it is in Christ crucified. Jesus the suffering Lamb of God, is the embodiment of saving and life-giving truth. And this truth is the " law of the Spirit." By law, we mean a governing power or authority. This is true in a civil sense, law being that authority by which government is sustained and its ends effected. So by the law of the Spirit is meant that authority and power by which he effects His great work of salvation from all sin. And that authority is truth as it is revealed in the holy passion of the Son of God. Armed with the death and blood of Christ, the Holy Spirit can save a sinner from all his sins and fill him with the life of God.

That truth " is sharper than any twoedged sword," and it reveals the thoughts and intents of men's hearts. " It is the power of God with salvation to all that believe." The saints are to be sanctified by it. " Sanctify them through Thy truth; Thy Word is truth."

Here, then, is the " sword " of the Spirit. This, then, the Spirit's agent. He saves through the belief of the truth.

II. Another law referred to here, is the "law of sin and death."

This is sin's power and authority over the lives and souls of men. It is not sin in act, or deed, or sin in the outward life, that controls and masters man. It is not outward sin that enslaves and kills men. Outward sin is only the fruit of inward sin. Man's weak point is not in act and word, but is at the heart. It is the heart that is "faint." The inner man is the corrupt tree, the outward is only the fruit. The outward life is only the corrupt stream that flows from the fountain of uncleanness within. Human nature breaks at the heart. It is here that it is weak, and it is here that sin's power is located. Here is sin's throne, and here he sways his sceptre over the entire man. Many a converted soul is grieving over a weak and faulty life outwardly, when the cause of failure is at the heart. Thousands of God's children are trying to conform the outward life to the standard of holiness, while the heart is unholy and impure and makes the outward holy life impossible. It is not God's way. It is a hard way; a slavish way. Many try it and give up altogether, or drop to a defeated life, a half-hearted life; a life without victory and conquest.

Now this evil and corrupt state of heart is sin's power, sin's authority, sin's law. It exists in the hearts of converted people who have not had the "second grace." It is working "death" or seeking to, to all the works and graces of the Spirit wrought in the soul at conversion. It seeks to poison the whole life of God in the soul. It is the power that is controlling the human race, and has been, through the centuries. It is this that drags man down from the innocency and tenderness of childhood, to the stolid, torpid, indifferent condition of many adult persons who are not converted. It is this that masters the drunkard. It is this that enslaves the temper and passion.

Men say that they cannot give up this evil or that. It is simply a confession that they are slaves; that sin has mastered them; that they cannot control themselves. The world of unsaved people know that they are drifting hellward and deathward, yet they are helpless so far as their own power is concerned. Sin is working death. If they do not let Christ save, they will sink to hell. Sin will damn them; not so much the sin of the outward life, as sin of the heart. This is also the chief cause of backsliding among Christians. This it is that cools the first love, weakens the faith, inflames ungodly desires and ambitions, and leads the soul astray. It fills the Christian's life with looseness and the church with worldliness. It discounts true holiness and spirituality, and looks to worldly methods to bring in the kingdom of Christ, instead of depending on the Holy Ghost. It works death; "It is the law of sin and death."

In vain do we multiply agencies and increase organizations; in vain do we point at great conventions and Christian gatherings; in vain do we shout that the world is better and the church purer than ever before; if we overlook sin's power and corruption, and fail to urge the church to the fountain of cleansing, that she may wash herself and be pure as the bride of the Lamb

FREEDOM FROM SIN AND THE LAW. 411

from inward infidelities as well as outward sins. If we fail to do this we shall be defeated.

III. The text speaks of another law.

"For what the law could not do," etc. This is the moral law of God embodied in the ten commandments, and in principle embracing the law of ceremonies and rites among the Jews.

This law is the standard of universal moral rectitude. It is the law that governs angels, and that governed unfallen Adam.

This law is as pure and holy as the thought of God, and yet the text says it cannot save; "It is weak through the flesh." I suppose it would save if we could keep it without the help of grace. Angels are justified by it, as Adam was before he sinned.

But fallen man without grace cannot keep it. He possibly might keep the letter of the law, yet this is not at all probable:— but it is impossible for him to keep the spirit of it. Christ says the ten commandments are "Thou shalt love the Lord thy God with all thy heart," etc., which is precisely what is meant by Christian perfection, and what no unconverted man can do.

Yet the law is without sympathy and knows no pity, and it never forgives; it never pardons sin; it has no mercy on the offender. "The soul that sinneth" against the law by the law must die. One transgression of the law prevents the soul ever being saved by the law. But instead it is hunted and pursued and condemned by the law to eternal death. If there is no hope but the law the sinner is doomed. God out of

Christ is a consuming fire. Wherever law obtains and rules alone the sinner is lost. If mercy does not interpose he is lost forever.

Converted persons not yet wholly sanctified do not "love God with all their heart, soul, mind," etc.; and their failure to do so results in heart-wandering, apostasies and infidelities, which are so common among Christians, and so painful to sincere believers; costing repentance, tears and contritions, and weakening the whole life, and threatening utter apostasy.

But it may be asked, "Does the entirely sanctified soul meet all the obligations and requirements of the holy and pure law of God? Are not the effects of the fall such, even, when the soul is cleansed from all sin and filled with perfect love, that it is impossible to meet all the requirements of the law of God faultlessly?" We answer, "Yes, it is impossible in a legal sense to keep the law thus perfectly, but in Christ 'love is the fulfilling of the law.'" And "love out of a pure heart" is the end of the commandment. That is, if we love God with all the being and love the neighbor as the self, are thus wholly devoted to God and given to Him, we are accounted, in Christ, as having perfectly kept the law. In our devotion to God and fidelity to Him, we go as far as our beings, dominated and impelled by love, can take us. We have done all we can. It is our best. Wherein we fall short, wherein we lack, wherein there is defect; Christ completes, Christ finishes. He is ours, and He bridges and spans the distance between what we are and do and what the law in its strictness demands of us. In that sense He is our righteousness. In that sense He has fulfilled the law for us. So that we are complete in Him, and in Him only. Hence the holiest and purest man is constantly dependent on the blood of Christ, and cannot stand a moment without it. But, thank God, we may have it every moment, and hence may be entire and wanting nothing.

1. But why can we not be saved by the law? Because it is weak through the flesh. The word "flesh" used here by the apostle, sometimes means the physical body, but here it evidently does not. The apostle says that the law cannot save; that it is weak through the flesh. He does not mean that it is weak through the body or physical nature, but through, or by means of, a fleshly or carnalized state of heart. The word "flesh" sometimes means the body, of course, but often it refers to a carnal and impure state of heart, and is identical with carnality or inbred sin;—this is the meaning of the apostle in this place. And he says that man is weak and unable to keep the law because he is carnal and corrupt in heart. This, then, is man's weak point; and as we noticed before, it is where human nature breaks. It is not in the outward life that he gives way; the heart corrupted by sin gives way first, and the outward wrong is but a result of inward failure. Christians bemoan their outward failures and breaks, whereas the cause of it all is corruption of heart. The apostle does not say "They that are in the body cannot please God," but he does say, "They that are in the flesh cannot please Him."

2. But God sent His own Son in the likeness of

sinful flesh, and for sin, condemned sin in the flesh." Christ looked like a sinner. "He was numbered with the transgressors." "He made His grave with the wicked." They said He had a devil. But God sent Him as a sin-offering, "to condemn sin in the flesh." Christ is the sin-offering. He is the atoning victim. He is the Lamb of God that takes away sin. In His death a provisional salvation is made for all sinners, and from all sin. For "He condemned sin in the flesh." That is, He condemned sin in the fleshly, or carnal state of the heart. He condemned sin in carnality; or, original sin. The word "condemned" here, means to pass sentence upon; to order executed, or put to death; to exterminate, to destroy. The verb "condemned' is in the aorist tense, and implies a single act, once for all time. That is, in the atoning death of Christ there is provision made for the utter extermination and destruction of the carnal mind, and that in an instant of time.

The blood of Christ in its saving virtue compasses all the need of man's moral nature. So that He may be free from sin's power and control by the destruction of sin itself, and being free from sin he is also free from the law.

Now, there are different kinds of freedom. There is the freedom that comes by the repeal of law, so that obligation no longer exists. Then there is a kind of freedom that comes from trampling all law underfoot. It is the freedom of mobs, anarchists and rabbles. It is the kind of freedom that the sinner boasts of. Then there is the true freedom, that which comes from harmony with the law. It arises from a state of heart in sympathy with the law, the law exists in all its force, but the heart is in perfect accord with it.

This is the freedom of the one fully saved from sin. And being in perfect sympathy with the law, that soul does not feel the law. It knows no oppression. Its neck is not galled by any yoke. It is not forcefully restrained by any command. It is not crushed by any burden. To it "His commandments are not grievous," but instead, "His yoke is easy, and His burden light." "The righteousness of the law is fulfilled" in that soul. The Spirit of life by His law, has made it "free from the law of sin and death" by virtue of Jesus' blood. All lawlessness and unrighteousness have been destroyed, and it stands blameless in the eyes of the law. It is in harmony with God, with itself and with all that is right. It can go anywhere and no evil thing can touch it, and no good thing will harm it. It is free.

XXXIII.

SALVATION.

JOSHUA GILL, BOSTON, MASS.

"For by grace are ye saved through faith; and that not of yourselves: it is the gift of God: Not of works, lest any man should boast. For we are His workmanship, created in Christ Jesus unto good works, which God hath before ordained that we should walk in them" (Eph. 2 : 8-10).

"ARE there few that be saved?" was demanded of our Lord. And He said unto them, "Strive to enter in at the strait gate, for many I say unto you, will seek to enter in, and shall not be able," which goes to show that Jesus was more interested in the practical side of salvation, than in the speculative. What we mean by the practical side, is not the mere perfunctory round of religious duties, for if there is anything that Jesus condemns unsparingly it is Phariseeism. Nothing is clearer than that religion is one thing, salvation another. A man may have religion and not have salvation. There are many religions; there is only one salvation. One religion is as good as another if it is only a question of words. Salvation is of Jesus Christ. "Neither is there salvation in any other; for there is none other name under heaven given among men whereby we must be saved."

In discussing salvation, we must first discuss sin, for the question arises at the very beginning, What is the need of salvation? What danger threatens? What calamity has overtaken us? Physical salvation may be from fire, water, famine, sickness and impending death. Spiritual salvation is from *sin*. The Bible does not speak of salvation from hell, though hell is a place sinners are liable to fall into. A man struggling in the water, will die if he is not saved from the water. So Jesus everywhere teaches that sin ultimates in death,— eternal death. "Lust when it hath conceived bringeth forth sin, and sin when it is finished bringeth forth death." But sin is the present danger. Sin kills. Jesus saves from sin, as said the angel, "Thou shalt call His name Jesus, for He shall save His people from their sins."

Sin is discussed in all the books, the Bible included, under two heads. There is the root and the branch, the fountain and the stream, the tree and the fruit, the disease and the symptoms. For example, we have in the Bible these two definitions of sin: "Sin is the transgression of the law," "All unrighteousness is sin." Unrighteousness is the sin principle, deeply imbedded in the heart; transgression of the law is the manifestation of that principle in outward life. Unrighteousness is the root, transgression the branches. Unrighteousness is the fountain, transgression the stream.

All philosophical discussions of sin, treat of it under the two heads of sin original, and sin actual, corresponding to the Scriptural ideas of tree and fruit.

Actual sin is sin committed, original sin is sin in the nature. Actual sin is the overt act, original sin is the bent of the nature, the desire, the motive, the affinity. The sin principle is called original sin, because it is "a natural corruption and tendency to sin inherited from Adam," who committed the first sin.

Every church from the beginning has stated in its creed, this doctrine of original sin. The ninth article of the Church of England is perhaps, the clearest and most comprehensive of all, but they all teach substantially the same: " Original sin standeth not in the following of Adam [as the Pelagians do vainly talk], but it is the fault and corruption of the nature of every man, that naturally is engendered of the off-spring of Adam, whereby man is very far gone from original righteousness, and is of his own nature inclined to evil, so that the flesh lusteth always contrary to the spirit; and therefore in every person born into this world, it deserveth God's wrath and damnation. And this infection of nature doth remain, yea, in them that are regenerated; whereby the lust of the flesh, called in the Greek *phronema sarkos*, which some do expound 'the wisdom,' some 'sensuality,' some 'the affection,' some 'the desire of the flesh,' is not subject to the law of God. And although there is no condemnation for them that believe and are baptized, yet the apostle doth confess that concupiscence and lust hath of itself the nature of sin."

Now if sin is what we have described it to be, salvation, to be salvation, must provide for the deliverance of man from its dominion and indwelling. It shall be our object to show that this is exactly what the gospel proposes to do. "Behold the Lamb of God which taketh away the sin of the world." And in this connection we ought to notice that the Bible makes a distinction between *sins* and *sin*. And this distinction runs on parallel lines with the distinction between actual sins ann original sin, or sins committed and sin in us. The question then arises as to the plan of salvation. How does Jesus save us from these two forms of sin?

First of all, let us insist that the sufferings and death of Christ form the basis upon which the whole superstructure of salvation rests. "We see Jesus, who was made a little lower than the angels, for the suffering of death, crowned with glory and honor; that He by the grace of God should taste death for every man." Let us also not forget that the efficient agent in the consummation of the work is the Holy Spirit who guides into all truth, regenerates and sanctifies.

Pardon is God's remedy, in the gospel, for sins committed. "Let the wicked forsake his way, and the unrighteous man his thoughts; and let him return unto the Lord, and He will have mercy upon him; and to our God, for He will abundantly pardon." "If we confess our sins He is faithful and just to forgive us our sins." Pardon and forgiveness are used interchangeably in the Bible, though strictly, pardon is a governmental term, while forgiveness is personal. God always had a spirit of forgiveness towards sinners. It was that which prompted Him to give His Son to die for them. Pardon, being governmental, is issued to penitent sinners who believe in Christ. "In whom we have redemption through His blood, even the forgiveness of sins." Pardon (or forgiveness) cancels the penalty of the broken law.

Pardon has accomplished a great work for us when it has delivered us from the sanctions of a violated law. But if the gospel left us there, we should relapse at once into actual sins. So the gospel provides a regenerating power. Regeneration and the new birth are used synonymously, but they really stand related as cause and effect. They describe that work of the Holy Spirit wrought in the heart of a believer, by which the power of sin in him is broken and he becomes a "new creature" — a "new man." The characteristic feature of the "new man," made new by the regenerating power of the Holy Spirit is, the non-commission of sin. "Whosoever committeth sin," says John's epistle, "transgresseth also the law." "Whosoever is born of God doth not commit sin, for His seed remaineth in him; and he cannot sin because he is born of God." "He that committeth sin is of the devil."

The new birth imparts power to keep God's law, for "love is the fulfilling of the law." "The love of God is shed abroad in our hearts, by the Holy Ghost, which is given unto us."

We find, then, that the gospel provides for the pardon of past transgressions, which is equivalent to the wiping out of the "old score," the canceling of the penalty of sin. And it also provides for the renewing of the heart in righteousness, by which we become "partakers of the divine nature, having escaped the corruption which is in the world through lust." By the power imparted in the "new birth" we are able to keep God's law of love. The fact that we do keep this law is the proof of our being born again. If we do not keep it, that fact demonstrates that we are still "in the gall of bitterness and in the bond of iniquity."

However much pardon and regeneration may do for a man, the work of salvation cannot be said to be complete until the sin principle is killed. This does not take place in regeneration, according to the English creed: "This infection of nature doth remain, yea in them that are regenerated." To this the Scriptures agree. St. Paul speaks of the Corinthian brethren as being "babes in Christ," and "carnal." There was among them "envying strife, and divisions," which demonstrated that they were still "carnal." At this point the "Creeds of Christendom" agree. A brief examination of what St. Paul means by the word "carnal" may serve to throw some light on this question. "Carnal" is from "*carnis*"—flesh. Hence in St. Paul's writings "carnal" and "fleshly" mean the same. The word "flesh" has two meanings in Scripture. The first is the literal meaning, as in 1 Cor. 15: 39, where the apostle speaks of the flesh of men, of beasts, of fishes and of birds. The second is the figurative meaning, as in Rom. 8: 8, where he says, "They that are in the flesh cannot please God." In the same chapter he declares that the "carnal [fleshly] mind is enmity against God." According to the thought of the church the "carnal mind," while modified and suppressed in regeneration, is not wholly destroyed. It is the sin principle, the root, the fountain, the lust which "conceives and brings forth sin."

Does the gospel provide for the utter extinction of this *substratum* of evil in the human soul? Or must we carry "lust" and "carnality" in our hearts to the grave, and perhaps to heaven? No one believes that any element antagonistic to God, as carnality is, would be tolerated for a moment in heaven. And the soul not yet delivered from carnality would be still unsaved, for Jesus came to "save his people from their sins." He is "the Lamb of God that taketh away the sin of the world." He came to "destroy the works of the devil."

It must be, therefore, that the gospel proposes the death of " the old man; " for St. Paul says: "Knowing this, that our old man is crucified with Him that the body of sin might be destroyed, that *henceforth* we should not serve sin." Hence St. Paul preaches the privilege of present deliverance from " the body of sin," from " the old man." And again he says, " They that are Christ's have crucified the flesh with the affections and lusts." Crucifixion means death, a death that has in some cases actually taken place. The same meaning must be attached to " mortify," where St. Paul says " Mortify therefore your members which are *upon the earth;* fornication, uncleanness, inordinate affection, evil concupiscence and covetousness which is idolatry." St. Paul also prayed for the Thessalonians: " The very God of peace sanctify you wholly; and I pray God your whole spirit and soul and body be preserved blameless unto the coming of our Lord Jesus Christ. Faithful is He that calleth you, who also will do it."

St. John declares the whole truth of the gospel when he says, "If we confess our sins He is faithful and just to forgive us our sins, and to cleanse us from all unrighteousness." Unrighteousness represents the inward state of the sinful heart. This may be cleansed. "Sins" may be pardoned,—"unrighteousness" may be cleansed. Again St. John declares that "the blood of Jesus Christ His Son cleanseth us from all *sin*." Notice, that "sins" are always to be forgiven or pardoned, "sin" is always to be cleansed. Jesus pronounced a blessing upon the "pure in heart." Even David prayed for a "clean heart."

Our conclusion is that "salvation" includes (1) pardon, whereby our guilt is canceled; (2) regeneration, by which the power of sin is broken, and divine life is implanted in the soul; (3) cleansing, which secures the eradication of remaining depravity, or the extinction of the sin principle. This is a perfect cure so far as sin is concerned. Many results of sin remain in the saved. Bodily redemption takes place at the resurrection. Infirmities of mind and body are necessary concomitants of the postponement of bodily redemption, but so far as sin as a principle controlling the will or the affections is concerned, the saved are free. They love God with all the heart, because God through grace has circumcised their hearts to love Him. They love their neighbors as themselves. They love their enemies. They always choose God's will as their rule of action. They are delivered from selfishness, for they have "the mind of Christ." Their motives, their desires, their purposes, their aims, their ambitions are all pure, for God has "purified their hearts by faith."

The word grace represents the unmerited favor of God. It is the source of salvation. The plan is God's. He originated it. His love inspired it. He paid the price. He gave His Son. Salvation is a free gift, "Not of works, lest any man should boast." Pardon is a gift; regeneration is a gift: cleansing is a gift. Still it is through faith. Faith is not something we do to merit or purchase salvation. It is simply receiving the gift. It is the expression of our appreciation of the gift. It is not something established by the arbitrary authority of God, the author of the gift. It is something made necessary, in the nature of things, to insure the giver from insult and waste. It is like the famishing multitude coming to the free soup house of a beneficent city government. Each brings a dish to carry home his supply, or at least sits down and eats to show his hunger and his gratitude. The city fathers do not give soup to have it thrown in the gutters. "By grace," shows God's beneficence. "Through faith," insures our honesty.

"We are His workmanship, created in Christ Jesus unto good works, which God hath before ordained that we should walk in them." Good works are not necessary to salvation. Salvation is a free gift. But good works are necessary as a demonstration of the genuineness of our faith. The fruit of a tree does not make the tree, but the tree makes the fruit. Jesus says, "Make the tree good and his fruit good." "Can the fig tree, my brethren, bear olive berries? either a vine figs?" "Make the tree good," and the fruit will

H. L. GILMORE.   H. C. LAUB.
J. F. LARKIN.   I. D. WARE.

be good; but if the tree be corrupt, the fruit will be corrupt also. This is an irreversible law. The test, therefore, of salvation, is good works, for hereunto are we created in Christ Jesus.

All of the processes of salvation being gracious and not natural, we are led to the conclusion that they are instantaneously wrought. Growth in grace is a natural process. Just as a good tree, or a healthy tree, will naturally grow, so a good man, made good by grace, will naturally and inevitably grow. Hence there must be a wide distinction between growing in grace, and growing into grace. One species of animal or vegetable never grows into another. The nature of a tree can be changed only by grafting. So a man's nature can be changed only by gracious processes. But after he is changed, the law of growth is there, by nature, and he will expand and grow in the direction of the gracious change that has taken place in him. Pardon and regeneration, therefore, are instantaneously wrought. Sanctification (or cleansing) is an instantaneous process. They are all by grace, through faith. "And if by faith, why not now?" asked John Wesley. "Behold *now* is the accepted time," "behold *now* is the day of salvation." No one can prove that the "now" of the Bible extends beyond death, and it may be demonstrated that many do fall into such chronic habits of sin or indifference, as to render it probable that their "now" is past already. "Grieve not the Holy Spirit of God whereby ye are sealed unto the day of redemption."

XXXIV.

"THE DOUBLE-MINDED."

W. A. DODGE, ATLANTA, GA.

"A double-minded man is unstable in all his ways" (James 1: 8).

THERE are but two minds in the world, — one is the mind of Christ, the other of Satan. Sinners have but the evil, while the fully saved have only the mind of Christ. And yet St. James tells us that there is a "double-minded man." The true meaning of the text is looking two ways. One looks forward, the other backward. Christ said: "No man, having put his hand to the plough, and looking back, is fit for the kingdom of God" (Luke 9: 62).

The mind of Christ looks forward, while the mind of Satan looks backward. God put his seal of condemnation on this look-back mind in his command and dealing with Lot's wife. The angel said, "Escape for thy life; look not behind thee" (Gen. 19: 17). In going out, Lot's wife, not forgetting but remembering the things left behind, turned and looked back, and she became a pillar of salt (Gen. 19: 26).

Paul in telling his experience uses this very same figure. In his letter to the church at Philippi, when telling them that he had given up all for Christ, that he

W. A. DODGE.

might attain unto the resurrection of the dead, he says that in the sense of the glorified resurrected state he had not attained, then adds, "This one thing I do, forgetting those things which are behind, and reaching forth unto those things which are before, I press toward the mark for the prize of the high calling of God in Christ Jesus. Let us therefore, as many as be perfect, be thus minded" (Phil. 3: 13–15). He plainly shows that only the sanctified have the one mind that looks forward. The statement of our Lord, that while the man had taken the gospel plough he was looking back, shows he had yet something in him that made him look back and that needed to be cleansed away, in order to have but the one mind that looks forward.

St. James says that this double mind makes the possessor vacillating. The civil war within the soul carries first one way and then the other. One mind says, "Read the Bible." The other says, "Read the newspapers." One says, "Go to church." The other says, "Stay at home." One says, "Hold family prayer," while the other says, "Go to bed." One says, "Support the gospel." The other says, "Look out for number one." This accounts for the irregularities in the lives of thousands of people that profess religion. To an interested observer this is one of the most painful of subjects to contemplate.

It is a sad fact that not one in a hundred that fail to go forward and obtain deliverance from the double mind, stand firm in their Christian experience.

Backsliding is always first in the heart before it is manifest in the life. Thousands are conscious of a decline in their heart life that never show it in their outer life. Loss of the fruits of the Spirit or declining in them is heart experience in backsliding. All that we ever found that were never conscious of a decline at some time in their Christian life, have belonged to that company known as the entirely sanctified, that subsequently to their conversion obtained the blessing of entire sanctification.

There are other results that come because of the presence of the double mind. This is demonstrated by the apostle in this epistle. Indeed, it seems to us that he wrote the letter to lead the Christians to whom he addressed it into the experience of heart cleansing. This is the golden thread that runs through all the apostolic letters, and in fact the whole Bible.

The fleshly mind of Satan makes us, 1. To repine at trials.

We are exhorted by the apostle James, first chapter and second verse, "My brethren, count it all joy when ye fall into divers temptations." The expression "divers temptations" means testings of all kinds. But instead of rejoicing, the carnal mind makes to murmur at them. Testings are needful experiences. They reveal what is and what is not in the heart. We have eye test, muscle test, ear test, and shall we not have spiritual tests? A test of faith on a plain "Thus saith the Lord" demonstrates to us whether there is doubt lingering in the heart or not. A test of love reveals to us the presence or absence of temper. Of humility, whether there is any pride lingering in the soul. Of liberality, if there be any covetousness remaining. Of submission, whether rebellion is to be found asserting itself or not. When testings come on these or any

THE DOUBLE-MINDED. 429

other lines, and we find the two opposite principles contending within, it should be taken as conclusive proof of the double mind remaining.

2. It makes us weak in the presence of temptation. "Blessed is the man that endureth temptation. . . . Every man is tempted, when he is drawn away of his own lust, and enticed" (James 1: 12, 14).

There is no sin in a temptation. If there is, Jesus our Lord was a great sinner, and the Holy Ghost was accessory. He was tempted in all points like as we are, and the Holy Ghost led Him up into the wilderness to be tempted of the devil. As long as the double mind remains, there is danger of yielding. The Master said, "The prince of this world [Satan] cometh and findeth nothing in me." No double mind, hence no disposition within to yield to the suggestion of evil from without. No lust to draw Him away and entice. God has promised that we shall not be tempted beyond that we are able to resist. By the mouth of the apostle James he announces, "Blessed is the man that endureth temptation."

It is charged by some that the sanctified claim freedom from temptation. This is one of the tricks of the enemy. Of all people they are the ones that Satan tries his skill on the most.

Freedom from temptation is proof conclusive that we do not belong to the number of the justified. For why should Satan trouble himself about those that are his already?

An infidel master berated his Christian servant for complaining at his tribulations and trials, saying, "You a Christian and have so many conflicts. I am not a professor of religion, but do not have any of the things to trouble me of which you complain." The servant could not answer, until one day while out hunting, and the master had fired into a flock of wild duck, killing one and wounding another. The master cried out, " Run, Charley, run, don't let him get away." The faithful servant soon returned bearing the wounded duck in his hand, saying, " Massa, I see how it is now. You say you has no trials, tribulations, and I has dem. It's 'cause you is de debil's dead duck, while I is de Lord's lame duck, and de debil he all de time try ketch me." If you want all the black ranks of darkness turned loose on you, get the blessing of entire sanctification. If you want to get where you can meet these legions of the pit, though hoofed and horned, marching in solid phalanx against you, and be enabled to stand against all their fiery darts, get the blessing of full salvation. To all such the divine pledge is given, that as their day is, so shall their strength be.

3. This double-mindedness makes us respecters of persons. " If there come into your assembly a man with a gold ring, in goodly apparel, and there come in also a poor man in vile raiment; and ye have respect to him that weareth the gay clothing, and say unto him, Sit thou here in a good place; and say to the poor, Stand thou there, or sit here under my footstool: are ye not then partial in yourselves, and have become judges of evil thoughts?"

Alas, alas! who has not seen this many times repeated! The mixed state makes our love heterogeneous, *i. e.*, to love those that think, feel, talk, and act as we do; while the sanctified mind alone makes our love homogeneous, *i. e.*, God-like, loving all men alike, whether good, bad, or indifferent. God loved and gave His Son to die for an African or Chinaman, as well as an Anglo-Saxon. The sanctified heart can and does put the arms of its faith and love about the lowest and meanest of Adam's race, as well as the best. The want of this state makes thousands shun the slums and with folded skirts to walk by the fallen in the ditch.

4. It makes to talk two ways. "Out of the same mouth proceedeth blessing and cursing [or scolding]. My brethren, these things ought not so to be. Doth a fountain send forth at the same place sweet water and bitter?" (James 3: 10, 11). The word "curse" should be rendered "scold," for Christian people do not swear, but how often do we find them to be regular old scolds. Mr. Wesley said that he would no more fret and worry than he would curse and swear. A sanctified heart has a sanctified conversation and a sanctified tone to the voice. St. James says such is "not from above, but is earthly, sensual, devilish;" while the conversation that is born of the heavenly mind is pure, peaceable, gentle, easy to be entreated, full of mercy and good fruits, without partiality and without hypocrisy. To the face the double-minded will frequently use flattery, while behind the back find fault. While the heart is double, with only one tongue with which to talk, the conversation will be double, for these two opposite minds cannot talk the same way. These things ought not so to be, and they are not in nature, but, alas, it is so with the double minded.

The difficulty is not with the tongue, but the trouble is farther back and deeper down. "Out of the heart proceed evil thoughts," etc. " Out of the abundance of the heart, the mouth speaketh." " As a man thinketh in his heart, so is he." It is not the stream that needs to be purified, but the fountain. A sanctified heart will have a sanctified conversation.

5. It produces inward conflicts.

" From whence come wars and fightings among [or within] you? Come they not hence, even of your lusts that war in your members?" (James 4: 1).

Paul in his letter to the church at Galatia, 5: 17: " For the flesh lusteth against the Spirit, and the Spirit against the flesh: and these are contrary, the one to the other: so that ye cannot do the things that ye would." Who can describe the unceasing conflict that goes on day and night in the heart of the double-minded? No language can portray it. Day and night the battle rages. And if at any time the hostilities seem to cease, and the conclusion is reached that the civil war within is at an end, never to be resumed, how soon it is discovered to be only a temporary suspension, in order to open again on some new line! When these battles are renewed from time to time, the cry is often extorted, as from Paul, " O wretched man that I am! who shall deliver me from the body of this death?" (Rom. 7: 24), — but fail to go into the experience of the next verse, which exultantly exclaims, " I thank God through Jesus Christ our Lord."

The blame for war within is often laid to the charge of environments, when they come, as St. James says, from within. Of course there are many ways in the outer life through which it finds expression, but the real trouble is the lust within.

Can it be thought by any that have any knowledge of God and His plan of salvation that this is the very best that can be done for us? The apostle James, 4:6, says that "He giveth more grace." Yea, to all such let it be said that they need not live in this state of double-mindedness where the civil war rages forever.

How may we be delivered? This is an important question, and one that we would hesitate to answer, were it not so plainly given in this same epistle.

1. Submission to God.

The apostle knew that this is the hardest victory to win. The carnal nature never likes to submit to another and especially to God, for "it is enmity to God, and is not subject to the law of God, neither indeed can be." "God resisteth the proud, but giveth grace to the humble. Submit yourselves therefore to God" (James 4:6, 7).

When God can, with full consent of the human heart, enter this citadel of man's being, He can begin a work that will tell in time and eternity. But nothing can be done until God has the right of way. To do this, our plans and opinions must be surrendered, if they are antagonistic to God's plans. How the personal pronoun "I" will go down under this requirement!

2. Resist the devil.

When this last ditch is being surrendered to God, the enemy of all good will reinforce the carnal nature with all the army of hell to defeat the work of cleansing. To him we must learn to say an eternal "No" that will be repeated all the way to the grave. He knows that in the clean heart there is not an inch of territory for his occupancy. He knows that henceforth all his attacks must be from without, with no sympathy from within. He will be willing to compromise on anything short of full salvation. He will agree to repression, growth in grace, death-bed sanctification or purgatorial cleansing, yea, anything to keep us out of the blessing of entire sanctification here and now.

3. "Draw nigh to God" (James 4:8). Here is the place for poor double-minded souls to come. All human effort to remove this carnal mind is a failure. God alone can do this. Any effort of our own to cast it out is putting our trust in an arm of flesh. It will do no good to accept God's plan theoretically; for Satan knows that nothing short of an experimental getting to God will bring deliverance. It is a pity that the untold multitude of converted Christians have never learned that the removal of the carnal mind is a divine work, and that they must come to God, who alone hath power to cleanse the heart.

4. "Cleanse the hands" (James 4:8). Hands in the Bible stand for actual deeds, and in this place for actual sins. Who has not learned from bitter experience that to do wrong, either by committing forbidden sin or omitting commanded duty, is the common experience of converted people! Hence sinners are not asked to be holy, but "repent," while backsliders are exhorted to return unto the Lord. The experience of entire sanctification begins on the plane of a clearly justified experience and not of an unpardoned sinner or a backslidden believer. If, since conversion, the believer has committed known wilful sin, or neglected plain duty, he needs pardon, and his hands are not clean. Hence the exhortation, or rather command, "Cleanse your hands, ye sinners."

The sin of the unsaved, either in the church or out, is the sin of transgression, while the sin of the double-minded, for the most part, is that of omission, but in either case it is sin; and to be delivered from either one or the other, or both, pardon must be sought and obtained.

If your hands are clean, then are you ready for the next step, which is —

5. Heart purity. "Purify your hearts, ye double-minded" (James 4:8).

Clearly does the apostle teach that a state of double-mindedness is a state of heart impurity, while on the other hand a clean heart has only the one single mind of Jesus in it. In the sense of self heart purification that is impossible.

The Ethiope cannot change his skin, nor the leopard his spots. But there is a sense in which this is true. Salvation in this is co-operative, as well as in conversion. Man's part and then God's. In justification, man repents and turns to God, then God forgives and regenerates. In full salvation, man consecrates and trusts, then God cleanses and fills with the Holy Ghost. Hence the Lord, by the mouth of Moses, said to Israel: "Sanctify yourselves therefore, and be ye holy. . . . I am the Lord which sanctify you" (Lev. 20:7, 8).

St. James shows that this is not a side issue, but adds "Be afflicted, and mourn, and weep; let your laughter be turned to mourning, and your joy to heaviness. Humble yourselves in the sight of the Lord."

What a thorough work! No healing slightly the hurt of the daughter of Zion. Here is a going to the bottom, and an applying the balm of Gilead by the Great Physician, that He may fulfil the promise succeeding these directions: "And he shall lift you up." O blessed lifting! O wonderful deliverance! Who that ever drank this cup of gall does not remember it? And then, when the cup of salvation, full and complete, is placed to the lips of the soul and the poor thirsty one drinks of its sweets, can he ever forget it? How unthankful ever to forget or deny it!

If you are converted and not sanctified, your heart is not yet right with God, but in a state of transition. Do not stop when you get the mind of Christ, which you do in regeneration, but press on until the mind of Satan is taken out of you, which is done in entire sanctification.

T. E. ROBINSON.

XXXV.

THE UNHINDERED GOSPEL.

T. E. ROBINSON, ALHAMBRA, CAL.

"Finally, brethren, pray for us, that the Word of the Lord may have free course, and be glorified, even as it is with you" (2 Thess. 3: 1).

DECEPTION and opposition were threatening the Thessalonian church, and Paul raises a note of warning against the man of sin, and calls their attention to the fact that he had spoken of these things before, and at the conclusion of some masterly reasoning, utters the urgent request of the fifteenth verse, "Therefore, brethren, stand fast, and hold the traditions which ye have been taught, whether by word, or our epistle," followed by his prayer for them, and his request, "Finally, brethren, pray for us, that the Word of the Lord may have free course, and be glorified." In the onward flow of the gospel there are four prominent factors to all success: the Spirit, the Word, the membership, and ministry. The two former are referred to in the previous chapter as the Spirit that sanctifies and the truth to be believed.

There is nothing more absolute in heaven than that the Holy Spirit, the personal Holy Ghost, seeks with infinite wisdom and love the salvation of man, having due regard to the divinely appointed fact of his free moral agency. Coercion of a soul in the polity of heaven is impossible, because out of harmony with the divine plan of Him who was pleased to create man with the power of finite purpose and will.

To reason, invite and entreat, then, is the relation occupied by the Holy Spirit regarding man's salvation; and all Scripture and reason and experience affirm that this relation is sustained along every possible avenue, in harmony with infinite justice, wisdom and love. And yet, my fellow sinner, we stand in the presence of the awful fact that the will of man may refute all efforts of this blessed divine agency. Listen, I pray, to the words of Paul in the last chapter of this first epistle, " Quench not the Spirit." Let us turn a moment and view the second factor of this holy agency. The Word of the Lord, revealed truth relating to God and man, time and eternity, power and responsibility, probation and eternal destiny, — these fundamental truths rising into the horizon of our consciousness appall us with their magnitude, are further enhanced as we gaze upon the history of man as created by God, as depraved by disobedience, as redeemed by the atonement, and his salvation is made to turn upon his own decision of acceptance or rejection of this heaven-revealed truth.

In the operation of the unerring Spirit and the straight lines of revealed truth, we look in vain for anything left undone, and bow with acknowledged defeat in the presence of the searching challenge, " And now, O inhabitants of Jerusalem, and men of Judah, judge, I pray you, betwixt me and my vineyard, what could have been done more to my vineyard that I have not done in it?" But we must turn now from the infallible to the fallible, from the Spirit and the Word to man. Universal nature is harmony itself, the stars are never late, the sun never refuses to shine. All things material seem in perfect time and tune; in this sphere weak man plays no part; but as we turn from the physical to the moral, distortion and discord greet our eye and ear on every side. Here man is a factor, and man has failed to play his part. The Father's great design in the gift of His Son must fall far short of its divine intent. "In Christ may all be made alive." Paul has no doubts to express concerning the Spirit and the Word. "We have confidence in the Lord touching you;" but pray for us, that the Word may run free. He directs their prayer to the point of hindrance. Let us consider it. Was not that which was written aforetime written for us? "I know thy works, that thou hast a name that thou livest and art dead." Does not this terrible language appeal to us in a manner that would cause us to forget Sardis, and turn to ourselves? Are we not making the vital mistake of placing the essence of Christianity in its machinery, in the letter and not in the spirit? Hath it not happened to us that our feasts and new moons are become an abomination? Are not our objective doings offered in place of the subjective sacrifice of a humble and contrite heart?

Do we not shrink from meditation of that searching request of Paul to the Romans, not to be conformed to the world, but to be transformed by the renewing of the mind? Between these two words lies a moral death line, where the body is presented "a living sacrifice, holy and acceptable unto God," a line which, when crossed, brings us to the higher spiritual, with a mind dead to the world and like that which was in Christ. Beloved, let us claim our privilege to this actual, full, complete experience — proving what is this will of God concerning us, " the good, the acceptable, the perfect." Why should not the church move as one mighty sacramental host to the highest lines of reasonable service, claiming the fullness of the blessing of the gospel of Christ? Where the few chosen in Sardis stand, there is room for the whole church, minister and people. This host is composed of individuals. Each must pass the line of crucifixion for himself, and for himself possess by faith the land; the death must be his, and the song and victory shall also be his. Why stand upon the brink? Your captain bids you go forward to triumph and success.

Hail the day when through every heart the Word of the Lord shall run free course. We have failed to obtain the blessing of Abraham because we have staggered at the Word. We have seen in it the instrument "sharper than any two-edged sword, piercing even to the dividing asunder of soul and spirit, and of the joints and marrow — a discerner of the thoughts and intents of the heart;" and we drew back in our consecration, because we would not consent to the death of self; and the Word that kills and makes alive, that purifies and fills, was denied free course; and the full joy of the peace that passeth understanding could not flow into our experience. Beloved, this we do at a loss, a loss incalculable to ourselves and others. Would there be so rich a man in the whole world as he who should possess all the land despoiled by river and rail because it lacked free course? It has always been considered both a difficult and costly undertaking to find such right of way through the country, and thousands have stood persistently blind to the blessing which plainly said, "For brass I will bring gold; for iron, silver; for wood, brass; and for stones, iron." Have you and I not stood amazed at such blindness, and expressed our amazement? Yet this was but a mote, and the beam was in our own eye. The Holy Spirit was pleading with us that the Word might have free course in us, and in our blindness we raised our puny arguments against the high claims of the Spirit that leads, and thus most of our Christian life has been spent in the back country, while it might have been ours to live in the very front of all spiritual blessing and aggressiveness. Our lives have not been the success we desired. We have fallen below our own ideal. We have not been at our best, nor met the expectation of the church; and the Master must have been disappointed in us.

Shall we not here and now act the part of wisdom, pay the price and obtain the blessing? No contract ever brought such remuneration as that which gives self fully for the Holy Ghost fully. Fully possessed of the Spirit, our hesitant speech shall be made eloquent, our lips to tremble with holy fervor, and all our effort shall prove to be in demonstration of the Spirit. Full, definite, enthusiastic experience in us will carry the Word with irresistible power to the hearts of others.

Our late beloved Bishop Simpson, preaching in Memorial Hall, London, spoke for half an hour in a calm manner and without gesticulation. Then, while picturing the death of Christ on the cross, and describing His atonement for the sins of the world, the bishop stooped as if laden with an immeasurable burden, and rising to his full height seemed to throw it from him, crying, "How far? 'As far as east is distant from the west, so far hath He removed our transgressions from us.'" The effect was tremendous. The whole assembly rose to its feet and remained standing for several moments, when one by one the people sank back into their seats. A professor of elocution present was asked by a friend what he thought of the bishop's elocution. "Elocution," he replied, "that man doesn't want elocution, he's got the Holy Ghost." Blessed Holy Spirit, through us "send forth thy light and thy truth." Give us this knowledge of which it is said, "The wind is in the wings of its messengers, and eyes in the wheels of its chariots; whose commander is one with bow in hand, sitting on the white horse of the apocalypse, going forth to conquer, a knowledge of whose glory shall cover the earth as the waters cover the sea." And the power, and the glory, and the wisdom, and the blessing shall be thine, for ever and ever.

FOUND AT LAST! .·. .·. .·. .·.

THE CREAM OF ALL BOOKS!!

A small-priced Song Book for Protracted meetings and Conventions.

GOOD NEWS IN SONG.

142 PAGES. 223 HYMNS. NO DUPLICATES.

There is Nothing Like it in the Market.

PRICES . · . · . · . ·

Single	- .25	**Hundred**	- - -	$20.00
Dozen	$2.40	**Thousand**	- - -	150.00

Among this collection of hymns will be found a large number of the latest and most popular pieces. There are also over eighty of the old standard hymns of the church, so that this book is adapted to all congregations. In fact, we are confident that this new edition contains more good music, with new and old reliable standards, than was ever before crowded between two covers at anything like the price. Ninety-two hymns have been added in this edition.

Large Discount to Evangelists.

We print name and address of evangelists on cover when not less than 100 copies are ordered.

TRY + IT

THE McDONALD & GILL CO.,

36 Bromfield St., Boston. 57 Washington St., Chicago.

THE ONLY AUTHORIZED COPYRIGHT AND COMPLETE EDITION OF

THE CHRISTIAN'S SECRET OF A HAPPY LIFE.

(Containing Three Chapters not in any other Edition.)

BY HANNAH WHITALL SMITH.

The most practical, helpful guide to the Christian life extant.

Price, Handsomely Bound in Gilt Cloth, $1.   Plain Cloth, 75c.   Paper Cover, 50c.

McDONALD, GILL & CO.,

36 Bromfield Street, BOSTON, MASS.

57 Washington Street, CHICAGO, ILL.

HALF ✢ A ✢ MILLION.

SONGS OF
JOY AND GLADNESS No. 2.

W. McDonald, J. Gill, W. J. Kirkpatrick, J. Sweney.

7,000 Copies Sold Before they were Printed.

The success of SONGS OF JOY AND GLADNESS No. 1 is unparalleled, having reached a circulation of nearly half a million copies in six years. All this has been accomplished without advertising the book in any paper except our own, *The Christian Witness.* These two facts and a growing demand for a new book seemed to warrant the publication of No. 2. In issuing No. 2 the publishers are persuaded that in every particular it is the equal of No. 1. It contains the latest and best compositions of its compilers, while its reprints are among the most popular in use. It is replete with new pieces, which are destined to make the book a favorite in all Christian circles.

· · PRICES · ·

	MUSIC.	WORDS.
Single, prepaid,	$ .40	$ .15
Single, not prepaid,	.35	
Dozen, not prepaid,	3.60	1.20
Hundred, not prepaid,	30.00	10.00
Leather, red edge, prepaid,	.75	
Morocco, gilt edge, prepaid,	1.00	

Special Rates to the trade and evangelists.

McDONALD, GILL & CO.,

36 Bromfield St., Boston.   57 Washington St., Chicago.

THE

CHRISTIAN WITNESS

and Advocate of Bible Holiness.

JOSHUA GILL,
ISAIAH REID,
G. A. McLAUGHLIN,
} Editors.

SIXTEEN PAGE WEEKLY.   **$1.50 PER YEAR.**

To Clergymen, $1.00 per year. Special terms to Agents.

The WITNESS, while devoted primarily to the spread of Scriptural holiness, aims, at the same time, to keep its readers posted in general religious news, as well as the work in Foreign Mission fields. The WITNESS is pronounced for Self-supporting Missions. Bright, crisp, sharp, newsy, always readable and profitable. It aims to furnish soul-food rather than worldly literature. A whole page is devoted to the children and young people. It is *The Young Disciple* rejuvenated on a small scale. Another department is a corner for Young Preachers, in which we give hints, sketches of sermons, and exegeses of texts in brief for the assistance of young preachers and evangelists.

SAMPLE COPY FREE.
THE CHRISTIAN WITNESS CO.,
36 Bromfield St., Boston.   57 Washington St., Chicago.

www.ingramcontent.com/pod-product-compliance
Lightning Source LLC
Chambersburg PA
CBHW031936080426
42735CB00007B/156

Voice of Triumph.

he cut on the front side of this sheet shows the title page
ır new song book,

THE VOICE OF TRIUMPH.

It contains the cream of our old books, and over a hundred new pieces. Messrs. Kirkpatrick and Sweney are our very best song writers, and we have had permission to select freely from their valuable collection.

This book is as near perfect as any book ever published.

═══PRICES.═══

	Music.
Single, prepaid	$0.40
" not prepaid	.35
Dozen, "	3.60
Hundred, "	30.00
Leather, red edge, prepaid	.75
" gilt edge, "	1.00

Special Rates to the Trade and to Evangelists

THE McDONALD & GILL CO.

36 Bromfield St.,   57 Washington St.,
   BOSTON, MASS.   CHICAGO, ILL.